To Maureen + Mort,
with much love,

Billy

REVISION AND AUTHORITY
IN WORDSWORTH

REVISION

AND AUTHORITY

IN WORDSWORTH

The Interpretation of a Career

WILLIAM H. GALPERIN

upp

University of Pennsylvania Press
Philadelphia

The author gratefully thanks the Rutgers University
Research Council which aided in the publication
of this volume.

Library of Congress Cataloging in Publication Data

Galperin, William H.
    Revision and authority in Wordsworth : the interpretation of a
career / William H. Galperin.
        p.   cm.
    Includes bibliographies and index.
    ISBN 0-8122-8140-3
    1. Wordsworth, William, 1700–1850—Criticism and interpretation.
2. Authority in literature.   I. Title.
PR5888.G25   1989
821'.7—dc19   88-30325
                                                         CIP

FOR MY PARENTS
ROSE AND GABRIEL
AND FOR TINA

CONTENTS

ACKNOWLEDGMENTS

Parts of Chapters 1 and 2 originally appeared in different form in *Victorian Poetry*, *ELH*, and *Criticism*. I am grateful to the editors of these journals for allowing me to reprint this material. The following publishers have also granted me permission to quote from the following works: Oxford University Press for *The Poetical Works of William Wordsworth*, edited Ernest de Selincourt and revised by Helen Darbishire (1952–59), *William Wordsworth, The Prelude or Growth of a Poet's Mind*, edited Ernest de Selincourt and revised by Helen Darbishire (1959), *The Letters of William and Dorothy Wordsworth: The Early Years*, edited by Ernest de Selincourt and revised by Chester L. Shaver (1967), and *The Prose Works of William Wordsworth*, edited by W. J. B. Owen and Jane Worthington Smyser (1974); Cornell University Press and Harvester Press for *"The Ruined Cottage" and "The Pedlar" by William Wordsworth*, edited by James Butler (1979); Cornell University Press for *"Poems, in Two Volumes," and Other Poems, 1800–1807 by William Wordsworth*, edited by Jared Curtis (1983); W. W. Norton for *William Wordsworth, The Prelude, 1799, 1805, 1850*, edited by Jonathan Wordsworth, M. H. Abrams, and Stephen Gill (1979); and Methuen and Co. for *Lyrical Ballads: The Text of the 1798 Edition with the Additional 1800 Poems*, edited by R. L. Brett and A. R. Jones (1968).

The present study is an outgrowth of a dissertation written under the direction of George Landow and the late James Boulger. I am grateful for their advice, encouragement, and unflagging support, both during my graduate years at Brown and in the years that followed. During these years I received support and encouragement from a number of friends and colleagues, including William Vanech, David Curtis, Gabriel Miller, Morton Schoolman, Tom LeClair, Leslie Chard, Mark Levy, David Robinson, Doug Holm, Gideon Bosker, Karen Brooks, Roger Porter, Kathleen Nicholson, William Ray, and Peter and Linda Parshall. Hazard Adams and Robert Gleckner were also very generous and gracious at this time.

More recently, I am grateful to the American Council of Learned Societies for vital support, financial and otherwise, during the interval when the present study was largely conceived. The NEH Summer Seminar for College Teachers I attended in 1982 at Stanford University, under the direction of Anne Mellor, was very instrumental in helping me to refine and sharpen the scope of my study. In addition to Professor Mellor, from whose advice, encouragement and professional example I continue to benefit, I want to thank several other members of the seminar: Theresa Kelley, Richard Matlak, Paul Privateer, and Douglas Wilson.

More recently still, I am grateful both to the Rutgers University Research Council and to the Rutgers University Faculty Academic Study Program for support leading to the completion and publication of the present study. I also want to thank fellow Rutgers Romanticists William Keach (now at Brown), William Walling and Susan Wolfson for advice, support and energetic conversation. Susan Wolfson and Peter Manning read the entire manuscript with scrupulous care and professional disinterestedness. My indebtedness to them is especially large. Charles Berger and Stephen Melville also read the study and gave invaluable advice. Throughout the final stage of composition Timothy Corrigan, Richard Macksey and Richard Slotkin each proved a continued source of enlightenment and support. Finally, it is scarcely an exaggeration for me to say that without Christina Zwarg—my most sympathetic and demanding reader—this work would have never materialized. Such, of course, is the usual credit reserved for one's spouse, yet anyone who knows me will realize how poorly Tina has been served by convention.

William H. Galperin
Irvington, New Jersey

INTRODUCTION

We must remember that what we usually call literary history has little
or nothing to do with literature and that what we call interpretation—
provided only it is good interpretation—is in fact literary history.

Paul de Man

Wordsworth's career has traditionally been divided into two categories: an early, "romantic" period of greatness (1797–1807) and a
longer, "conservative" period of decline (1808–1850). This study
challenges that demarcation. It does so, however, by arguing that
some division of Wordsworth's career is ultimately warranted.

This contention will immediately strike many readers as paradoxical. How can we divide Wordsworth's career in the conventional
manner without implicitly admitting the superiority of the poet's
"great period" over the ensuing one? Some readers chastened by
the admonitions of poststructuralism and marxism have even suggested that the division of Wordsworth's career might be eliminated
altogether. Not only do they argue that Wordsworth's "great period" represents an aberration from an essential or ultimate Wordsworth who is very much a man of his time; they contend, still more
provocatively, that the aberrant sensibility on which Wordsworth's
"reputation" rests derives its energies from a conservatism achieving full expression in the later poetry. Whether by the "Jacobinism-
in-recoil" in which, as E. P. Thompson maintains, Wordsworth's
"great romantic impulse came to maturity"; or the "celestial" orientation that, as Paul de Man argues, betrays Wordsworth's affinity
with a more conventional order of hierarchies and correspondences; or the "ideology" which, as Jerome McGann and Marjorie
Levinson have recently proposed, called for the elision of revolutionary content in Wordsworth's poetry, it is typical of the "revisionist" approach to Wordsworth to excoriate the Wordsworth of
1797–1807 as a false messiah.[1]

My sympathics, it should be emphasized, are more with this latter
group than with those readers who see no possible relationship
between the early and late Wordsworth. But where the revisionists

increasingly use Wordsworth to disabuse the liberal, humanistic values seemingly encoded by the poems of the Great Decade (and on which Wordsworth's reputation rests), it is the purpose of this study to show that Wordsworth was necessarily the first to undertake this revision.

It is for this reason that I insist on the validity of demarcating Wordsworth's career. The alleged "anti-climax" in the aftermath of Wordsworth's Great Decade was not a betrayal of the poet's radical or romantic vision. It resulted instead from Wordsworth's exercise of poetic authority—yielding a revision of the earlier poetry that by turns anticipates and supersedes our contemporary, revisionist approaches to romanticism. The humanistic or individual authority for which Wordsworth has been long admired—and only recently reviled—was always unstable, particularly in the works where it is alleged to be humanized, radical, and unorthodox. Thus, the conservative personae of the later poems—far from forgetting their various progenitors—actually recall the authority of Wordsworth's earlier humanism. And in so doing they make clear what is already detectable in the early poetry: namely, the arbitrariness of authority in general. Wordsworth does not "become" an orthodox Christian in his later phase. Instead, his orthodoxy cancels the authority it supersedes so as to cancel *all* authority, including, of course, the authority of orthodoxy itself.

Attributing this critical capacity to Wordsworth's own texts— even if the text is ultimately that of Wordsworth's literary career— has both methodological and theoretical implications. These in turn relate generally to the question of interpretation. For in addition to reinterpreting Wordsworth's career, I derive my reinterpretation from the interpretation of individual poems. To so justify one interpretation by another may seem to some critics very precarious. But it is less precarious than the interpretations of Wordsworth which proceed from some a priori assumption—humanist, poststructuralist, or marxist—that does not take into account the central dynamic of Wordsworth's poetry, early and late, in which the energies of his self-criticism are located.

My way of reading Wordsworth may be clarified by E. D. Hirsch, Jr.'s recent response to a forum on the "politics of interpretation," where he distinguishes between two kinds of interpretation.[2] First, there is the "autocratic" mode, which originates with the reader or with a specific value of the reader's and "is not in principle revisable except by accidental change of preference." Second, there is what Hirsch terms the "allocratic" mode of interpretation, which "is revisable ex post facto on the basis of changing theories and evidence about a determinative historical event" (327–28). This latter mode, with its "possibility of being wrong," allows for "empirical progress," whereas the "autocratic mode," in "always [being] right," provides no progress at all (330).

My view, then, that Wordsworth's "anti-climax" contests his "climax" or great period is not an autocratic one but governed by the "determinative historical event" of Wordsworth's literary career. My argument that the alleged hardening of sensibility in the late Wordsworth is more nearly a poststructural critique of a humanistic, romantic sensibility, is not a "deconstruction" or critique of Wordsworth in the customary sense, but a submission, rather, to a principle of revisability that the *whole* of Wordsworth's career mandates. Thus, for all its deference to "Wordsworth," my way of reading may be similarly distinguished from the a priori interpretations which read the poetry from a more honorific perspective that credits Wordsworth's intentions. In the very way that I deconstruct Wordsworth *according to* Wordsworth, I am able to extend these principles of revisability to his individual poems which, in the *oeuvre* they comprise, warrant new interpretations as a measure of, and pursuant to, the poet's corrigibility.

Another way to talk about this approach would be to relate it to the critical innovations of the last thirty-five years. As most readers are undoubtedly aware, the last two decades have witnessed the introduction of theory—particularly poststructuralism—into the practice of literary study. The reasons for theory's sudden relevance are manifold, but in romantic studies the move to theory can certainly be seen as an undoing (or at the very least a refutation) of the "romantic reassessment" which reached a crescendo in the early 1960s. The "romantic reassessment," whose proponents have included such notable critics as M. H. Abrams, Harold Bloom, and Northrop Frye, remains one of the most important movements in modern literary studies. Not only did this movement identify romanticism as the place at which to begin talking about modernism; it was the movement most instrumental in overthrowing the New Criticism that had dominated literary analysis and canon formation in the twentieth century. Interest in the previously overlooked Romantics was both accompanied and justified by a new methodology that replaced the formalist desiderata of impersonality, ambiguity and aesthetic autonomy with other priorities, including intentionality, mythopoesis, and politics. The seemingly aristocratic disposition of a more formal mode of analysis—with its notable affinity for

Anglo-Catholic writing—gave way to a more Protestant or human-istic orientation, effectively reversing T. S. Eliot's injunction (to writers and readers both) that "tradition" maintain precedence over the "individual."[3]

It has been the function, then, of the varieties of poststructur-alism that have emerged in recent years (deconstruction, reception theory, feminist theory, psychoanalytic theory, etc.) to critique this humanistic reversal by pointing to, among other things, the bed-fellowing of tradition and the individual talent. However attractive the values behind the romantic reassessment, it is now argued that in granting the individual priority over tradition, this criticism merely replaced one form of authority with another form—that of the self. Unfortunately, it is also the tendency of much theoretically-based criticism to register its viewpoint by means of accusation, the effect of which has been to place the Romantics, their admirers, and romantic texts in virtually the same dock. Thus, an otherwise tanta-lizing mode of analysis is frequently undertaken at the expense of the very thing it sets forth to illumine, romantic literature.

What must be emphasized about my approach to Wordsworth, therefore, is that it comes less out of theory than out of the romantic reassessment. This is not to suggest that I have not been influenced by theory or that theory has not helped me to develop my ideas regarding Wordsworth. It is simply to observe that my reading of Wordsworth has been most strongly influenced by the largely sym-pathetic mode of analysis in which I first encountered Words-worth's poetry and to which theory has since proven anathema. The difference is that instead of resisting theory, as my critical position or as the legacy of my stance might appear to warrant, my readings, indeed my expansion of Wordsworth to include the poems hitherto ignored by the romantic reassessment, rush to meet theory in a new, hybrid way. While my emphasis on interpretation might seem to some readers either accessory or, even worse, vulnerable to theory, it is my purpose in this study to interpret Wordsworth in a way that essentially does the work of theory. Thus, I show why, in the after-math of two decades, theory has become so intrinsic to literary study: why deconstruction, for example, has been embraced by the literary rather than the philosophic community. For my particular maneuvers as a critic are, in the case of Wordsworth, literary ma-neuvers as well, which it is my function here to interpret.

Wordsworth's "career" is not the only "event" on which an inter-pretation such as this one may be founded. But its preference is perhaps best justified by remembering that the "determinative" event that normally governs our approach to Wordsworth—his major decade of 1797–1807—is a critical or interpretive invention. This invention, furthermore, reflects those humanistic values resuscitated by the romantic reassessment, and so attempts both to save Wordsworth from himself and, not coincidentally, to save criticism from Wordsworth. In rewriting Wordsworth into two poets (one memorable and the other not), criticism has done more than guarantee an after-life for Wordsworth's poetry; it has perpetuated its own existence through an autocratic or "idealist" approach to Wordsworth in which one a priori view—humanist, pantheist, deconstructionist, or new historicist—is continually set against another. Granting Wordsworth his six-decade history *as Wordsworth* replaces this autocratically constituted Wordsworth (from "whom" interpretations have proliferated) with a Wordsworth answerable to Wordsworth, and with a principle of revisability that extends to all his writings.

Such an approach to Wordsworth has a history as well. Prior to Matthew Arnold, in fact, who is ironically regarded today as the quintessential Victorian reader of Wordsworth, many Victorians, including Ruskin, were reluctant to segregate the earlier and later Wordsworth. Their reluctance may have had something to do with the imposing reality of the poet himself (who was very much alive and quite productive until the mid 1840s) as well as with the fact that literary interpretation, spurred on by biblical hermeneutics, was only beginning to take hold. Yet it is clear that such reluctance also operated as an argument "against interpretation," or for an *oeuvre* so continually corrigible that there seemed little point in polarizing Wordsworth's "early" and "late" phases. It is not that such critical discriminations could not have been made or were not made in the nineteenth century; it is that, unlike critics such as De Quincey who carried their romantic legacy well into the Victorian period, the majority of Victorians were sufficiently persuaded by the "completed" Wordsworth not to make any discriminations of period.

Indeed, the Victorian readers of Wordsworth do not constitute what Stanley Fish calls an "interpretive community," whose "members . . . necessarily agree because they . . . see (and by seeing, make) everything in relation to that community's assumed purposes and goals."[4] It is precisely their lack of community, in fact, the way Wordsworth's poetry prevents the Victorians from becoming a recognizably "autocratic" unit (or from being galvanized into "communities" with recognizable biases and aims), that most accurately describes their interpretive posture toward him. Until Arnold effectively delivered the "humanistic" Wordsworth in his famous preface to *The Poems of William Wordsworth* (1879), Wordsworth's readers were more various than opposed in their approaches to his poetry. This is particularly evident in the hyperbolic certainty with which Wordsworth, frequently in independence of what he says, is assumed by the majority of nineteenth-century readers to matter.[5]

There is some of this hyperbolic certainty in Arnold too, notably his claim that Wordsworth's poetry is "at bottom a criticism of life."[6] Yet this very claim is a good example of the autocratic position of Arnold and of the "interpretive community" he would help found. Summoning a "Wordsworth" who embodies values sufficiently humanistic to make "his powerful and beautiful application of ideas to life" (46) his most impressive feature, Arnold charges his contemporaries for failing to discriminate "Wordsworth," as he defines him, from the poet of encyclopedic relevance. Thus, he begins his preface by blaming the "vogue," which had gone so far as to replace Wordsworth (whose "English fame was [earlier] secure") with Tennyson. It is the disturbing laxity of Arnold's contemporaries—the way the "public" remains "undetermined" about Wordsworth—that concerns Arnold and proves the basis for his interpretable, canonical Wordsworth (37). That praise is ancillary to blame here, that the threat posed by Arnold's contemporaries is in a way more considerable to him than Wordsworth's achievement, cannot be overestimated. It confirms the view that, even if Wordsworth's early poetry can be called humanistic, the whole of Wordsworth's poetry is neither stable nor determinate enough to support the humanism by which only certain of his poems may be deemed "first-rate" (42).

Arnold's hermeneutics create a "Wordsworth" able to sustain the very values on which that "Wordsworth" tautologically depends. And this strategy bears "assumptions current in [nineteenth-century] hermeneutics," by which, as Tilottama Rajan observes, the reader is made "coproducer of the text." Curiously, it is not doubt over "the presence and location of meaning in relation to the written text" that helps to enfranchise the reader in the hermeneutic configuration; it is more "an anxiety about the self-sufficiency of the linguistic system and its subset, the textual system."[7] Despite the "disestablishment of authoritative meaning" implied in the hermeneutic stance toward reading, this position, Rajan shows, actually represents a counter-revolution against just such an upheaval. Whatever responsibility hermeneutics confers on the reader is granted, she submits, in the interest of saving the text by advancing "the author [as] the locus of a fixed meaning and . . . a grounding center" (578–79). Thus, by very dint of the subversions it both initiates and portends, nineteenth-century hermeneutics "confers a certain liberty on [the reader] only to take it away" (579).

If the allocratic (or "undetermined") attitude of the majority of Victorians to Wordsworth might be said, therefore, to be innocent of the anxiety of hermeneutics, the autocratic position of Arnold and the critics after him reflects the influence of hermeneutics, specifically the *influence of anxiety*, on interpretation. In narrowing Wordsworth's achievement to a certain, interpretable thing, Arnold does more than adopt an authoritarian position; he constructs an arbitrary, authoritarian Wordsworth who governs his reader's viewpoint. It is both ironic and necessary that the Wordsworth so subjected to a "supplement of reading" (in Rajan's phrase) loses authority over himself, becoming now the property of his readers.

In contrast to this "Wordsworth," the Wordsworth answerable to himself is committed to a process of *devaluation*, prompting suspension of the very criterion—romantic humanism—by which his poetry has been defended and, more recently of course, deconstructed. As we shall see, in fact, the peculiar susceptibility of the earlier poetry to poststructural, even feminist critiques more accurately reflects a susceptibility of Wordsworth to Wordsworth. This is even truer of the irony that characterizes the later renunciations of authority in poems such as the *Sonnets Upon the Punishment of Death* or "Yarrow Revisited." Effectively wresting responsibility from the poem's speaker, such irony would have been impossible were there no authority to renounce or, earlier, to assimilate. The authority that Wordsworth eventually renounces was never his own and always detachable—refuting the charge of apostasy that autocratic readers, convinced of the centrality of the Wordsworth's humanism and the primacy of his imagination, have invariably leveled against him. The completed Wordsworth reveals that authority is never totally assimilable, that like the "sense of God" it is always inherited or imposed by agency of writing. It is the task of the interpreter— duly sanctioned by Wordsworth's career—to show how these various claims to authority are merely claims and, in the early poetry especially, always removable.

This removability, which moves Wordsworth from poem to poem, is apparent in the way a "constitutional" Wordsworth is, throughout the "golden decade," written over by a "professional" Wordsworth,[8] creating an ever increasing gap between the "self" and the poetical self. This gap becomes clear both in *The Prelude* (1805), whose speaker is quite literally the "character of the Poet," and in contemporary lyrics that similarly attest to the discrepancy between the "self" and its alleged sublimity. It becomes the function of *The Excursion* (1814) (which is usually taken to mark the beginning of Wordsworth's "decline") to contend with this discrepancy by dismantling the self and by relieving it of its archetypal, authoritarian function. No sooner is the character of the Poet introduced in *The Excursion* than he relinquishes his professional dispensation to the Wanderer—and after him, to the Solitary and the Pastor, who also represent authority. This succession of authority from the Poet to others proceeds less from Wordsworth's "assurance" of "his identity as a poet" (Rzepka 98–99), than from his sense that poetic identity is always a creation of the self in the image of something else.

This self-reflexive displacement is especially apparent in Wordsworth's later poetry. Beginning with *The Excursion*, these poems do more than rescue the self from poetry; they gradually save poetry from the authority of the self. This rescue leads by turns to a revolution in poetic language, where the authority formerly ascribed to the "Poet" is relinquished so completely that it cannot be reconstituted elsewhere. The apparent orthodoxy of the later poetry, notably the *Ecclesiastical Sonnets*, is in this way of a piece with those orthodoxies it supersedes and destabilizes, most importantly the romantic (or, if you prefer, secularized) humanism for which Christianity, historically, was a pretext. Thus, while the culmination of this "revolution" against authority involves, as I have suggested, Wordsworth's recourse to irony, it is to irony of a very special sort: where meaning is less the province of an authorized reading than of the "disestablishment of authoritative meaning" that only the vitiation of speaking—of what a poem says and ostensibly means—accomplishes.

This view of Wordsworth's career may be distinguished from two important readings which might appear to anticipate it: Frances Ferguson's *Wordsworth: Language as Counter-Spirit* and Kenneth R. Johnston's *Wordsworth and "The Recluse"*. Ferguson argues that poetry and "language" adulterate and/or alienate "consciousness" sufficiently to allow Wordsworth to become a reader of himself. Yet withal, she subscribes to conventional periodization: such alienation, she contends, yielded "Wordsworth's famous 'decline,' " which "resulted from the asceticism of his poetics . . . pronounced from the outset of his poetic career."[9] The idea that "the difference[s] between poems of [Wordsworth's] different periods are ones of degree rather than kind" (xv) is provocative and a significant amendment to the accepted view of Wordsworth's career. But it is impeded, at the same time, by a refusal to acknowledge *any* development in Wordsworth by which degree and kind are, more plausibly, intermixed.

The difficulties of this approach are especially apparent in Ferguson's reading of *The Excursion*, for she views the poem primarily as recapitulating issues of authority in the poetry that precedes it. The speaker's resignation of his role as poet and his casting of himself as an auditor are important only in that they prevent Wordsworth's "identification" of "himself and the Wanderer" from "becom[ing] fixed and absolute" (204). Other lines of authority are similarly rendered problematic, and studied within a critical perspective that accords equal weight to the claims of self and self-reflexivity—in effect, the hypostatic legacy of Wordsworth's earlier period.

Without denying the value of Ferguson's work, one may still ask whether *The Excursion* looks only one way—in this case, backward to previous instances of self-reflexivity in Wordsworth's poetry—or whether it also looks forward to a point where authority may be renounced? That is, does not *The Excursion* ultimately pressure Ferguson's dialectic of language and consciousness enough to portend a revolution in poetic language and poetic consciousness? In refusing to observe Wordsworth in his entirety, or worse, in only looking backward from the later Wordsworth, Ferguson is disposed to reassert the primacy of Wordsworth's humanistic period, whose synthesizing tendencies include and (in that way) recuperate the first full indication of the inadequacy of that orientation.

The spirit of Ferguson's interest in synthesizing the claims of self and self-reflexivity finds a counterpart in Johnston's study.[10] Johnston's point of synthesis is (with some irony) the never-completed *The Recluse* in conjunction with which "almost all of [Wordsworth's] greatest poetry was [either directly or indirectly] written." Thus, although Wordsworth "could not make *The Recluse*," *The Recluse* (which included both *The Excursion* and the posthumously published *Prelude*) "made Wordsworth the poet he is" (xxi).

It is just as easy to argue the obverse of this view: the fragmentary state of this long philosophical poem "containing views of Man, Nature, and Society" is a reflection, most immediately, on the inadequacy of the dialectic (with its projected synthesis) on which Wordsworth's "greatness" depends. And one might argue further that in minimizing the impact of poems such as *Lyrical Ballads* that are not expressly part of *The Recluse*, Johnston minimizes the effects of *their* impact—the development and the dismantling of authority both during and after *The Recluse*—all of which seriously impedes the dialectic of "a truly humanistic poetry" (227).[11]

Although, as Johnston shows us, plans for *The Recluse* were in effect almost from the inception of the Wordsworth-Coleridge relationship, and undoubtedly inform the first efforts to write *The Prelude* in 1799, the thirteen-book *Prelude* of 1805 comes from another place altogether: from a development that between 1797 and 1804 oversaw the creation of the poetical self in the image of authority. Not only does this process account for the evolution of the sublime self in Wordsworth, which achieves ever more confident expression in poems leading to *The Prelude;* it accounts also for the recognition, as early as *The Prelude,* that such identity is at best a representation of something else. Johnston notes a disquietude in *The Prelude* over Wordsworth's radical humanism (119–216), but his determination to find a synthesis in Wordsworth keeps him from appreciating how such disquietude is underwritten by Wordsworth's appropriation of authority; for this is what creates discrepancies *within* the self pursuant to those *between* the "self" and the rest of the world. As a result, when he reads *The Excursion,* Johnston views the Wanderer and the Solitary as adversaries in a dialectic of self and society rather than as counterparts, or representations of the "self," that together enact a movement against dialectic commensurate with the renunciation of individual authority that follows.

Any study of a poet's career, much less of Wordsworth's, is bound to be selective, and mine is no exception. Because I devote considerable attention to the *The Excursion* and the poems written after it, I am especially selective in treating frequently discussed earlier poems. My study does not concern works written before 1797, including *Descriptive Sketches, An Evening Walk, Salisbury Plain,* and *The Borderers* (which was completed in early 1797), nor many of the "major" lyrics, those poems contemporary with or written shortly after *The Prelude,* that initially appeared in *Poems, in Two Volumes* (1807). Although these poems are regarded as essential to understanding Wordsworth's evolution into a mature poet, they are not as crucial to his overall development as the poems in the 1798 *Lyrical Ballads,* the poems composed between and 1799 and 1802, and *The Prelude* and *The Excursion.*

Indeed, I begin my study with *The Excursion* primarily because this poem has the unique and paradoxical distinction of being both the first document of Wordsworth's "anti-climax" and, for the fifty years following its publication, the poet's acknowledged masterpiece. Beginning with *The Excursion,* moreover, allows us to follow the Victorian precedent in looking backward and forward simultaneously: backward to the poems that lead to *The Excursion,* and forward to the later poems to which *The Excursion* and the earlier poems alike are a prelude.

The poems Wordsworth wrote after *The Excursion* are quite numerous and even more difficult to distinguish among than the preceding poems. Thus, my choice of representative texts—beyond such obvious selections as the *River Duddon* and *Ecclesiastical* sonnets—is bound still more by claims of expedience. All of this is most unfortunate, since at almost every turn in the later Wordsworth, whether in the memorials of the various tours or in any of the miscellaneous sonnets, we encounter something that speaks immediately and powerfully to the question of artistic and cultural value.

It seems appropriate, therefore, to end this introduction with one such instance—the sonnet "Malham Cove" (composed in 1818)—which provides a model for the revisability I am proposing:

Was the aim frustrated by force or guile,
When giants scooped from out the rocky ground,
Tier under tier, this semicirque profound?
(Giants—the same who built in Erin's isle
That Causeway with incomparable toil!)—
O, had this vast theatric structure wound
With finished sweep into a perfect round,
No mightier work had gained the plausive smile
Of all-beholding Phœbus! But, alas,
Vain earth! false world! Foundations must be laid
In Heaven; for, 'mid the wreck of IS and WAS,
Things incomplete and purposes betrayed
Make sadder transits o'er thought's optic glass
Than noblest objects utterly decayed.

Because it resorts to a form—the sonnet—and to a content—the foundation of Heaven—that are more traditional than original, it is common to read "Malham Cove" as evidence of Wordsworth's conservatism. And, indeed, the poem's emphasis on failure and the concluding *sententia* ("Things incomplete . . ."), for which the cove is presumably an example, make it a very traditional kind of utterance. Nevertheless, there is about "Malham Cove" a demonstrable or nonauthoritative irony to which these conventional elements are at once crucial yet accessory. What the poem ultimately exposes, by recourse to the myth of origins, is the arbitrariness of its "tradition," so to speak: the odd complementarity of tradition and the individual talent. The opening question about the mystification of place— the cove's mythological origins—becomes a means, indeed, not only to contest this myth, but, more important, to reveal the self-aggrandizement of all mythmaking. The rather "conservative" belief here in a "perfect[ion]" unrivaled on "earth" leads finally, then, to a demystification of heavenly perfection as the reification of earthly desire.

The two suggestions—of heavenly perfection and of the myth of heavenly perfection—are important, for together they render impossible a single authority. Although the failure of the cove to form "a perfect round" is apparently a figure of earthly imperfection, this surmise derives its authority from a mythology similar to that of the giants. Whether the cove was constructed by giants, or whether it recalls an even greater gigantism "in Heaven," the actual or the merely visible (Malham Cove) is in each instance subsumed by a vision or act of mind. That transit "o'er thought's optic glass" allows Wordsworth to introduce another way of telling in order to show how willful, or how similar in their "aim," the secular myth and the myth of "Heaven" remain.

Operating between "IS and WAS," within a movable present uninformed by an intentional structure, this new way of seeing eschews the "false world" whose "foundations must be laid / In Heaven." The ironic hinge by which the two myths are now linked—"must"—can be read in two ways: as a token of exasperation at the very preposterousness of the foundational giant-myth, as well as part of the recognition that foundations— insofar as they exist—are necessarily "in Heaven." In the first reading, the speaker derides the vanity in the initial mythopoesis, the presumption of those who create giants to create coves. The second reading proves more difficult; for in this reading "Heaven" does win a victory. But it is a Pyrrhic victory, since the faith professed is, as the speaker warrants, in something invisible.

To assume that Wordsworth uses Christian orthodoxy or earthly vanity simply to oppose the presumption of the secularized giant myth limits the poem's adversariness. Wordsworth's point (enforced, in a peculiar sense, by the very artifice of his diction as well as by the untraditional aspects of this sonnet with its several enjambments) is that Imagination can no more be excoriated in the name of Christianity than Christianity can be excoriated in the name of Imagination. Wordsworth reveals how the two mythologies are in the end quite similar, how each involves impositions of order in repetition of the authority each promotes.

As for the world viewed, it is fragmented, disordered, a "wreck." But so long as the world can make "transits o'er thought's optic glass," it cannot be mystified (or imagined) into ruin, into an "objec[t] utterly decayed." What "IS" is incomplete without being synecdochical: a fragment with no prospect of completion, no wholeness—past, passing, or to come— of which it is visibly a part. What is there and visible is now contrary to narrative, to the foundational visions that " 'mid the wreck of IS and WAS" now cause, indeed are the only cause for, "sad[ness]."

The sad transits of thought with which "Malham Cove" concludes nicely characterize the peculiar difficulty of the later Wordsworth, particularly the retrospection and circumspection that keep the poet from assuming a more forthright or authoritative stance. But this must not be reckoned an undecidability on Wordsworth's part. The speaker's sadness, if anything, remains a subjective correlative for the poem's irony, whose resistance to meaning makes clear, at the same time, the meaning of that resistance. The sadness at the poem's close may be vague to a point—and less determined certainly than simple *contemptus mundi;* but the poem clearly bears both the freight and onus of referentiality, if only as expiation for the *sententia* it has abandoned. It might have been easier for the speaker of this and other late poems to behold the world thoughtlessly; it is Wordsworth's greater achievement to think and to communicate his "thoughts" in a nonauthoritative manner.

NOTES

1. E. P. Thompson, "Disenchantment or Default? A Lay Sermon," in *Power and Consciousness,* ed. Conor Cruise O'Brien and William Dean Vanech (New York: New York University Press, 1969), 149–81; Paul de Man, "Intentional Structure of the Romantic Image," in *Romanticism and Consciousness,* ed. Harold Bloom (New York: W. W. Norton, 1970), 65–77; Jerome J. McGann, *The Romantic Ideology: A Critical Investigation* (Chicago: University of Chicago Press, 1983); Marjorie Levinson, *Wordsworth's Great Period Poems: Four Essays* (London: Cambridge University Press, 1986). A notable modification of this view, which sees not only a consistency, but something akin to a persistent radicalism, throughout Wordsworth's career, is David Simpson's *Wordsworth's Historical Imagination: The Poetry of Displacement* (London: Methuen, 1987). Although Simpson's study appeared after my book was drafted, I am able to show where it anticipates or otherwise relates to my study.

2. "The Politics of Theories of Interpretation," in *The Politics of Interpretation,* ed. W. J. T. Mitchell (Chicago: University of Chicago Press, 1983), 321–33.

3. See, in particular, Eliot's "Tradition and the Individual Talent," in *The Sacred Wood* (London: Methuen, 1960), 47–59. An especially succinct

manifesto of the "romantic reassessment" (and rebuttal of Eliot) is Harold Bloom's "Prometheus Rising: The Backgrounds of Romantic Poetry," in *The Visionary Company: A Reading of English Romantic Poetry*, 2d ed. rev. (Ithaca, NY: Cornell University Press, 1971), xiii–xxv, which accords with Bloom's well-known "influence" theory in employing the Romantics so as to humanize Eliot's dialectic. A similar clarion call was sounded earlier in the series of English Institute essays characteristically titled *Romanticism Reconsidered* (New York: Columbia University Press, 1963) edited by Northrop Frye.

4. *Is There a Text in This Class?: The Authority of Interpretive Communities* (Cambridge, MA: Harvard University Press, 1980), 15. For Fish's defense of interpretation see, especially, 305–71.

5. Eschewing any specific analysis of "On the Power of Sound" ("It should be read entire, and I shall not quote a line"), Margaret Fuller concludes her discussion with the following: "What more to the purpose can we say about Wordsworth, except—read him." (*Papers on Literature and Art, Part I* [New York: Wiley and Putnam, 1846], 98.)

6. "Wordsworth," in *English Literature and Irish Politics*, vol. 9 of *The Complete Prose Works of Matthew Arnold*, ed. R. H. Super (Ann Arbor: University of Michigan Press, 1973), 46.

7. "The Supplement of Reading," *NLH*, 17 (1986): 576–77.

8. I take these terms from Charles Rzepka, *The Self as Mind: Vision and Identity in Wordsworth, Coleridge, and Keats* (Cambridge, MA: Harvard University Press, 1986), 51. Because of his largely psychoanalytic view of the development of Wordsworth's poetic identity, Rzepka uses the designations "professional" and "constitutional" interchangeably.

9. *Wordsworth: Language as Counter-Spirit* (New Haven, CT: Yale University Press, 1977), xv.

10. *Wordsworth and "The Recluse"* (New Haven, CT: Yale University Press, 1984).

11. According to Johnston, "the philosophy informing *The Recluse*," and the fortuitous basis for what amounts finally to a dialectical or synthetic structure, shifts "from an initial phase in which human mental consciousness is presented in strongly ambivalent tension with its socio-physical contexts . . . ; through a dialectically contrary stage in which, in the form of the artist's creative imagination, it acts as if radically independent of material limitation . . . ; to a tertiary compromise between acts of mind and their necessary containment and conservation in the social, educational, and religious institutions of human civilization" (15).

ONE

Wordsworth's Anti-Climax and the Critical Tradition

That Wordsworth's "anti-climax" remains a critical judgment and largely an issue of taste is something few would dispute. Nevertheless, the effect of critical practice since Matthew Arnold has been to obscure this fact by placing the onus for Wordsworth's decline on Wordsworth's poetry, especially the poems after 1810. The term "anti-climax" comes from H. W. Garrod, who dubbed the last four decades of Wordsworth's career "the most dismal anti-climax of which the history of literature holds record."[1] Willard Sperry's *Wordsworth's Anti-Climax*[2] ponders the problem but does not contest the issue, attributing it to a variety of extra-poetical influences, ranging from Wordsworth's disappointment as a revolutionary, to Annette Vallon, to the deleterious effect of Francis Jeffrey's criticism of *The Excursion*.

Wordsworth, of course, wrote much that, regardless of the measures employed to judge it, is less than what Arnold would call "first-rate." But to narrow his achievement only to the "golden decade" of 1797–1807 raises certain questions about excellence and about literary value. The belief, moreover, that there are essentially two antithetical Wordsworths during the Great Decade alone, or two extremities between which criticism may steer a course in crediting Wordsworth's achievement, has had the additional effect of making the canonical Wordsworth all things to all people; one aspect of a career has been magnified and made to appear comprehensive in lieu of the more palpable comprehensiveness of the poet's achievement overall.

A more useful approach requires that we first acknowledge the interrelation and mutual dependency of the two Wordsworths in the "two Wordsworths" critical tradition. Regardless whether

Wordsworth is, as M. H. Abrams phrases the issue, "an affirmative poet of life, love, and joy," or an "equivocal . . . self-divided poet whose affirmations are implicitly qualified (if not annulled) by a pervasive sense of mortality and an ever-incipient despair of life,"[3] these characters are two sides of the same coin. Wordsworth, "the great poet of natural man and the world of all of us," is in the long view no different from, nor any less a humanist, than the antinatural Wordsworth, "whose profoundest inclinations are toward another world that transcends biological and temporal limitations" (4).[4] In either "Wordsworth" there is a radicalism characteristic of what Hazlitt, and Abrams after him, have called the "spirit of the age."[5] The assumption that Wordsworth consistently found "God" in nature is a variation finally on the putatively contrary argument that for Wordsworth (as for the other Romantics) God was in the mind of man, or at the very least in the mind that half perceives and half creates. In either stance, power and authority are in a world imagined, where order and chaos are, in effect, self-born.[6]

The question must be asked, then: is Wordsworth's widely perceived anti-climax the sign of a hardened or otherwise ossified sensibility? Or does this category, to the contrary, reveal that the standards for judging the breadth of Wordsworth's achievement are more narrow, more arbitrary, than criticism has recognized? Is the uncanonical Wordsworth merely a bad writer or is he an antihumanistic writer whose writings pose a challenge to posterity and to literary value? My questions are not without precedent. Prior to Arnold's construction of the Wordsworth canon, in fact, the majority of Wordsworth's admirers, particularly those not the poet's contemporaries, made no consistent distinction between what have become the canonical and the anticlimactic Wordsworth. Behind the reluctance to make this distinction was of course the reality of Wordsworth himself, who as long as he was alive and working required deference at the cost of more rigorous discrimination. Yet the absence of a canonical dispensation in the nineteenth century stems equally from "the authentic anti-Romanticism" of the succeeding generation of writers, whose antiromanticism we are just beginning to appreciate.[7]

That the Victorians were "anti-Romantics," both as writers and critics, is a commonplace in literary history and criticism. Nevertheless, the efforts of many Victorianists to distinguish Victorian writers from their predecessors, who sought similarly to be different from what Lamb disparagingly termed the "past century," have had recourse to nearly identical claims for difference, originality, and modernity, long associated with the critical treatments of the "romantic assertion."[8] One of the most visible indications of this critical tendency has been the effort to install the Victorians, formerly the "last Romantics," as the first Moderns.[9] In contrast to the judgments of Eliot and Leavis, who saw nineteenth-century writing, and Victorian writing in particular, as a falling off from "the prestige of the Romantic achievement,"[10] the Victorians, it is increasingly argued, actually anticipate and supplant Eliot in their preoccupation with the loss of faith and with the deficiencies in both self and society that made new belief difficult.

The impulse to rescue Victorian writing from the belatedness to which it had been consigned by Eliot and, more recently, by Romanticists such as Harold Bloom is a laudable one.[11] Yet such efforts generally occlude the equally powerful struggle with both modernity and the attendant mystifications of authority and originality long evident in the Victorian reception of Wordsworth's poetry. In refusing, that is, to distinguish between the canonical and the antihumanistic Wordsworth, or, contrarily, to denigrate the poet's anti-climax, the Victorians were neither generous nor especially imprecise. They were reluctant merely to claim a difference between romantic notions of authority, located in the mind of the imagining subject, and the more conventional, or conservative, conceptions of authority whose "intentionality" romanticism appropriates. Thus, the Victorians fail to promote a specific orientation—be it revolutionary or conservative—and by this inadvertent deconstruction emphasize the undecidability and the ironic counterspirit characteristic of Wordsworth's poetry in general.

Arnold underscored this tendency when he charged that contemporaries such as Leslie Stephen had "prais[ed] Wordsworth for the wrong things," not realizing that "poetry is the reality, philosophy the illusion" ("Wordsworth" 48). He had in mind the way Stephen and other "Wordsworthians" adopt Wordsworth as a moral authority or spiritual guide. But Arnold was also responding, if not altogether wittingly, to the transparency of his contemporaries' "wrong"-ness: more than ill-conceived, their praise of Wordsworth was intentionally that way. Here, for example, is Ruskin's hyperbolic defense of Wordsworth:

> [He] has a grand, consistent, perfectly disciplined, all grasping intellect—for which nothing is too small, nothing too great, arranging everything in due relations, divinely pure in its conceptions of pleasure, majestic in the equanimity of its benevolence—intense as white fire with chastised feeling. . . . I believe Coleridge has very little moral influence on the world;

his writings are those of a benevolent man in a fever. Wordsworth may be trusted as a guide in everything, he feels nothing
but what we all ought to feel—what every mind in pure moral
health *must* feel, he says nothing but what we all ought to
believe, what all strong intellects *must* believe.[12]

Obvious questions are provoked by Ruskin's final assertions: does
the writer actually believe what he is claiming for Wordsworth, or is
it more that Ruskin wants to believe such things precisely because
they are unbelievable?

On the one hand, summoning Coleridge, Ruskin means to distinguish an earlier, romantic orientation from a more contemporary
one, and one for contemporaries to follow. What Arnold might see
as a Victorian mystification or appropriation of Wordsworth is from
another perspective an attempt to redefine both Victorianism and
Wordsworth so that they are characterized less by the contemporary
ideals of "Wordsworthianism" than by a gap or difference that
removes that ideal to the realm of the impossible. There is in
Ruskin's hyperbole, no less than in the now forgotten comments of
Frederick William Faber, to whom *The Excursion* remained an *Odys-
sey* sprinkled with Christianity, an ironic undercurrent in which
Wordsworth is no longer an example to be imitated.[13] Instead,
Wordsworth becomes an example *already imitated* in the way Ruskin
praises him for the wrong things: Ruskin's excess and hyperbole are
now a language adequate to the problem or to the achievement,
following Wordsworth, of representing a problem that cannot be
solved or changed or circumscribed by more specific or determinate
means.[14]

To appreciate the determined wrongness, the irony, of Ruskin's
argument, one need only examine the non-ironic judgments of his
contemporaries such as Arnold and Walter Pater, both of whom
used Wordsworth in the hope of disabusing what they necessarily
took too literally. In Pater this corrective yields a distinction between
"being" and "doing," to the way Wordsworth's best poetry "reveals
an intimate consciousness of natural things which weighs, listens
and penetrates" so that the "the end of life is not action but contemplation."[15]

It is for this reason, submits Pater, that Wordsworth "chooses to
depict people from humble life":

They are on the whole more impassioned . . . than other men:
it is for this direct expression of passion that he values their

humble words. In much that he said in exaltation of rural life, he was but pleading indirectly for that sincerity, that perfect fidelity to one's own inward presentations, to the precise features of the pictures within, without which any profound poetry is impossible. . . . (51)

Wordsworth, and other poets who have been like him . . . are the masters, the experts, in this art of impassioned contemplation. Their work is not to teach lessons, or enforce rules, or even to stimulate us in noble ends; but to withdraw the thoughts for a little while from the mere machinery of life, to fix them, with appropriate emotions, on the spectacle of those great facts in man's existence. (62)

It may seem that Pater has simply reversed Ruskin's argument, substituting one desideratum for another. Yet unlike Ruskin's claims for Wordsworth, which do not appropriate the un-Wordsworthian (specifically the Coleridgian), Pater's argument is more clearly dialectical in presenting Wordsworth's poetics as a counter-poetics to other poetry and poets. Without a poetry of "doing," one that serves "to stimulate" or "to teach," there can be no poetry of being—no poetry to "weigh," to "listen," to "penetrate." Where Ruskin's claims are absolute to the point of undecipherability, Pater's are more measured and tailored to an orthodoxy to which didactic poetry is continually (and necessarily) antithetical.

A similar argument is advanced by Arnold in the preface to his edition of Wordsworth's poems. At first discriminating between Wordsworth and "the vogue" of Tennyson, which had developed at Wordsworth's expense, Arnold then distinguishes the Wordsworthian from the un-Wordsworthian. He does this in the manner of Pater, but elaborates the un-Wordsworthian by further distinguishing "Wordsworth's best work" from the "mass of [his] inferior work . . . imbedding the first-rate work and clogging it, obstructing our approach to it, chilling, not unfrequently, the high-wrought mode with which we leave it" (42). For the most part Arnold, like Pater, prefers the poems of 1797–1807 to the "work before and after this golden prime" (42). However, this is also a matter of reading Wordsworth properly and for the right reasons. Unlike the majority of his contemporaries, who "lay too much stress on what they call [the poet's] philosophy," Wordsworth's "greatness," according to Arnold, lies not in any particular system, but in the "powerful and beautiful application of ideas to life,—to the question: How to live" (46–48). Correspondingly, the texts of Wordsworth's that fail to do so such as *The Excursion* ("a tissue of elevated but abstract verbiage, alien to the very nature of poetry" [49]) fail because they do not transform "philosophy" or "doing" into the work of reality or "being."

Despite his efforts to distinguish reality from abstraction, "life" for Arnold remains, no less than the abstractions it opposes, a representation: a "life" that, following its application to ideas, is somehow truer, more commensurate with the experience of the real, than either the real *or* the abstract, both of which apparently elude the "powerful and beautiful" controls of art. Arnold, in fact, perpetuates the wrongheadedness he excoriates by privileging a certain kind of poetry—a poetry informed by the very "reality" it informs in turn—over another version of art that Wordsworth has also produced but which Arnold, against the judgments of his contemporaries, elects not to acknowledge.[16] Arnold, in other words, proposes more than a reduction of the Wordsworth canon to an arbitrary standard; he seeks a diminution of Wordsworth that associates the bulk of his writing with what both he and Pater disparagingly deem "the vogue."

The bearing of this "Arnoldian" Wordsworth on our present-day sense of the poet, and on the values that foster our perception of Wordsworth's achievement, is evident enough. Just as the twentieth century has consigned Wordsworth to the ten years designated as "golden," so it has magnified the contracted or canonical Wordsworth in order to represent and defend the largely humanistic values of the golden decade. The struggle to save a humanistic poet, for whom the "real" is represented, created or contemplated, from the "conservative" successor, whose opposition to his own authority protests the arbitrariness of "man's existence," is no longer much of an issue these days, particularly among the poet's admirers. But this does not mean that the tension is no longer a tension or that forgetting it has not also involved creating something in its place. Rather, as we see in A. C. Bradley's famous Oxford lecture of 1903, the conflict was forgotten because it had to be, because it was inimical finally to the myth of originality and authority that modern criticism, more than Wordsworth himself, has been determined to uphold.[17]

Bradley's claims for Wordsworth's "strangeness" (101) and for the paradoxical disposition of his poetry strike Abrams ("Two Roads" 3–4) and others as a crucial corrective to the cozier, Victorian Wordsworth promoted by Arnold, Pater and Ruskin. But this view of Bradley serves only to remove him from his Victorian legacy. Bradley tries, for example, to enlarge the Wordsworth canon constricted by Arnold by incorporating the *Poems Dedicated to National Independence and Liberty,* most of them composed after 1810. Though he does nod to Arnold by noting that in their "increasing use of theological ideas," these otherwise "characteristic" poems herald "the decline of Wordsworth's poetic power," Bradley also observes the way the "patriotism of these *Poems* is equally characteristic" of Wordsworth. The "love of country" inherent in them reflects both the ideals of "natural kinship" customarily associated with the poet as well as a "moral" imperative for the defense of national liberty, which Wordsworth did not regard as "stereotyped or narrow" or especially militaristic (116–18).

Bradley's departure from Arnold's canon and Arnold's values is not total. He believes in the poet's decline, which he attributes, with Arnold, to an "increasing" prevalence of "ideas" that are more imposed than applied. However Bradley shows a tendency to complicate this view by exposing Arnold's representational sleight of hand, where ideas and life combine to make "poetry . . . the reality," in the failure of the later poems to perform this trick. There is no difference, Bradley implies, between the characteristic pantheism of Wordsworth's earlier poetry and the moral and patriotic agenda "equally characteristic" of the poet's stance in general.

Bradley, to be sure, is aware of this particular conflict, and he attributes it to the generally paradoxical nature of Wordsworth's poetry. Yet what Bradley was in no position to realize is that the paradoxes in Wordsworth have less to do with Wordsworth than with the competing modes of reading him. To suggest that the jingoism of the poems on liberty has its root in the more expansive ideals of natural kinship is to read Wordsworth as the Victorians read him—with a certain charitable irony that makes his poetry less "determined" in the end than it sometimes appears. However, by invoking the notion of narrowness in assigning a negative value to the increasing use of theological ideas, Bradley reflects another way of reading that promotes certain liberal values (or applications) at the expense of other values which, he admits, are continuous in Wordsworth's poetry.

Nowhere is this tension more apparent than in Bradley's treatment of Wordsworth's "originality"—"the 'mystic,' 'visionary,' 'sublime' aspect of [his] poetry"—as involving the "apprehen[sion of] all things . . . as the expression of something which, while manifested in them, immeasurably transcends them" (100, 127–29). Two aspects to this observation are crucial: the competing myths of origins, in which the beholder Wordsworth at once rivals and imitates what he beholds, and the wavering conceptions of identity against which the initial rivalry appears almost a conspiracy. Where the first conception posits identity in the "expressive" transcendent as well as in the "apprehending" subject who perceives it "in all things," the second conception—as the very slide from "mystic" to "visionary" to "sublime" suggests—is altogether less certain about who is seeing whom and how. Where godhead in the one is conferred in imitation of the beheld, it is in the other taken from the beholder in imitation of "something." By calling the transcendent the "expression of something," Bradley not only destabilizes the transcendent as "something" other than transcendental; he also suggests how the very notion of an "other" in Wordsworth mystifies the apprehending/expressive subject.

It is not important whether Bradley realized the incompatibility of these two views, that he had exposed the narcissistic completeness, and consequent narrowing, of Wordsworth's achievement. It is important that, unlike Arnold and the majority of critics after him, Bradley consciously refers Wordsworth's "visionary feeling" to "the intimation of something illimitable, over-arching or breaking into the customary 'reality' " (134). It is customary to regard such a statement as fundamentally humanistic, especially since it holds imagination as a way to the illimitable. Yet this is also a view threatened by intimations of rupture. For the tension in Bradley's argument derives less from the paradoxical nature of the poetry *per se* than from a critical confusion—effectively a deconstruction— that turns the Arnoldian, humanistic Wordsworth into an argument against himself.[18]

This sense of contrariness in Wordsworth is familiar in the Wordsworth criticism of our time, as evidenced by such influential studies as David Ferry's *The Limits of Mortality* (1959) and Hartman's *Wordsworth's Poetry 1787–1814* (1964). Yet to the extent that Wordsworth is contrary in these readings he is also something of a problem, implying that a more univocal Wordsworth would be a better poet than the multivalent one. The "enmity to man," for example, that Ferry's Wordsworth "mistook for love" turns out not only to be Wordsworth's "genius"; it remains the source, Ferry observes, of "confusions" whose necessary banishment "banished his distinctive greatness as well" (173). Thus, despite situating itself "against the 'Arnoldian' tendency to take Wordsworth's vocabulary of feeling at face value" (ix), there is throughout *The Limits of Mortality* a nostalgia for what Arnold, according to Ferry, unfortunately misconstrued:

Wordsworth's failure to be a poet otherwise reconciled to life made him into a poet whose characteristic genius inevitably spelled his decline. Similarly, the conflict that Hartman describes between "apocalypse" and "akedah," between an imagination that eschews materiality and a desire to relinquish imaginative autonomy in deference to the natural world, not only promotes one aspect of Wordsworth at the expense of another (225–42); it yearns, like Ferry, for a Wordsworth who never was. Hartman's "Wordsworth" turns out to be a more revolutionary figure than Ferry's, whose conflicts continually contain the germ of his decline. Yet, like Ferry, Hartman betrays an affinity with Arnold by subordinating the real to the Arnoldian "real"—to a world, that is, whose continued idealization (or, in Hartman's case, annihilation) protects the poet from his less felicitous tendencies. By contrast, in succumbing to the real or to the primacy of natural law, Wordsworth not only resigns control, according to Hartman; he paves the way for what both critics are convinced is his "anti-climax."

In the determination to privilege ideas over reality, recent critical practice has paradoxically shown that the real in Wordsworth is not necessarily a condition of the "world," but rather a condition of the "word," or another idealization. And yet, for the majority of Wordsworthians there is still a distinction between the ideas Arnold described as "alien to the very nature of poetry" and the idealizations (or applications of ideas) by which the real in Wordsworth becomes what is "really life." This naturally makes it difficult for critics to see the continuities in Wordsworth's career: that the alleged primacy of Nature and later, of God, are reflexes of the primacy of man; that Wordsworth's love of nature points continually to his resistance to it; that the love of man requires, by definition, an oppositional stance of which separation and enmity are virtual conditions.

Indeed, by distinguishing between the romantic and the anticlimactic Wordsworth, modern criticism has sometimes created distinctions where none exist and, in doing so, has eliminated another poet—the hitherto conservative Wordsworth—whose refutation or blurring of these distinctions yields a less authoritative or more ironic Wordsworth such as Ruskin essayed to describe. The undecidability, therefore, customarily a feature of the Wordsworthian in many modern accounts, and more recently in the deconstructions of Paul de Man and others, though relevant in its general skepticism about authority, is not always helpful either—since it cannot grant Wordsworth the prerogative of his undoing. As its concurrence, in fact, with canonical practice reveals, the deconstruction of Wordsworth is often grudging in its assessment, chastising Wordsworth's authority as a humanist, which it deems preferable still to the renunciation of his authority that followed.[19]

The present study, then, means not only to make a "case" for the middle and later Wordsworth, but to "unmake" Wordsworth's anticlimax by recourse to what earlier readers very pragmatically took to be Wordsworth in general. Accordingly, I begin with "their" Wordsworth: *The Excursion.* Read as the first and most visible sign of Wordsworth's decline (as well as Wordsworth's masterpiece for nearly fifty years following its publication), this poem remains a glaring account of the way certain literary values have served to diminish a poem that clearly, and brilliantly, makes no appeal to them.

The chapters following my interpretation of *The Excursion* read Wordsworth's earlier poetry to show that even there, in the very works that modern criticism contends are first-rate, the values behind such critical contentions are frequently put to test. In the "lyrical ballads" leading to "Tintern Abbey," what is often deemed evidence of a particular imagination turns out, in conjunction with Wordsworth's notion of sincerity, to be a consequence of writing at a certain juncture in response to certain imperatives. More than Leslie Brisman, who has traced the tendency on the part of the Romantics to invent a past or origin in concomitant (or gradual) awareness of its fictionality, I argue that the self constructed in Wordsworth's early poetry was virtually invented for him.[20] By the time he was at work on *The Prelude,* in fact, identity and authority customarily seen as constitutive of Wordsworth's "high" romantic phase had so literally taken on lives of their own that Wordsworth could actually continue in one direction, toward an apotheosis of self, while revealing at the same time the dispensation under which he had become a figure of authority. By the end of *The Prelude* Wordsworth is moving in two directions at once: forward toward the fulfillment of an intentional structure, and backward toward an exposure of that structure's intentionality. This exposure constitutes a deconstruction of the self; and it is a deconstruction made inevitable by the various deferments inherent and acknowledged in Wordsworth's development.

It devolves to *The Excursion,* however, and to its ostensible hero the Wanderer, both to anatomize and clarify these deferments. For the tradition-minded Wanderer, who virtually supplants the poetical self, makes *The Excursion* as consistent with *The Prelude* as that epic was consistent with the works that preceded it. The difference is that where previously this consistency abetted Wordsworth's movement toward climax, its peculiarly deconstructive freight is openly marshaled in opposition to progress (which is nonexistent in *The Excursion*), making this development, as critics have rightly determined, an anti-climax. More than a falling-off, however, "Wordsworth's anti-climax" remains an increasingly unmediated challenge to poetical authority and its various underpinnings. In *The Excursion*, not surprisingly, it is the spoken, or at least those aspects of Wordsworth's writing that formerly masked and mystified the authority of the "man speaking," that are accessory, leaving us with a text which is recounted or heard as opposed to authored, and with a poem whose other "authorities"— the Wanderer, the Solitary, the Pastor—effectively merge to justify the "Poet"'s renunciation.

Nevertheless, there is still the problem of the represented, the "life" so previously dependent on the mediation of authority that Arnold was doubtless correct in designating much of Wordsworth's poetry "the reality." In contrast to the canonical lyrics that surround *The Prelude,* asserting ever-desperately the authority of the beholder over a *particular* beheld ("The Solitary Reaper," "I wandered lonely as a Cloud," "Composed Upon Westminster Bridge," "Elegiac Stanzas"), such reality, *The Excursion* makes clear, is merely poetry. Thus, the various epitaphs enlisted by the Pastor to support his conception of the world, are not only "lives" which resist his "application of ideas"; they are lives that do so by performing another function which, as *The Excursion* is disposed finally to concede, remains intentional or idealized simply by being oppositional.

It devolves to the poems *after The Excursion,* to works universally ignored by modern criticism, to justify their marginality by making poetry adumbrational or ironic rather than representational. This transformation is managed, in part, by a recourse to religion, which stands in ironic juxtaposition to the secularized authority it supersedes. In many of these poems, moreover, there is an increased emphasis on the visible or on the world seen, which centers similarly on the absence or renunciation of authority. The conservatism of the later Wordsworth turns out to be more than simply a typology (indeed the only one available) to contest a still earlier humanism; it is a reminder, more ironically, of a culturally sanctioned authority that, suddenly foregrounded, is less seductive, less mystificatory, than its previous interiorization. Wordsworth's conservatism or anti-climax, no matter how virulent—or how problematic its various evidence—remains a challenge to culture and, as canonical practice has confirmed, to both tradition and the individual talent.

NOTES

1. *Wordsworth* (Oxford: Clarendon Press, 1923), 138.
2. Cambridge, MA: Harvard University Press, 1935.
3. "Two Roads to Wordsworth," in *Wordsworth: A Collection of Critical Essays*, ed. M. H. Abrams (Englewood Cliffs, NJ: Prentice-Hall, 1972), 4.
4. Geoffrey H. Hartman's study, *Wordsworth's Poetry 1787–1814* (New Haven, CT: Yale University Press, 1964), culminated and conclusively articulated the tendency to read Wordsworth as a poet of oppositions already prevalent in the studies of F. W. Bateson (*Wordsworth: A Re-Interpretation* [London: Longmans, 1954]), John Jones (*The Egotistical Sublime: A History of Wordsworth's Imagination* [London: Chatto and Windus, 1954]), and David Ferry (*The Limits of Mortality: An Essay on Wordsworth's Major Poems* [Middletown, CT: Wesleyan University Press, 1959]): namely, a poet whose stance to nature was more a mystification on the part of criticism than on the part of Wordsworth, whose professed love of nature was, more properly, a love of nature reconstituted and thus a tribute to the poetic imagination.
5. M. H. Abrams, "English Romanticism: The Spirit of the Age," in *Romanticism Reconsidered: Selected Papers from the English Institute*, 26–72.
6. The recent deconstruction of Wordsworth is clearly enabled by granting the poet his humanistic stance, which is observed afterwards to founder on its inherent contradictions. For example, Paul de Man's "Wordsworth and Holderlin" (in *The Rhetoric of Romanticism* [New York: Columbia University Press, 1984], 47–65) explores the way the "two tendencies" toward "infinitude" and a more human "temporality" are brought to conflict in the very instances in Wordsworth's poetry where "the moment" would be "[reconciled] with eternity."
7. Michael Timko, "The Victorianism of Victorian Literature," *NLH*, 5 (1974): 610.
8. See, for example, R. A. Foakes, *The Romantic Assertion: A Study in the Language of Nineteenth-Century Poetry* (London: Methuen, 1958).
9. Two of the most influential studies that discriminate between the Victorians and the Romantics by way of promoting the modernity of Victorianism are Jerome H. Buckley's *The Victorian Temper: A Study in Literary Culture* (Cambridge, MA: Harvard University Press, 1951), which stresses the antiromanticism of the period, and E. D. H. Johnson's *The Alien Vision of Victorian Poetry* (Princeton, NJ: Princeton University Press, 1952), which underscores the "public-private" dichotomy in Victorian writing. Studies by Albert J. LaValley, *Carlyle and the Idea of the Modern* (New Haven, CT: Yale University Press, 1968), and John D. Rosenberg, *The Fall of Camelot: A Study of Tennyson's "Idylls of the King"* (Cambridge, MA: Harvard University Press, 1973), continue to argue that the "modernity" of modernism is a "distortion" of literary history by which writers such as Eliot sought to distinguish themselves "from the all-dominating voice . . . of the nineteenth century" (Rosenberg, 1). More recently still, Carol T. Christ has explored antiromanticism as the aspect of Victorian "poetics" most visibly sustained in the

Modern period (*Victorian and Modern Poetics* [Chicago: University of Chicago Press, 1986]). In a rather curious twist, Robert Langbaum argues in *The Poetry of Experience* (New York: W. W. Norton, 1963) that romanticism is a "modern tradition," yet redefines the romantic agenda so that it is more properly a "movement toward objectivity" and thus a prelude to Victorian writing.

10. F. R. Leavis, "Poetry and the Modern World," in *New Bearings in English Poetry* (London: Chatto and Windus, 1932), 20.

11. Bloom, like most Romanticists, naturally agrees with Leavis on the primacy of romanticism in the nineteenth century (which, unlike Leavis, Bloom privileges), arguing that poets such as Browning and Tennyson were not altogether successful in following the path of their "poetic precursors." (*The Ringers in the Tower: Studies in Romantic Tradition* [Chicago: University of Chicago Press, 1971], 145–94.)

12. E. T. Cook and A. Wedderburn, eds., vol. 4 of *The Works of John Ruskin* (London: George Allen, 1903), 392.

13. Frederick William Faber, *Sights and Thoughts in Foreign Churches and Among Foreign Peoples* (London: Rivington, 1842), 626–32. It is worth remembering, of course, that Ruskin's critical theories, and the appeal of those theories to his contemporaries, were founded less on his unflagging belief in the existence of some absolute than on an ever-growing doubt, which versions of art such as Wordsworth's provoked by ostensibly allaying. For the influence of Ruskin's religious concerns on his critical writing, see especially George P. Landow, *The Aesthetic and Critical Theories of John Ruskin* (Princeton, NJ: Princeton University Press, 1971).

14. For a different view of Ruskin's stance toward Wordsworth, see Elizabeth K. Helsinger, "Ruskin on Wordsworth: The Victorian Critic in Romantic Country," *SIR*, 17 (1978): 267-91. Conceding Ruskin's enduring admiration for *The Excursion*, Helsinger nevertheless emphasizes the extent to which Wordsworth also represented a flawed, romantic way of seeing for Ruskin, where too much feeling was brought to the perception of nature. In this way, Wordsworth—though influential in helping Ruskin to define his aesthetic position—performs a merely adversary *and not* a self-reflexive function.

15. *Appreciations* (New York: Macmillan, 1910), 43, 62.

16. Although David J. DeLaura is undoubtedly right in noting the differences in Arnold and Pater's Wordsworth ("The 'Wordsworth' of Pater and Arnold: 'The Supreme Artistic View of Life,' " *SEL*, 6 [1966]: 651–67), their similarities, as even he suggests, far outweigh their differences.

17. References to Bradley's essay are to the text of "Wordsworth" in *Oxford Lectures on Poetry* (London: Macmillan, 1909), 99–148.

18. For a related, albeit different, view of this problem, see Paul de Man, "Wordsworth and the Victorians," in *The Rhetoric of Romanticism*, 83–92. According to de Man, Arnold's attack on Stephen criticizes the attempt of his contemporaries to "domesticate" Wordsworth by making him a philosopher instead of a poet. Thus, while de Man correctly emphasizes the

Victorian awareness of "a certain enigmatic aspect of Wordsworth" (84), he nevertheless narrows this aspect to pertain only to the "self-reflecting, recollecting mind" (87), or to a "condition of consciousness" whose "totality," in spite of Arnold's humanistic claims, was a function, in language, of its "ever-threatening undoing" (87).

19. The extent to which a poststructuralist approach to romanticism, in this case de Man's, reflects a nostalgia for the very humanism it opposes is examined by Tilottama Rajan in "Displacing Post-Structuralism: Romantic Studies After Paul de Man," *SIR*, 24 (1985): 451–74. Rajan's own study, *Dark Interpreter: The Discourse of Romanticism* (Ithaca: Cornell University Press, 1980) is more direct in its effort to unite a poststructural orientation with a concept of intentionality by way of allowing poetic discourse the prerogative of contesting itself.

20. See especially Brisman's chapter on Wordsworth (*Romantic Origins* [Ithaca, NY: Cornell University Press, 1978], 276–361), which underscores the "shady dependencies [of] poetic origins" on the continued "conflict of power and weakness" (279).

T W O

The Excursion

Although "more than a third of the work [was] yet to come," it is not at all fashionable these days, or even pragmatic, to insist on the centrality of *The Excursion* in Wordsworth's poetry. From Coleridge to Hazlitt to Arnold to the present day, it has become the "tradition" of Wordsworth criticism to enlist the poem as a warning sign of Wordsworth's decline or as the work of Wordsworth's "we seldom go beyond" (Sperry 35). In a way criticism has been right to accord this terminal status to *The Excursion,* since the poem, very clearly, is determined to beleaguer—to be a difficult poem—rather than to satisfy. Such difficulty is regularly attributed to the increasing use of theological ideas or, more pointedly, to an increasingly Christian posture in the poem; almost no critic will admit that the poem is difficult because it also offends or proves a challenge to readerly sympathy. It is one thing to agree jocularly with Hartman that a daily reading of *The Excursion* be administered as punishment to "those famous misreaders of Wordsworth who say he advocates rural nature as a universal panacea" (320). It is quite another thing to admit to being punished by the poem for having mystified its author into one capable of reconstituting the grounds of faith. Criticism, in short, cannot accept responsibility for *The Excursion*'s failings any more than it is likely to attribute the success of the "Intimations Ode" to the satisfaction it offers in seeing a sense of entitlement, or self-worth, defended rather than challenged.

Coleridge's disparagement of *The Excursion* helps us assess why the poem has been such a problem. Coleridge wrote to Wordsworth in 1815 that compared to *The Prelude* "the excursion, as far as it was new to me, had disappointed my expectations." These had centered on the "hope" that *The Excursion* would be "the *first* and *only* true Phil[osophical] Poem in existence" in which "the matter and arrangement of *Philosophy*" would be primary and "the Totality of a

System [would] not only [be] capable of being harmonized with, but even calculated to aid, the unity (Beginning, Middle, and End) of a *Poem.*" *The Excursion* "disappointed" because it failed to "point out . . . a manifest Scheme of Redemption" or to reconcile art to what is already an idea of life.[1]

Coleridge, it is generally argued, was disappointed by *The Excursion* because the project of which the poem remained the first real installment—the philosophical poem that in finished form was to be called *The Recluse*—was one he had conceived himself and had merely elected Wordsworth to fulfill.[2] Yet this expectable dissatisfaction must also be weighed against two complaints, which together shed light on the tautology inherent in the poem's failure to have represented what was already, in effect, "a *Poem.*" First, there is Coleridge's sense that the poem was "new" and consequently something of a shock; second, and more noticeable, is his stated preference for *The Prelude. The Prelude,* of course, was at the time unpublished and known only to members of the Wordsworth circle. Hence, Coleridge's judgment against *The Excursion,* unlike the reviews of Jeffrey and Hazlitt, remains the first criticism of *The Excursion* both to prefer Wordsworth's personal epic to its sequel, and to hold *The Excursion* in opposition to the romantic orthodoxy of its precedent and, in the projected design of *The Recluse,* its prologue.[3] The "newness," in other words, that for Coleridge remains a source of surprise necessarily recalls the familiarity of a "scheme" whose belatedness is confirmed by a conception of Nature that was already art, already an application of ideas to life, before Wordsworth failed to make it so. And indeed, Coleridge's adamance about *The Excursion*'s failure points ultimately to the poem's accomplishment— which was to render old or belated what, prior to *The Excursion,* was putatively "new."

That *The Excursion* proved more a challenge than a declension— or was a challenge simply in being a declension—Coleridge would never admit. However, for the generation following him who eventually read *The Prelude, The Excursion* occupied an altogether different place in Wordsworth's poetry. For these readers, the majority of whom did not distinguish Wordsworth's climax and his anti-climax, *The Excursion* remained, even after the publication of *The Prelude* in 1850, the poet's magnum opus. It is customary to attribute this popularity to the characteristic narrowness of Victorian orthodoxy, which not a few defenses of *The Excursion* in our time have actually contrived to emulate. Yet the literature about *The Excursion* between 1826 and 1860 indicates an altogether different picture: one in which the poem takes on an encyclopedic, or what Ruskin hyperbolically (again) termed a "thoroughly religious," function countered only by the occasional complaint that *The Excursion* is not systematic enough in offering an alternative theology or, just as infrequently, that it is not strong enough in its defense of traditional Christianity.[4] Between the extremities of tradition, on the one hand, and romanticism (as perhaps distinct from romantic poetry) on the other, *The Excursion* steers a course that throughout much of the nineteenth century is characterized by a diffuseness, or lack of a trajectory, rather than by those commitments it is simultaneously charged with failing.

Committed, in any case, to a humanistic agenda, Romanticists and Wordsworthians alike have preferred to follow the advice of Pater and others in "forgetting" poems such as *The Excursion*[5] and by forgetting in the process what *The Excursion,* more than any of the poems preceding it, remembers: that the romantic claim to difference or to "newness" is a mystification that necessarily masks the poet's affinity with an authoritarian past. For as *The Excursion* shows (and as its admirers, I believe, have always understood) the efforts, following Coleridge, to distinguish among Wordsworth's poems are efforts in the long run to save Wordsworth from himself by enfeebling him or by determining what his poetry can and cannot do. The interpretation of *The Excursion* that follows not only seeks to approximate what the Victorians, unencumbered by romantic humanism, variously saw in the poem; it seeks to reveal what Wordsworth, in earlier becoming a humanist, gradually discovered about that position.

*　*　*

No interpretation of *The Excursion,* not even one that would reconstruct the "Victorian" sense of the poem, can proceed without first considering its relationship to *The Prelude.* Posthumously published in 1850, the latter had little impact on the established consensus that *The Excursion* was Wordsworth's masterpiece. It is only in our century, again, that Coleridge's initial complaint has become legion—as we customarily reverse the relationship between a "preparatory poem" and the work that in fact made *The Prelude* a prelude.

This reversal involves more than making *The Excursion* synonymous with Wordsworth's anti-climax; it represents a restriction of the Wordsworth canon so that *The Prelude* is no longer the poem first alluded to in the preface to *The Excursion:* the "subsidiary [history]" of "the origin and progress of [the Author's] powers. . . .

to the point when he was emboldened to hope that his faculties were sufficiently matured for entering upon the arduous labour which he had proposed to himself."[6] Eschewing this decidedly tentative description, along with the more explicit complaint to Beaumont in 1805 that *The Prelude* "seemed to have a dead weight about it,"[7] students of romanticism have transformed *The Prelude* into a more forceful culmination—"a creative breakthrough" that, in Abrams' view, "amply justified Wordsworth's claim to have demonstrated original genius" and whose hero, as Karl Kroeber reads him, "is the prototype of the contemporary hero: the man who fights against his culture."[8] That these judgments are only partly accurate, or accurate insofar as they pertain to the "representational" aspects of *The Prelude,* is not the point. The point is that the excursus of *The Excursion* from all this actually reduces *The Prelude* to the subsidiary, belated and arguably unpublished status that Wordsworth accorded it, and more important, institutes a gap, a rupture, that critics as early as Coleridge have rushed to cover.

Immediately noticeable is the way *The Excursion* discredits the agenda of which *The Prelude,* as personal epic, remains the fullest representation. The poem's narrator appears as the central character of Book I only to resign his role to the Wanderer, an old pedlar of Calvinist disposition who subsequently narrates the tale of Margaret and is usually regarded as a mouthpiece for Wordsworth. Not much is generally made of this resignation, much less that the speaker just prior to his resignation is a "character of the Poet" very much like the hero in *The Prelude.* Nevertheless, by transforming the poet's role in this way—that is, allowing the "Poet" to defer to the Wanderer—Wordsworth suggests two (almost contradictory) things about the inadequacy of the poetic stance: its inability to order nature in a secularized, unorthodox way, and how, in failing, the Poet *follows* the eminently imitable example of the Wanderer. The inadequacy that the speaker initially displays in his vulnerability to the natural scene in the poem's opening cuts two ways: backward against a romantic orientation, where the will to power is now tantamount to empty posturing; and forward (or still further backward) toward a more Christian or "conventional" orientation the inadequacy of which had given rise to a more secular, if no more adequate, replacement. Although the Wanderer appears to supersede the "Poet" in the section appropriately called "The Wanderer," it is in memory and imitation of a more recent supersession, whose authority, as it were, the Wanderer merely reclaims.

Readers familiar with *The Excursion* may complain that I am making too much out of a poetical scheme that was sketched out over a decade earlier in the unpublished *The Ruined Cottage*. Yet the poem of 1797–98 (and its addendum *The Pedlar* composed in 1802) are qualitatively different from the published version in *The Excursion*. And this is evident in the figure of the Wanderer who, as E. P. Thompson describes him, "commences as a self-taught Cumbrian shepherd boy, fond of the songs of Burns [and] ends as a literary product of the Scottish kirk" (175). This trajectory, I submit, is neither accidental nor, as Thompson implies, unfortunate. Rather, it underscores the circularity and persistence of the very narrative (hence "literary product") to which Thompson's values must assign a beginning and an end. The Wanderer of 1814 is undoubtedly more Christian than the Pedlar of the 1790s. But this only connects him more forcefully to his prototype who, in either the "Poet" or the figure of Margaret, represents an equally entrenched orthodoxy where the "self," as Thompson suggests, has essentially replaced God. While the Christianity of *The Excursion* clearly adulterates the humanistic spirit of the earlier poems, it also recalls the adulteration that *is* humanism and is responsible for the Poet's default.[9]

The most noticeable index of the Poet's default in *The Excursion* is his silence, which in the aftermath of *The Prelude* serves a purpose altogether different from its function in *The Ruined Cottage*. Earlier, silence was a way to "ventriloquiz[e]" through the Pedlar en route (as we shall see) to achieving a poetic identity.[10] In *The Excursion*, however, silence both signifies and justifies the resignation of self by allowing Wordsworth to connect the Wanderer with the tragic, more subjective, figure of Margaret. Having taken it upon himself to create order independent of the customary religious and cultural guides, Wordsworth entered a situation—as he came to recognize—in which order, a desired object, made him a victim of both tradition and selfhood—and not of the chaos and mutability he had sought to order. Thus, if Book I centers on the Wanderer and the character of Margaret, it depends on the vulnerable Poet for its *raison d'être*, especially regarding Margaret, whose over-constant yearning (more evident now than in *The Ruined Cottage*) continuously recalls ideas whose "application" "life" assiduously resists.

The extent to which Man and Nature are at strife in *The Excursion* reflects, as its first lines suggest, the extent to which man has reappropriated the authority he earlier consigned to the world:

'Twas summer, and the sun had mounted high:
Southward, the landscape indistinctly glared
Through a pale stream; but all the northern downs,
In clearest air ascending, shew'd far off

A surface dappled o'er with shadows flung
From many a brooding cloud; far as the sight
Could reach, those many shadows lay in spots
Determined and unmoved, with steady beams
Of bright and pleasant sunshine interposed.
Pleasant to him who on the soft cool moss
Extends his careless limbs along the front
Of some huge cave, whose rocky ceiling casts
A twilight of its own, an ample shade,
Where the wren warbles; while the dreaming Man,
Half conscious of the soothing melody,
With side-long eye looks out upon the scene,
By that impending covert made more soft,
More low and distant! Other lot was mine;
Yet with good hope that soon I should obtain
As grateful resting-place, and livelier joy.
Across a bare wide Common I was toiling
With languid feet, which by the slippery ground
Were baffled; nor could my weak arm disperse
The host of insects gathering round my face,
And ever with me as I paced along.

    Upon that open level stood a Grove,
The wished-for Port to which my steps were bound.
Thither I came, and there—amid the gloom
Spread by a brotherhood of lofty elms—
Appeared a roofless Hut; four naked walls
That stared upon each other! I looked round
And to my wish and to my hope espied
Him whom I sought; a Man of reverend age,
But stout and hale, for travel unimpaired.
There was he seen upon the Cottage bench,
Recumbent in the shade, as if asleep;
An iron-pointed staff lay at his side. (1–37)

Admirers of *The Ruined Cottage* find little noteworthy in these lines save a "verbosity," they charge, at variance with poetry. However, just as the earlier poem derives its effect from numerous and sometimes insignificant details, so "The Wanderer" does as well. Here, the details attenuate the *concordia-discors* of the initial text—no longer a point of origin but one of departure. In line 2, for example; *The Excursion*'s Poet observes that "the landscape indistinctly glared," a revealing comment to be sure, yet never more so than in conjunction with *The Ruined Cottage*'s "uplands feebly glared" (2). The earlier description is more particular, less universal, hence a less authoritative description and less concerned with the consequences of subjectivism and the resultant enmity between the speaker and the natural world. If the speaker of *The Ruined Cottage* is affected by the natural scene, even perturbed by it, if nature is discomforting, even hostile, nature in 1798 is still nature and the Poet a representative man. Their difference is both evidence of an active universe and a precondition for their reconciliation at the poem's close.[11]

In 1814 the antagonism is more acute, the emphasis less on nature (or on nature's authority) and more on the way nature is perceived. The dissociative "but" at line 3 replaces the more conjunctive "and" of 1798, and the shadows "flung" now from "many a brooding cloud" in place of shadows "dappled o'er" (5) warn that nature in *The Excursion* either wears the Poet's face or none at all. Having failed to bring order to chaos by means of individual perception, the Poet must admit a chaos of which he is creator and victim. Hence the "brooding" clouds and "indistinct" landscape, the variousness without and, as the dreaming man points up, the vulnerability within.[12]

Part invention, part convention, even part parody, the dreaming man is the figure on whom the introductions to both poems turn and through whom their differences are readily apparent. In the *The Ruined Cottage*, which promotes the authority of nature through the pantheistic mystification of "One life," the dreamer prefigures both the Pedlar and the Poet-to-come (all three, in fact, eventually assume the same physical posture), so that any difference between the dreamer and the Poet is primarily one of mood rather than orientation. Compared to their counterparts in *The Excursion*, both men see things in similar ways and effectively share the same experience:

> far as the sight
> Could reach those many shadows lay in spots
> Determined and unmoved, with steady beams
> Of clear and pleasant sunshine interposed;
> Pleasant to him who on the soft cool moss
> Extends his careless limbs beside the root
> Of some huge oak whose aged branches make
> A twilight of their own, a dewy shade

Where the wren warbles while the dreaming man
Half-conscious of that soothing melody,
With side-long eye looks out upon the scene,
By those impending branches made more soft,
More soft and distant. (6–18)

The repetition of "pleasant" prior to the introduction of the dreaming man is an act of perception in *The Ruined Cottage,* appropriately prefacing the shared, almost Keatsian idyll that follows. By contrast, the simple insertion of a period in line 9 (replacing the conjunctive semi-colon of *The Ruined Cottage*) inaugurates a countermovement away from the dreamer—and from the Poet's ability to perceive what earlier he perceived. Thus, despite the tension that necessarily exists between the two men in the initial text, *The Excursion* significantly exacerbates matters by making pleasantness a speculation rather than an experience—the unnatural evidence of loss rather than of power. Possible only at a "distan[ce]," within the confines of some atavistic cave rather than in the unmediated presence of nature, such order remains a mixture of memory and desire, a "wished-for" end that will not be reached so long as it is the Poet's prerogative to do so. For the dreamer, by contrast, and following him the Wanderer, order is possible through a kind of arrested development: by the agency of narratives so thoroughly usurpatory that perception is rendered passive to the point of dreaming. But for the Poet, a Romantic incapable of ordering the natural world, of annihilating all that's made to a green thought, the alternative is a more pervasive annihilation, supplanting requital with desire, uniformity with difference, presence with absence.

In *The Ruined Cottage,* the differences separating the Poet and dreamer help to unite the Poet with the reader. The poet's discomfort is mostly sensory, the accessibility of which assists in the movement from isolation to community. No sooner is the Poet attacked by nature then he is distracted from that affliction by a recognition of nature's vitality. Mere physical discomfort defers to aural and intellectual fascination, which enlivens rather than subdues. The Poet hears and only then imitates nature's more active example. Likewise, the isolated ruin and the alienation its discovery provokes ("I found . . . I looked . . . I saw") are quickly overcome by the appearance of the Pedlar who, as both Nature's pride and her embodiment ("[a]s dear to me as . . . the setting sun"), provides a more human, more relational correlative to the active universe.

In *The Excursion* the Poet's authority is more pronounced, his subjectivism more thoroughgoing, so that roughly the same experience actually accentuates the gap between self and community or between subject and object. Less assimilable, things in *The Excursion* are predictably more identifiable. Where earlier "brotherhood" was demonstrated (and, with respect to the reader again, cultivated), now it is merely observable and more discrete—an independent order that the detached Poet measures simply by measuring himself. "Other lot was mine" he confesses at line 18, and with this direct borrowing from *The Ruined Cottage* comes the disclosure of his desire: a response to the distance now separating him from community, placing both in sharper relief. Wishing, hoping, and seeking have literally replaced the earlier acts of finding and recognizing because the objects upon which they seize are, for the Poet, nonexistent. Brotherhood in *The Excursion*'s first book depends entirely upon its absence, upon the discord everywhere apparent. The ruin, for instance, which in *The Ruined Cottage* seemed part of nature, is described as a "roofless hut," evoking the dual image of harmony-in-absentia, of a wished-for, therefore nonexistent, brotherhood. So, too, the abiding harmony that earlier subsumed the ruin, making it no more remarkable than surrounding nature, is firmly rejected in *The Excursion,* where the ruin is simultaneously a token of the Poet's individuation and belated proof of the not-me, the "other lot," that defines his sense of self and is defined by it in turn.

For this very reason, the Wanderer's appearance is more remarkable in *The Excursion* than the Pedlar's was in the early poem. Where the Pedlar appears in advance of being "sought," the Wanderer is presented as the Poet's "wish" ("*I* looked round / And to *my wish* and to *my hope* espied / Him whom *I* sought" [emphasis added]), whose immediate fulfillment proves the otherness, the opposition, which grounds their "fellowship." For this reason, too, the Wanderer is absolutely vital to the book appropriately titled after him, and the biography of him that follows, as necessary to *The Excursion* as it was expendable in *The Ruined Cottage.* Without the Wanderer and the vision he embodies we would not see that the Poet, and the vision *he* embodies, are equally the result of a narrative or intentional structure, whose application to the world as vision is scarcely an autonomous gesture. Indeed, the ultimate discrepancy between narrative and life as documented in Book I proves testimony to the inadequacy of narratives in general, and to the very selfhood, which is neither so autonomous nor so authoritative as we may want to believe. Although initially the obverse of the man speaking, the Wanderer is, in the manner of the speaker, evidence of the Poet's disaffection with himself and a means, in conjunction with Margaret, to justify the speaker's systematic withdrawal.

In spite of the fact that passages from *The Pedlar* eventually found their way into the "Childhood" books of *The Prelude*, critics have been right in noting the similarity between the revised version of that biography in *The Excursion* and earlier, autobiographical statements in Wordsworth's other poems.[13] Where criticism has perhaps failed has been in its determination to assign a negative judgment to the way a formerly secularized narrative becomes in the Wanderer's biography a Calvinist narrative of glorification. It is the purpose of "The Wanderer" to challenge such judgments by showing that there is no difference between a humanistic or romantic narrative (whose glorification of imagination clearly borrows from its precedent), and the Calvinist narrative whose precedent in this instance is the humanistic narrative.[14] The difference is that where the secularized narrative is already in default, it devolves to the Wanderer to show why it was destined to be so, and why, prior to humanism, it was necessary to magnify the self by some other means.

Thus, just as the "poetic spirit" in *The Prelude* is characterized in the way the "babe . . . upon his mother's breast" is permitted to sustain his "blessed[ness]" by becoming the symbolic father in whose omniscient gaze he is observed (II, 240ff.), so the Wanderer owes his grace to parentage by the Church, which conflates the roles of mother and father. The Wanderer's yearnings since childhood "that the winds might rage / When they were silent" (309–10) are not only self-fashioning in the manner of similar "visitations" in *The Prelude*; they are also self-mediating, or the result of "an habitual piety" (132) and of the environment that makes piety possible:

> The Scottish Church, both on himself and those
> With whom from childhood he grew up, had held
> The strong hand of her purity; and still
> Had watched him with an unrelenting eye.
> This he remembered in his riper age
> With gratitude, and reverential thoughts.
> But by the native vigour of his mind,
> By his habitual wanderings out of doors,
> By loneliness, and goodness, and kind works,
> Whate'er in docile childhood or in youth
> He had imbibed of fear or darker thought
> Was melted all away: so true was this,
> That sometimes his religion seemed to me
> Self-taught, as of a dreamer in the woods;

Who to the model of his own pure heart
Framed his belief, as grace divine inspired,
Or human reason dictated with awe. (427–43)

The apparent conflict here between the agency of the church and
the agency of the individual heart does not belie the irony inherent
in their interchangeability. Wandering from the mother church,
particularly in her role as mediator, the "self" becomes its own
church and teacher, making the Wanderer's religion tantamount
to self-worship or, as Wordsworth suggests, "his religion."[15]
Moreover, it is the "Poet," not the Wanderer, who makes this connection, who recognizes that just as the romantic "self" has been, for
better or for worse, a representation of God, so God, as the interchangeability of "grace divine" and "human reason" (442–43) further signifies, may be a mystification of the self which only the self
may demystify.

For the Wanderer who believes in God, who does not realize that
to serve the "Church" he must necessarily forsake it, there are no
contradictions. Rather, the "fever of his heart" is inevitably "soothed" by his decision to become a pedlar in the "perseverance" of
which (and in the performance of "kind works") he obtains "pro-
vision for his . . . wants" (412) and peace of mind:

Happy, and quiet in his chearfulness,
He had no painful pressure from without
That made him turn aside from wretchedness
With coward fears. He could *afford* to suffer
With those whom he saw suffer. (396–400)

Although it appears that the Poet is praising the Wanderer at the
Poet's own expense (the lack of painful pressure from without
contrasts implicitly with the Poet's pressure from within), it is not
because the Wanderer has succeeded where the Poet has failed; it is
rather that the Wanderer is another version of the man speaking,
whose admiration of the Wanderer is therefore ironic and self-
reflexive. That the Wanderer "can *afford* to suffer / With those
whom he [sees] suffer" (the "afford" is emphasized in *The Excursion*
where in *The Ruined Cottage* it is simply a matter of fact) suggests that
he does not suffer at all, that he has been girded by the Church (in
ignorance of its contradictions) from the subjectivism that leads to
suffering.

The Poet, for his part, understands these contradictions. Realizing that the belief in God is the belief in self, he recognizes too that the difference between him and the Wanderer is proof of their similarity. Thus, as the Poet proceeds to demonstrate through the Wanderer's account of Margaret, the ability to suffer as the Wanderer does remains a measure of the same authority, the same selfhood, by which suffering is either nonexistent and affordable, or a function of the failure of imagination to make it so.[16]

Revealing the similarities in the men who narrate it—the narrator who narrates because he can afford to suffer and the one who listens because he is already suffering—the story of Margaret is also the means by which another difference, born of the recognition of their similarity, is gradually disclosed. This difference underlies the qualitatively different function of the Margaret story in *The Excursion*. Although it focuses ultimately on the Wanderer, whose efforts at resolution continue the Poet's initial efforts to order the natural scene, the story is more immediately about Margaret. It is Margaret now who, in objectifying subjectivism, represents the Poet's growing detachment from a "self" concurrently aligned with the Wanderer.[17]

The basic details of the Margaret story are familiar to readers of Wordsworth. Abandoned by her husband Robert, who in the aftermath of famine, unemployment, and near-disabling illness joins a "troop of soldiers" out of sheer desperation, Margaret lingers "in unquiet widowhood" (908) for nine years (five in *The Ruined Cottage*) before collapsing under the crushing weight of rural poverty. Vulnerable to both nature and culture, she has no stays, social or familial, against a confusion in which one imperial affliction—blight—is supplemented by another—empire. Still, in the very way she is vulnerable to the authority of these forces, Margaret—in *The Ruined Cottage* at least—is equally in the sway of forces whose harmonizing tendencies (culminating in her reintegration in death) are meant to compensate for her individual tragedy.

In *The Excursion* Margaret's own authority and consequent self-victimization are the issue, much as they were the issue in the poem's very first lines. Margaret, it is now observed, "was a Woman of steady *mind*" (my emphasis),

> Tender and deep in her excess of love,
> Not speaking much, pleased rather with the joy
> Of her own thoughts: by some especial care
> Her temper had been framed, as if to make
> A Being—who by adding love to peace
> Might live on earth a life of happiness.

Her wedded Partner lacked not on his side
The humble worth that satisfied her heart. (544–52)

Significant in this passage, pursuant to the equation of "mind" and "being," are the phrases "excess of love" and "joy of her own thoughts," their relationship to earthly "happiness," and finally the fact that Margaret's "wedded Partner" was able to satisfy "her heart." The constituents of a particular self or "temper," these elements provide also for its particular interest. Desire (excess of love) is central to Margaret's personality as it has been for the Poet, making its satisfaction (the joy of her own thoughts) the only possible condition for a "life of happiness." And this is because the fulfillment of Margaret's narrative and measure of her completeness, like the Poet's before her, remains a "wished-for" end that, while furnished from "without," nevertheless originates within. The same holds true for Robert, who has similarly achieved his heart's satisfaction:

> She with pride would tell
> That he was often seated at his loom,
> In summer, ere the Mower was abroad
> Among the dewy grass,—in early spring,
> Ere the last Star vanished.—They who passed
> At evening, from behind the garden fence
> Might hear his busy spade, which he would ply,
> After his daily work, until the light
> Had failed, and every leaf and flower were lost
> In the dark hedges. So their days were spent
> In peace and comfort. (554–64)

That the measure of Robert's completeness is *work* does not suggest that his marriage to Margaret is inadequate; it simply reminds us that "peace and comfort" are closely related to desire, whose satisfaction is hardly continuous. While the account of Robert's disappointment is no different really from the account in *The Ruined Cottage*, the effect now is to see Robert as his own worst enemy rather than as a victim of presumably alterable conditions. In an age of the imperial self, no afflictions—natural or social—are as great as those visited upon the self by the self, vulnerable here to the ravages of desire.[18]

All the same, it remains for Margaret to demonstrate the problem frankly and unsparingly. Speaking to the Wanderer in the summer following Robert's departure, she observes:

                    I perceive
You look at me, and you have cause; to-day
I have been travelling far; and many days
About the fields I wander, knowing this
Only, that what I seek I cannot find.
And so I waste my time: for I am changed;
And to myself . . . have done much wrong. (797–803)

Margaret's knowledge of "what" she desires is exceeded only by her knowledge that the object of her desire, and the only fulfillment of her narrative, cannot and will not be regained. She realizes that she has "changed," understands the reasons for her change and, most importantly, acknowledges that she is the author of her transformation. Equally disturbing, then, is her final assertion:

But I am now in mind and in my heart
More easy; and I hope . . . that heaven
Will give me patience to endure the things
Which I behold at home. (808–11)

In light of all she has related, "[easy] in mind and . . . heart" cannot possibly mean peace of mind. What it suggests is a slackening of hope that can no more be confused with a slackening of desire than Margaret is capable of resigning her authority to "heaven." While she may resign herself to widowhood, Margaret never relinquishes her role as Robert's wife, nor does the object of her desire and the measure of her completeness ever change. "She linger[s] in unquiet widowhood; / A Wife and Widow" (908–09) and even grows to love "this wretched spot" (946), which she allows paradoxically to sink into decay.

Essentially, Margaret (far more than her counterpart in *The Ruined Cottage*) is so "self-occupied" that "all outward things / Are [to her thinking mind] like an idle matter" (832–34). Robert's significance, for instance, has less to do with his obvious attributes than with the fact that, deracinated or not, he is the object of Margaret's desire and the satisfaction of her heart. Her children are a somewhat different matter and because they fail to strike a responsive chord in their mother's "mind," they are either sent away, in the case of the eldest, or else forgotten. No matter how much everything in Margaret's life is reduced to idle matter, her real tragedy lies not in the various physical consequences of her self-occupation. It is in the fact that "matter" so requires Margaret to be animated that having once "[t]urned inward" (70), there is no way that Margaret can defend herself *or the world* from the ravages of subjectivism and desire.

To argue, therefore, that the ruined cottage is an outward token of Margaret's inwardness, still more to equate the two, deprives *The Excursion*'s first book of its significance. Surely both Margaret and her cottage are the victims of forces that are uncontrollable and disturbingly similar in their effects. But while the hut is ravaged by forces of external nature (following its neglect), Margaret's ravishment remains the consequence of her own nature. If there is a correspondence between Margaret and the ruined cottage, it is not that they are synonymous but that they are sequential, that the forces responsible for their decay confirm how "the external World" "to [the individual Mind] / Is fitted" ("Prospectus," 63, 65–66). And it is in conjunction with this rather grim inversion of the Wordsworthian notion of correspondences (and the uniformitarian ideals inherent in *The Ruined Cottage*) that we must evaluate the book's close: both the Wanderer's remarks on the consolation Margaret's tale affords and the Poet's response, before and after.

For the Poet, as I have suggested, Margaret is not only a representation of himself and thus the subject of the story of which he, not the Wanderer, is the ultimate narrator; she is simultaneously a displacement or dramatization of the poetical self, showing his reluctance (in recognition of their similarity) to continue to imitate her example by assuming the burden of narration. Hence, the Poet responds to the Wanderer's tale with a strange sense of "comfort . . . while with a brother's love" he recalls "bless[ing] her—in the impotence of grief" (958–59). Given the ambiguity about who is impotent, we must rely on the poet's "blessing"—his ability to bless—as evidence that he has evolved from Margaret's "brother" into a less aggressive, less authoritarian figure, whose power is based on self-knowledge rather than in a self whose autonomy precludes comfort.

The Wanderer is clearly a different matter and, like the subject of his story, from whom he is typically removed, it is the imposition of his authority, his application of ideas to life, that makes him vulnerable (in the Poet's eyes) to their frustration.[19] Enjoining the Poet to grieve "no more," the Wanderer continues with a preemptive conclusion:

Be wise and chearful; and no longer read
The forms of things with an unworthy eye.
She sleeps in the calm earth, and peace is here.
(969–71)

Later, of course, Wordsworth would amend this direct borrowing from *The Ruined Cottage* to include the more pietistic assertion that Margaret "had ofttimes felt / The unbounded might of prayer; and learned, with soul / Fixed on the Cross, that consolation springs, / From sources deeper far than deepest pain" (*Poetical Works*, V 39). However, as it is Wordsworth's purpose now to anatomize the failure of a more romantic or secularized imagination, it is altogether fitting that the Wanderer is observed to succeed where the Poet had earlier failed. For success of this order is by now extremely qualified; nothing about the Wanderer's reading of the world corresponds to the world as it is—neither his presumption of the Poet's distress, which is in fact "comfort," nor his generalization of "peace" from a contingent calm. Like the pietistic comments later added, which examine the problem from a more ironic vantage (given Margaret's own agnosticism), it is difficult to construe these too-abrupt judgments as Wordsworth's own. They are merely the most recent attempt to reconstitute the world according to a structure of desire.

For the Poet, Margaret, and Robert such intentionality is a matter of will and is inevitably disappointed. For the Wanderer, in contrast, who has been girded by religion, or by the culture of the Church, from the realization that "his religion" represents his imposition, such disappointment is inconceivable. Accordingly, it devolves to the Poet, in whose initial image both Margaret and the Wanderer are recreated, to connect the Wanderer's faith with his will and to be "admonished" *with the Wanderer* in a manner he simply (and indeterminately) calls "thus" (989). For "thus" at this point is nothing less than *The Excursion* thus far, during which the Poet has been admonished by Margaret, by the Wanderer, and most importantly, by an affinity with both figures sufficient to recall their failure to heed their own exempla.[20]

* * *

The remaining eight books of *The Excursion* recount a four day journey during which the Wanderer and a noticeably withdrawn Poet next encounter the Solitary, a former revolutionary disillusioned by both personal and political disappointments, and the Pastor, who endeavors with the Wanderer to "correct" the Solitary's "despondency." That this correction is more asserted than demonstrated, or recounted in such a way that it is only asserted, is often cited as a liability in the poem. Still, it is clear, if only on the evidence of Book I, that such liabilities are very much in keeping with the general scheme: unlike "growth" in *The Prelude*, progress is not progress in *The Excursion*, but a series of doublings or repetitions.

As the Wanderer begins by repeating the Poet (who is already a repetition of Margaret), so the Solitary continues by repeating the Wanderer, whose orthodoxy he reiterates, and reiterating, deconstructs. "Religion," which is imposed on the Wanderer in such manner as to be "self-taught" is no less an imposition for the Solitary, whose more secularized, more romantic beliefs are equally predetermined. The difference is that while the Solitary's narrative is purely one of "desire," founded on the promise of a "world where," he suggests, "hope and memory [are] as one" (III, 418), the Wanderer is disposed to privilege his Christian faith as if its value were independent of his desire, hope, and memory. In recounting the Solitary's involvement in the French Revolution following the deaths of his wife and children, the Wanderer finds it nearly impossible to "trace the change" or to "tell / That [the Solitary] broke faith with those whom he had laid / In earth's dark chambers, with a Christian's hope!" (II, 261–63). The assumption that the Solitary is still Christian is an important irony, for in a way he is. And this is shown in the Wanderer's disappointment, which reveals, by parallel example, that the broken faith he describes is really a kept faith: a fidelity to "hopes," which in both the Wanderer and the Solitary are demonstrably self-born.

It remains the Solitary's role (as it had earlier been the roles of both the Poet and Margaret) to emphasize this doubleness by disclosing the authoritarianism endemic in his more secularized position. In the same way that the Wanderer's Calvinism makes it impossible for him to accept his own authority as a perceiving subject, so the Solitary's authority in "colour[ing] objects to his own desire / As with a Lover's passion" (II, 292–93) reflects (unbeknownst to the Wanderer who makes this observation) how little these desires are his own. Just as "Society became," in the Solitary's words, "my glittering Bride" (III, 754), so these very prospects— based, as they are, on a continued appropriation of woman by man—are consummations consumed by the very "society" or culture the Solitary would transform.

The most telling instance of this consummation is the Solitary's vision of "glory beyond all glory" at the close of Book II. Climaxing the story of an "aged Pensioner," the vision is neither about the community's rescue of the old man nor the Solitary's experience of community. As the experience confirms, the Solitary is as removed from the community as the lost man:

A single step, that freed me from the skirts
Of the blind vapor, opened to my view
Glory beyond all glory ever seen
By waking sense or by the dreaming soul! . . .
The Appearance, instantaneously disclosed,
Was of a mighty City without end!
Fabric it seemed of diamond and of gold,
With alabaster domes, and silver spires. . . .
The vapours had receded, taking there
Their station under a cerulean sky.
O, 'twas an unimaginable sight!
Clouds, mists, streams, watery rocks and emerald turf,
Clouds of all tincture, rocks and sapphire sky,
Confused, commingled, mutually inflamed. (860–90)

The uniqueness of this vision, which the Solitary achieves only by departing from his immediate community, is ironically so familiar, even so trite an evocation of the sublime, as to cast aspersions on his autonomy. Although different undoubtedly from the experience of other members of the party, the language describing this "sight" is less than original. Quite literally "an unimaginable sight," it remains so in the way all imaginings, according to the poem, are unoriginal: that is, subsumed, like the Solitary's millenarian hopes, by a structure of desire (or in this case Biblical history) that must culminate in an ending without end. As a result, the Solitary's larger "despondency," as his reaction to the sight confirms (" 'I have been dead . . . / And now I live! Oh! wherefore do I live?' " [910–11]), owes comparatively little to the particular events to which it is attributed: the deaths of his family and his disappointments in both France and America. Like Margaret's despair or the Poet's bafflement early on, such despondency obtains from the failure of vision to persist, or from the failure of the actual to accommodate an intentional structure.[21]

This point is reiterated even more dramatically in the ensuing sections of *The Excursion* devoted to the "correction" of the Solitary's despondency. Where it has been the Solitary's purpose to expose the cultural legacy inherent in individual authority, it becomes the Wanderer's purpose, in his role as culture's minister, to grant his own authority the status of conventional wisdom. The difference is that the Solitary is now vulnerable to the inadequacy of the actual, whereas the Wanderer remains protected from the actual and can afford to suffer for his failure to see how the conceptions of the real in which he professes faith are effectively, if only provisionally, his own." While the Solitary exposes the tradition in individual talent, the Wanderer demonstrates the individuality or subjectivism that tradition in his case fortuitously masks.

Not realizing, of course, the proximity of the Solitary's dilemma to his own orientation, the Wanderer begins his task of "correction" in Book IV ("Despondency Corrected") by misconstruing the source of the former's despondency, and worse, by actually offering its source as the solution: the "[o]ne adequate support" for the "calamities of mortal life" is "an assured belief / That the procession of our fate, howe'er / Sad or disturbed, is ordered by a Being / Of infinite benevolence and power" (IV, 10–15). The Solitary, of course, is already a believer, albeit one who has modified the Wanderer's conception by wresting authority from the "Being" of whom the latter speaks. Thus, the Wanderer's persistent efforts in Book IV to distinguish "intense / And overconstant yearning" (171–72) from "belief / In mercy carried infinite degrees / Beyond the tenderness of human hearts" (186–88), not only create false distinctions by privileging such "etherial hopes" (135) over "yearning"; they reveal that the authority in whom the Wanderer believes is effectively himself—a yearning subject—raised to a higher level.

By construing the Wanderer and the Solitary as adversaries in a "true spiritual debate" (Hartman, *Wordsworth's Poetry* 300), we overlook their peculiar kinship as well as the way each of them, in the presence of the other, gradually becomes his own adversary. As his inability to correct the Solitary's "despondency" confirms, the Wanderer does less to remedy the Solitary's problem than to "correct" or reinscribe "despondency" as a tendency toward secularization that shows the spirit of this age to be much like that of any other. Correspondingly, the presence of the Solitary lets us appreciate how, in comparison to him, the Wanderer is a case of arrested development, whose recourse to the "infancy of society" as an exemplary moment in history is an outward token of his inability to grow up. Hazlitt, who had other problems with *The Excursion*, had particular praise for the Wanderer's recourse to "distant Ages of the world" (860), and it is easy to see why.[22] The distant ages that the Wanderer represents are clearly forerunners of the present—worlds in which man, like the Solitary, "perceive[d], / Within himself, a measure and a rule" (820–21) and

> heard, upon the wind, the articulate Voice
> Of God; and Angels to his sight appeared,
> Crowning the glorious hills of Paradise. (647–49)

Yet for Wordsworth, whose quarrel is with the present and its repetition of the past, the Wanderer is not the spokesman that Hazlitt took him to be; his nostalgia, if anything, suggests an imperviousness to the continuity of history. Accordingly, the models whom the Wanderer enjoins the Solitary to imitate in Book IV, those who most successfully keep desire within the parameters of hope, are "infant minds"—those of the "Shepherd-lad" and the "curious child" listening to a seashell. Committed, like the Wanderer, to a narrative not explicitly his own, the Shepherd boy is a mere conduit of that narrative. The sundial that he inscribes "[o]n the green turf" (815) proves a pattern rather than a reappropriation; although "Imagination . . . is left free," it is also "girded by a zone / That, while it binds, invigorates and supports" (832–38). The willingness to serve, to subordinate himself to history, girds the shepherd from the dissonance of modern times and ensures that he "lives and breathes / For noble purposes of mind [as] his heart /Beats to the heroic song of ancient days" (843–45).

The curious child by the seashore is a more dramatic instance of the reversal where, in the regressive orientation, faith is demonstrably a reversal of subject and object. "[A]pplying to his ear / The convolutions of a smooth-lipped Shell," the child, as the Wanderer describes him, hears "murmurings from within . . . whereby . . . the Monitor expresse[s] / Mysterious union with its native Sea" (1144–51). Although "within" in this description means "within the shell," the oceanic feeling of infancy within the "infant mind" suggests the relationship of "the Universe itself . . . to the ear of Faith" (1152–53), and so offers a parallel that is remarkably ironic. Rather than proving the Wanderer's point, the example leagues faith and hope with infantile wish fulfillment, which originating "within" does not yet distinguish greatest things from least suggestions.

When, however, the Wanderer turns to the Solitary, and from the infancy of society to the present, it becomes clear that the years that have brought the philosophic mind have also brought a distinction between subject and object (and a concomitant transfer of authority) sufficient to compel the faithful to "build up greatest things / From least suggestions" (*Prel.* XIII, 98–99). The Wanderer is perfectly correct in asserting that the Solitary "[a]dore[s]" and "worship[s] . . . when [he] know[s] it not" and is otherwise "[p]ious beyond the intention of [his] thought" (1159–60); for, as in the case of the two children, the acuity of this observation is in the way the Wanderer, in virtual imitation of the Solitary, is deconstructive beyond his own intention. "Has not the Soul, the Being of your

Life," he queries, "[r]eceived a shock of awful consciousness"
(1167–68); without awaiting a reply, he ventures an example:

> —the solitary Raven, flying
> Athwart the concave of the dark-blue dome,
> Unseen, perchance above the power of sight—
> An iron knell! with echoes from afar
> Faint—and still fainter—as the cry, with which
> The wanderer accompanies her flight
> Through the calm region, fades upon the ear,
> Diminishing by distance till it seemed
> To expire, yet from the Abyss is caught again,
> And yet again recovered! (1189–98)

This example illustrates, of course, that "Nature" necessarily "fails
. . . to provide impulse [to glorify the Eternal]" (1176–80) or to
"yield / Far-stretching views into Eternity" (1199–1200). An ordi-
nary sensory perception, the flight of the raven prompts an unex-
ceptional—though in this case mystified—image that coordinates
sight and sound with an empirical narrative tracing the progress of
an object that has disappeared from view. "Beyond the [speaker's]
intention," the use of the experience as evidence of "awful consciousness" reiterates (following an inadvertent reference to the
bird as "solitary . . . wanderer") what we have learned from the
Solitary: such "shocks" are at once projections of the self upon the
world, and projections of another world or structure of desire upon
the self. Imparting "[a]uthentic *tidings*" of the "invisible" (1155, my
emphasis) such experiences, the Wanderer shows, are tidings of
both self and cultural occupation, and so testify to what he appropriately deems "the Mind's *excursive* Power" (1275).[23]

* * *

Ah! how different is it to render account to ourselves of ourselves and
to render account to the public of ourselves.[24]

Emerson on The Excursion

With virtually half *The Excursion* still remaining, Wordsworth has
said all he is going to say about the bedfellowing of tradition and
individual authority and their bearing upon the romantic stance he
has abandoned. And yet, were it not for the last five books of the

poem, it is doubtful that *The Excursion* would have received either the approbation it garnered for nearly half of the nineteenth century or the critical opprobrium of the twentieth. The poem's second half does more than supply additional proofs of argument and continued justification of the Poet's withdrawal; it provides a release from proof, or from authority of the usual kind, that in turn becomes the basis for a different kind of art. This retreat from poetical authority, even such self-reflexive authority as the Poet now maintains, begins early in Book V ("The Pastor"), where the Poet offers "fervent thanks / For [his] own peaceful lot and happy choice":

> A choice that from the passions of the world
> Withdrew, and fixed me in a still retreat,
> Sheltered, but not to social duties lost,
> Secluded, but not buried; and with song
> Cheering my days, and with industrious thought,
> With the ever-welcome company of books
> By virtuous friendship's soul-sustaining aid,
> And with blessings of domestic love. (48–57)

It may be that compared to Margaret, whose abandonment and early death comprises Book I, or to the Solitary, whose "wandering course of discontent" has claimed attention since then, the Poet is indeed happy. Yet, in terms of *The Excursion* thus far, such happiness is more accurately a sleep and a forgetting, whose proper index remains the self-portrait of the speaker in the "ever-welcome company of [his] books." Situated comfortably in his own library, the Poet has not merely made himself over into a reader; he has negotiated this transformation by becoming a poet who actually imitates the reader. He may have forgotten what it means to be the Poet, but he transfers the meaning to us so that we represent what—in declining to an auditory role—the Poet has aspired to all along. Despite the fact that *The Excursion* is represented as the Poet's recollection of a five day journey, this framework had finally to be de-emphasized if only because memory, however passive, is itself a tyranny to which the reader, among others, has been subject. In accepting the invitation to "forgetfulness" (and "sleep") at the end of the preceding book (1335), Wordsworth does two related things: he foists memory upon the reader and, in so doing, ensures a new seat of his authority. By retaining authority in this particular way—that is, *through* the reader—Wordsworth simultaneously forgets that authority and, in the words of Wallace Stevens, moves "beyond forgetfulness" to "a cure of ourselves."[25]

Trading roles with the reader in Book V rings a change upon the earlier exchange in Book I, where the Poet deliberately assumed the auditory role. That exchange placed the Poet in consort with an implied if somewhat passive reader and placed both of them in opposition to the Wanderer. The exchange in Book V, by contrast, comes at a juncture when the futility of that opposition is such that the kinship of the Solitary and the Wanderer extends to include the ostensibly excluded or opposed Poet. Wordsworth, it is important to note, waits until *after* the Wanderer has unwittingly "corrected" or deconstructed the Solitary's "despondency" before instituting this shift of alliances. Like his kinship to Margaret, whom the Poet blesses retrospectively with a "brother's love," his nostalgia for the Wanderer, the Solitary, and more recently, for a reader in his own image, had also to be forgotten. Thus, it devolves to "forgetfulness" to enable "a new syntax" in which the "syntax of . . . description" will, in Earl Wasserman's axiom, be consistent with that of "the moralizing."[26]

Contriving through "varying degrees of negation" to "impe[l] the reader to seek" what Wolfgang Iser has called "a positive counterbalance," forgetting in *The Excursion* creates a need that neither the Poet nor his poem can strictly satisfy.[27] Having previously resigned his roles both as the Wanderer's "tried Friend" and as "silent" partner to the poem's other characters, the Poet must go one step further: he must resign that resignation, or "withdr[aw]" from his withdrawal to a state of peace and happiness. Only by returning to his library can the speaker resign his authority sufficiently for the reader to set the poem "in motion," eliciting "responses" (as Iser calls them) which may or may not be those "awaken[ed]" in the speaker himself (275).

Yet lest the reader resist this "awakening," or be tempted to take the part of one or another of the poem's participants, Wordsworth provides a further provocation in the unlikely figure of the Pastor. His appearance at this juncture reminds readers of their prerogative to reject all of the poem's orientations for the sake of something better. The Pastor is introduced, presumably, to answer the Solitary's complaint by "giv[ing] us, for our abstractions, solid facts; / For our disputes, plain pictures" (V, 623–24). Yet the failure of his epitaphs in Books V, VI, and VII to answer the Solitary in the way the Pastor wants simply repeats earlier failures: the Wanderer's inability to apply his abstractions to Margaret's life; and the failure in Book II of the Solitary's "vision" to persist. Thus, the Pastor's epitaphs place a counter, representational pressure on their "subjects" by making them more idealized, more a testimony to the prevalence of desire, than they need be. Whether it is the widower who refuses to remarry (*Excursion* 301–04); or the botanist who "[l]oved fondly, truly, fervently . . . and sued in vain" (*Excursion* 254–57); or Ellen who, like Margaret, is deserted (*Excursion* 294–97); or another widower whose memory of his wife is rekindled, then disappointed, by a granddaughter who dies (*Excursion* 338–41); or the "patriarch" who survives his entire family including grandchildren (*Excursion* 321–23); or the ill-requited Priest who, even in old age, "[r]etained a flashing eye, a burning palm, / A stirring foot" (*Excursion* 314–20); or the initial "matron" whose "anxious duty" it was to will her "Husband home" (V, 747–49), the Pastor transforms all the inhabitants of the churchyard, as a group—and more importantly as an argument—into "scattered subjects which compose / Earth's melancholy vision" (V, 931–32).

Indeed, to the extent that the sixteen epitaphs in *The Excursion* demonstrate Wordsworth's theory of the genre in his famous essay on the subject, it is by counterexample: they perform an "anatomical" rather than "monumental" function in their "dissect[ion of] the internal frame of mind" (*Prose Works*, II 57). The epitaphs in *The Excursion* are truly "negations," reminding the reader that while life may often be subjected to various idealizations, the representation of life requires a different kind of memorial—and memory—less in keeping with the intentions of a given authority.[28] This memorial is broached in the concluding books of *The Excursion*. Here, Wordsworth changes the timescape, grounding it more deliberately in the present, and renews attention to sensory particularity. Together these changes yield a provisional movement away from ideas and from the representation ideas inform.

The movement, in fact, is so provisional that it is not until the rather prosaic description of the Pastor's house and surrounding landscape in Book VIII that we discover a temporality distinctly different from the surrounding poem. This transformation is immediately followed by a description of the Pastor's wife and daughter, which is followed by a description of his son and a friend:

> suddenly the door
> Opening, with eager haste two lusty Boys
> Appeared,—confusion checking their delight.
> —Not brothers they in feature or attire,
> But fond Companions, so I guessed, in field,
> And by the river-side—from which they come,
> A pair of Anglers, laden with their spoil.

One bears a willow-pannier on his back,
The Boy of plainer garb, and more abashed
In countenance,—more distant and retired.
Twin might the Other be to that fair Girl
Who bounded tow'rds us from the garden mount.
Triumphant entry this for him!—for see,
Between his hands he holds a smooth blue stone
On whose capacious surface is outspread
Large store of gleaming crimson-spotted trouts;
Ranged side by side, in regular ascent,
One after one, still lessening by degrees
Up to the dwarf that tops the pinnacle. (552–70)

Already the sense of time has begun to dissolve: what begins as a recollection suddenly becomes, with the painstaking and deliberate description of the boys' catch, a transcription of events at the advent of their perception. The description of the trout has a non-grammatical, non-representational immediacy consistent with a tendency to describe rather than narrate. This tendency similarly informs the preliminary and seemingly fastidious distinction between surmise ("so I guessed") and actuality.

Nevertheless, it is not until the ninth (and concluding) Book that the meaning of *The Excursion*, which simultaneously proves an obstacle to meaning, is disclosed. The discourses of the Wanderer and the Pastor are interrupted by a chance event:

Forth we went,
And down the Valley on the Streamlet's bank
Pursued our way, a broken Company,
Mute or conversing, single or in pairs.
Thus having reached a bridge, that overarched
The hasty rivulet where it lay becalmed
In a deep pool, by happy chance we saw
A two-fold Image; on a grassy bank
A snow-white Ram, and in the crystal flood
Another and the same! Most beautiful,
On the green turf, with his imperial front
Shaggy and bold, and wreathed horns superb,
The breathing Creature stood; as beautiful
Beneath him, shewed his shadowy Counterpart.
Each had his glowing mountains, each his sky,
And each seemed centre of his own fair world:

Antipodes unconscious of each other,
Yet, in partition, with their several spheres,
Blended in perfect stillness, to our sight! (436–54)

To call this moment an interruption of "happy chance," of
course, is to overlook the fact that its vision of completeness confirms what the Wanderer and Pastor have asserted all along and
what the Solitary, at an earlier time, similarly believed: that life
in the here and now is informed by a larger, providential scheme.
Yet it is on this very proximity, on the way sight supports these
surrounding narratives, that its difference (or deferral) turns.

Accordingly, Wordsworth not only presents the sight as an accidental interruption; he allows it to be interrupted in turn by the
Pastor's wife, who exclaims:

"Ah! what a pity were it to disperse,
Or to disturb, so fair a spectacle,
And yet a breath can do it!" (455–57)

Reflecting on both the sight and the Wanderer's discourse, she
confesses to "sometimes feel[ing]"

That combinations so serene and bright,
Like that reflected in yon quiet Pool,
Cannot be lasting in a world like ours,
To great and small disturbances exposed." (470–75)

It may be too ironic to view such words as final testimony against her
husband's (and the Wanderer's) authority; but the wife's ostensible
appreciation of the Wanderer ("I love to hear that eloquent old
Man / Pour forth his meditations . . ." [462–63]) seems also to
refute the evidential function of the fair "spectacle" she admires.[29]
For the "spectacle" *in her rendering* no sooner forges than it disperses
any link between the real world, with its various "disturbances," and
a more stable, heavenly "antipode."

Indeed, this counterevidence becomes even clearer when one
looks at the original version of the ram scene composed for, and
then deleted from, Book VIII of *The Prelude* in 1805. Here, amid
recollections summoned to counteract those of his residence in
France, Wordsworth recalls that

Once coming to a bridge that overlook'd
A mountain torrent, where it was becalm'd
By a flat meadow, at a glance I saw
A twofold image; on the grassy bank
A snow-white ram, and in the peaceful flood
Another and the same; most beautiful
The breathing creature; nor less beautiful
Beneath him, was his shadowy counterpart;
Each had his [glowing] mountains, each his sky,
[And each seem'd centre of his own] fair world.
A stray temptation seiz'd me to dissolve
The vision,—but I could not, and the stone,
Snatch'd up for that intent, dropp'd from my hand.[30]

The central difference of this passage, commensurate with the fact that it is the speaker alone who now observes the sight, is the urge to dissolve the vision. The urge, however, is suppressed, as well as expressed, for several reasons. First, Wordsworth wants to appropriate the view as a "vision." The experience, as the existence of the text verifies, is valuable as an act of mind that makes both poets—both the poet speaking and the Poet acting—"each . . . centre of his own fair world." Yet because this same text was suppressed, another possibility presents itself: the situation in *The Prelude* is precisely one in which the mind's appropriative powers are sufficiently legible to make the seer, like the Solitary, subject to his own story. Like the text itself, the urge to disrupt the vision is suppressed in the recognition that, having usurped the real for the sake of vision, the mind has put itself in harness.

In making the wife victim of a prior intentionality, similar to the Poet himself—whose vow "ne'er [to] . . . forget" the "moment" (588) is an index of how he has already magnified it—Wordsworth lets *the reader* reformulate what he himself had surmised ten years earlier: certain sights, however fleeting, however a part of unidealized reality, provoke the mind to idealization. The symmetry of the sight and the order it instills, particularly the pictorial character of the experience, clearly record an object less innocently than intentionally found. This is evident both in the structuring of the sight as picture and in its strategic placement in *The Excursion.* More than in *The Prelude,* then, where this tack is also abandoned, Wordsworth means to reveal the connection here between an artistic strategy and what, in either the example of the Poet who refuses to forget the sight, or his companions who are variously united in their understanding of the spectacle, is always a compelled activity. No matter how we interpret this "spectacle," in other words—whether as a subversion of human authority (as Wordsworth's strategy seemingly warrants) or as a promotion of some other orientation (as the various characters allow)—its opposition, as it were, is never far removed from its function. And this is echoed very nicely in the way the Pastor's wife privileges the sight by anticipating its disruption. Like the poets of *The Prelude* and *The Excursion*, whose oppositional stances are likewise responsible for preserving the sight, the resistance of the wife to her own resistance reveals in the end how "accidentality" (to use Coleridge's term) is in this case a version of intentionality.[31]

Consistent, then, with the contrary disposition of being an "[un]-forget[table] . . . moment," the ram scene at once breaks from an intentional structure yet fails, by that break, to be anything but intentional. And this accords with the circumspection of *The Excursion* as a whole, whose various orientations—most immediately the discourse into which the ram scene is deposited—are sufficiently repetitive *and* contradictory to make the poem, in Ruskin's altogether apt description, "thoroughly religious." Such qualities are not much appreciated by critics, who in the fashions of literary history enjoin us not to read Wordsworth as he can be read: as a poet whose early and late poetry, and ostensibly radical and conservative phases, are necessarily continuous. Having lost the ability to read Wordsworth as the non-Arnoldian Victorians read him—with a measure of irony—we no longer see that it is in the "thoroughly religious" nature of Wordsworth's poetry that religion and poetry are mutually contested. Nor do we see how the ironized Poet of *The Excursion* completes a trajectory in Wordsworth's development, in allowing for an enfranchisement of the reader, that Wordsworth's earlier poetry, the so-called "poetry of sincerity," necessarily (and ironically) forestalled.

NOTES

1. E. L. Griggs, ed., vol 4. of *Collected Letters of Samuel Taylor Coleridge* (Oxford: Clarendon Press, 1959), 570–76. In Coleridge's plan, *The Excursion* was to have concluded with "a grand didactic swell on the necessary identity of a true Philosophy with true Religion, agreeing in the results and differing only as the analytic and synthetic process, as discursive from intuitive, the former chiefly useful as perfecting the latter—in short, the necessity of a general revolution in the modes of developing & disciplining the human mind by the substitution of Life, and Intelligence . . . for the

philosophy of mechanism . . . which idly demands Conceptions where Intuitions alone are possible or adequate to the majesty of Truth" (575).

2. For a reading of *The Excursion* as central and of a piece with the remaining parts of *The Recluse* (including *The Prelude*), see Johnston, *Wordsworth and "The Recluse"*, 237–329. Johnston envisions *The Recluse* as a project that (while stimulated by Coleridge) is natively Wordsworthian. My view is rather different. In making *The Excursion* a crossroads in Wordsworth's career, I regard the poem as fundamentally removed from *The Recluse*. Furthermore, I regard the other—generally unpublished—*Recluse* fragments, particularly *Home at Grasmere* (1800–06) and "The Tuft of Primroses" (1808), as more peripheral to Wordsworth's development. In *Home at Grasmere*, which was completed shortly after *The Prelude*, Wordsworth reasserts the "paternal sway" (821) and "internal brightness" (886) (MS. B, in *Home at Grasmere* [*The Cornell Wordsworth*], ed. Beth Darlington [Ithaca, NY: Cornell University Press, 1977]) whose conjunction had been tantamount to demystification in *The Prelude*. As a result, their recovery in *Home at Grasmere* marks an effort (as I see it) to accommodate some other agenda. Similarly, the attempt in "The Tuft of Primroses" to reconstitute the Church by making a "Temple" (544) of nature and a Saint of the self— in short to ground a theology in individual perception—corresponds to Coleridge's ultimately conservative program. By the same right, the "Prospectus" to *The Recluse*, which initially concluded *Home at Grasmere* yet was published in the Preface to *The Excursion*, remains, for all its bravado, somewhat doubtful about this program and about Wordsworth's ability to fulfill it. The use of "would" in "I . . . [w]ould chaunt, in lonely peace, the spousal verse / Of this great consummation" (55– 57), in place of either "will" or "want," accords nicely with the suggestion (also in the "Prospectus") that "Paradise," far from being regainable in the way Coleridge would have wanted Wordsworth to demonstrate, is a "history only of departed things, or," worse, "a mere fiction of what never was" (47–51). (References to the "Prospectus" and "The Tuft of Primroses" are to the texts in E. de Selincourt and Helen Darbishire eds., vol. 5 of *The Poetical Works of William Wordsworth*, 2d ed. rev. [Oxford: Clarendon Press, 1959].)

3. Jeffrey's oft-cited review of *The Excursion*, beginning "this will never do," first appeared in the *Edinburgh Review*, 24 (November, 1814), 1–30. Hazlitt, whose "Character of Mr. Wordsworth's New Poem, The Excursion" was published in *The Examiner* (August 21, 28, and October 2, 1814), 541–42, 555–58, 636–38, clearly agreed with Jeffrey that the poem was too didactic, and that Wordsworth had allowed an "intense, intellectual egotism [to swallow] up every thing." Nevertheless, Hazlitt conceded that *The Excursion* was "an original and powerful performance" containing "many splendid passages." (P. P. Howe, ed., vol 19 of *The Complete Works of William Hazlitt* [London: J. M. Dent, 1933], 9–25.) For further discussion of the differing views of Coleridge and Hazlitt with respect to Wordsworth, see Roy Park, *Hazlitt and the Spirit of the Age* (Oxford: Clarendon Press, 1971), 206–36.

4. For discussions of the reception of *The Excursion* in the nineteenth century (especially its favor over *The Prelude*), see Herbert Lindenberger, *On Wordsworth's "Prelude"* (Princeton, NJ: Princeton University Press, 1963), 271–75. Ruskin's comment on the poem (which Lindenberger cites) is from a letter of 1851 (*Ruskin's Letters from Venice: 1851–52*, ed. J. L. Bradley [New Haven, CT: Yale University Press, 1955], 92). As a further index of the poem's popularity, at least two reviewers praised Tennyson's *In Memoriam* in 1850 for being similar to *The Excursion:* both in the ability to "address itself to its own time" and to expose "with equal zeal and efficacy, the poisonous weeds that are germinating in all directions, and choking the good crop" (Stuart F. C. Niermeier, "*In Memoriam* and *The Excursion:* A Matter of Comparison," *The Victorian Newsletter*, 41 [1972], 20–22). More generally, the summary comments in N. S. Bauer's recent bibliography, *William Wordsworth: A Reference Guide to British Criticism*, 1793–1899 (Boston: G. K. Hall, 1978), show quite clearly that *The Excursion* was not only regarded as Wordsworth's great poem in the Victorian period, but that there was great reluctance on the part of most of its admirers to define its greatness. At the same time, "romantic" critics such as De Quincey and John Wilson continued throughout the nineteenth century to criticize Wordsworth's poem on a variety of grounds, including its apparent lack of an alternative theology.

5. *The Renaissance* (New York: Mentor, 1959), xiv.

6. *The Poetical Works*, vol. 5, 1–2. References to *The Excursion* are to the 1814 version in *"The Excursion," Being a Portion of "The Recluse," A Poem* (London: Longman, Hurst, Rees, Orme, and Brown, 1814). Citations from *The Ruined Cottage* are from the version of the poem in MS. D. in *"The Ruined Cottage" and "The Pedlar"* (*The Cornell Wordsworth*), ed. James Butler (Ithaca, NY: Cornell University Press, 1979). References to *The Prelude*, unless otherwise cited, are to the 1805 version of the poem in *The Prelude: 1799, 1805, 1850*, ed. Jonathan Wordsworth, M. H. Abrams, Stephen Gill (New York: W. W. Norton, 1979).

7. E. de Selincourt, ed., *The Letters of William and Dorothy Wordsworth: The Early Years, 1787–1805*, 2d ed. rev., Chester Shaver (Oxford: Clarendon Press), 594.

8. Abrams, *Natural Supernaturalism* (New York: W. W. Norton, 1971), 74; Kroeber, *Romantic Narrative Art* (Madison: University of Wisconsin Press, 1960), 90.

9. According to both James A. Butler ("The Chronology of Wordsworth's *The Ruined Cottage* after 1800," *SP*, 74 [1977]: 89–112) and Mark Reed (*Wordsworth: The Chronology of the Middle Years, 1800–1815* [Cambridge, MA: Harvard University Press, 1975], 22, 665–66), "The Wanderer" was not composed, that is, adapted from *The Ruined Cottage*, until 1809 and possibly as late as 1812. Yet of the recent discussions of "The Wanderer"—Reeve Parker, " 'Finer Distance': The Narrative Art of Wordsworth's 'The Wanderer,' " *ELH*, 39 (1972): 87–111; Neil Hertz, "Wordsworth and the Tears of Adam," *SIR*, 7 (1967): 15–33; Peter F. McInerney,

"Natural Wisdom in Wordsworth's *The Excursion*," *TWC*, 9 (1978): 188–99; and Peter J. Manning, "Wordsworth, Margaret and the Pedlar," *SIR*, 15 (1976): 195–220—only Manning treats "The Wanderer" as a later poem. The others view *The Excursion* version in much the same light that critics have traditionally viewed *The Ruined Cottage* and thus, intentionally or not, treat Book I independently as a late eighteenth-century poem. By contrast, Hartman's reading of *The Ruined Cottage* (*Wordsworth's Poetry*, 135–40) takes a more modern, less uniformitarian view of the early poem and is much closer in many ways to my reading of Book I.

10. Complaining about Wordsworth's use of the Wanderer as a mouth-piece, Coleridge charged him with "ventriloquizing through another man's mouth" ("Table Talk" [July 21, 1832], *The Complete Works of Samuel Taylor Coleridge*, ed. W. G. T. Shedd [New York: Harper and Bros., 1860], 403).

11. The uniformitarian or pantheistic view of *The Ruined Cottage* detailed by Jonathan Wordsworth (*The Music of Humanity: A Critical Study of Wordsworth's "Ruined Cottage"* [London: Nelson, 1969], 102–53) and others shows Margaret's tragedy neutralized by a larger, more subsuming vision of natural calm. Concurrently, the poem's other participants—the Poet-narrator, the Pedlar-narrator, and the implied reader—are gathered, by the sympathy and compassion their concentricity affords, into a collective, essentially selfless self. Tragedy, in other words, is continuously opposed in *The Ruined Cottage* by the presence of a larger whole of which all the participants, but particularly Margaret, are "functioning parts." Other readings of *The Ruined Cottage* along these lines include: Paul D. Sheats, *The Making of Wordsworth's Poetry, 1795–98* (Cambridge, MA: Harvard University Press, 1973), 137–87; H. W. Piper, *The Active Universe* (London: Athlone Press, 1962), 106–23; Bateson, 123–45; Jones, 78–83, 87–90; and Philip Cohen, "Narrative and Persuasion in *The Ruined Cottage*," *Journal of Narrative Technique*, 8 (1978): 185–99. See also James A. Averill's comments interspersed throughout *Wordsworth and the Poetry of Human Suffering* (Ithaca, NY: Cornell University Press, 1980).

12. Many critics, including Jonathan Wordsworth and Reeve Parker, have noted the Poet's vulnerability, but it is viewed generally as a rhetorical device rather than an index of the poet's state of mind, indeed of the romantic state of mind, in the shadow of its development.

13. In the 1805 version of *The Prelude*, II, 416–34, and III, 122–27, 141–47, 156–57 derive directly from *The Pedlar*.

14. I am grateful to the late James D. Boulger for pointing out to me the Puritan-Calvinist resonance in the Wanderer's "perseverance" (I, 362) and, more importantly, in its salutary results—all products of a theology that divides Puritan experience into stages remarkably similar to those of the Wanderer's life. For further discussion, with reference to *The Excursion*, of the futility of separating "religion and Romanticism for very long" (384), see Boulger's *The Calvinist Temper in English Poetry* (The Hague: Mouton, 1980), 414–22.

15. Although allusions to the Pedlar's Christianity appear as early as

1804, their ironic purport would only increase over time. As I show in subsequent chapters, Wordsworth had by the time of *The Prelude* (around 1804) grown less assured of his own authority as a human subject, which had burgeoned in the preceding two years. For discussion of certain aspects of narcissism in Wordsworth's poetry, particularly as they bear on the relationship of selfhood to parentage, see Michael H. Friedman, *The Making of a Tory Humanist: William Wordsworth and the Idea of Community* (New York: Columbia University Press, 1979), 1–118; Richard J. Onorato, *The Character of the Poet: Wordsworth in "The Prelude"* (Princeton, NJ: Princeton University Press, 1971); and, with special relevance to my argument, Barbara A. Schapiro, *The Romantic Mother: Narcissistic Patterns in Romantic Poetry* (Baltimore: The Johns Hopkins University Press, 1983), 93–129.

16. In an altogether different argument, which allows nonetheless for an ironic dimension in *The Excursion,* William Howard ("Narrative Irony in *The Excursion,*" *SIR,* 24 [1985]: 511–30), argues that the narrator of the poem "speaks without the constant approval of his author" (524). Adopting a view of the poem that accepts the Wanderer's wisdom over and against that of the other participants—one that sees little difference, for example, between *The Ruined Cottage* and the version of that poem that became Book I—Howard continually diminishes the Poet for his "unimaginative description" of various phenomena (523), thereby restricting Wordsworth's irony to a very small part of the poem. My sense of the ironic dimension of *The Excursion* accords more with David Simpson's poststructural view of irony in *Irony and Authority in Romantic Poetry* (London: Rowman and Littlefield, 1979), where it is a means by which the reader is authorized to complete the "hermeneutic circle."

17. For a related view, see Susan J. Wolfson, *The Questioning Presence: Wordsworth, Keats and the Interrogative Mode in Romantic Poetry* (Ithaca, NY: Cornell University Press, 1986), 93–130; Wolfson stresses the "problematic kinship" of the poem's participants, both in Book I and later.

18. Although Simpson emphasizes *The Excursion's* link to Wordsworth's earlier poetry in its particular challenge to urbanization, he nevertheless observes that "any unified (or reified) image of the ideal country life is pre-empted in this poem," most notably "by the dramatic form itself, which invites us to regard each interpretation of events as the property of speakers with specific interests and priorities" (*Wordsworth's Historical Imagination,* 195).

19. See, again, Wolfson (*The Questioning Presence,* 109–15) who, in contending with the arguments of many of the poem's commentators, stresses the inconclusiveness, indeed the interrogative pressure, in the Wanderer's assertions.

20. See Simpson, *Wordsworth's Historical Imagination,* 201–02: "That [the memory of Margaret's fate] produces not just acceptance but 'happiness' seems to suggest a disjunction between the events as seen by others (including the troubled narrator) and as received by the Wanderer. It is by no means clear that the Wanderer has passed his first test in trying to convince

others . . . of the sufficiency of faith as an answer to the problems of earthly life."

21. I am indebted for my conception of romantic narrative to Paul de-Man's poststructural critique of romantic intentionality in "Intentional Structure of the Romantic Image." For the more humanistic approach to romantic narrativity, which de Man's analysis sets out to deconstruct, see both Harold Bloom, "The Internalization of Quest Romance," in *Romanticism and Consciousness*, 3–23, and Geoffrey H. Hartman, "Romanticism and 'Anti-Self Consciousness,' " in *Romanticism and Consciousness*, 46–56.

22. Unlike Coleridge, whose program for *The Recluse* involved the reconciliation of conventional theology with the more romanticized notions of subjectivism and imagination, Hazlitt's interest in *The Excursion*, particularly its recourse to "the religion of ancient Greece," was based on the way Wordsworth used the past to justify or otherwise describe the present: specifically, the "intercourse of imagination with Nature" and "the habitual propensity in the human mind to endow the outward forms of being with life and conscious motion" (*Complete Works*, vol. 19, 13). Thus by 1814, Hazlitt's agenda (and expectations for Wordsworth) were more humanistic than were Coleridge's. For a detailed analysis of Hazlitt's reading of *The Excursion*, and of the way Hazlitt's preoccupation with the poet's sublime selfhood "brings him closer to Bradley, and his successors in our own day, than to any nineteenth-century critic of Wordsworth," see David Bromwich, *Hazlitt: The Mind of a Critic* (New York: Oxford University Press, 1983), 158–85. Although Arnold can also be credited with having appreciated Wordsworth's genius along lines not unlike these, Bromwich is right to emphasize the persistence of Hazlitt's vision

23. See Wolfson, *The Questioning Presence*, 119–25, for another argument against Book IV's success in allegedly correcting the Solitary's despondency.

24. Ralph H. Orth and Alfred R. Ferguson, eds., vol. 9 of *The Journals of Ralph Waldo Emerson* (Cambridge, MA: The Belknap Press of Harvard University Press, 1971), 123.

25. "The Rock," in *The Collected Poems of Wallace Stevens* (New York: Alfred Knopf, 1954), 526.

26. *The Subtler Language* (Baltimore: The Johns Hopkins University Press, 1959), 184. The problem in the later eighteenth-century poem that Wasserman addresses in his chapter "Metaphors for Poetry" (169–88) is generally endemic to *The Excursion* thus far, in which there has been a "bifurcation" between the natural and the moral, or between what de Man, speaking of a similar problem, calls the "earthly" and the "celestial" ("Intentional Structure," 75). This problem is made manifest in the flight of the raven in which "Nature" is required, according to the Wanderer, "to glorify the eternal" (IV, 1176–80).

27. *The Implied Reader* (Baltimore: The Johns Hopkins University Press, 1974), xii. Iser regards this search for a "counterbalance" as a means to force the reader "to take an active part in the composition of [a work's]

meaning," which is precisely, I believe, what Wordsworth has in mind in *The Excursion*. Since Iser's study involves the role of the reader in fiction, "negations" for him are a means to force the reader to question social norms and regulations. Here, "negations," though equally leagued with human culture, are of a more metaphysical nature.

28. For a related argument, see Paul H. Fry, "The Absent Dead: Wordsworth, Byron, and the Epitaph," *SIR*, 17 (1978): 413–33. Although Fry contends that both "the part of *The Excursion* that was written in 1810" and the appended "Essay" seek equally to "modify, if not to undermine, the traditional polarity of the seen and the unseen in churchyard literature," he insists nonetheless that "the typical gestures of both the poem and the essay are not really incarnational or symbolic" but metonymic: "Wordsworth's epitaph writing is metonymy, the trope in which aspects of perception are made contiguous but not identical, and which exposes rather than conceals the temporality of written experience" (418–20). This "exposure," then, the way the Pastor's epitaphs *resist* his symbolizing intentions as a writer, aptly characterizes their function in the poem and, as David Bromwich perspicaciously observes, the function of the poem as a whole. Following the example of the epitaphs, according to Bromwich, "we may have to regard *The Excursion* itself as one enormous 'illustration' the connection of which with its own moral remains uncertain throughout" (*Hazlitt*, 170).

29. See Simpson, *Wordsworth's Historical Imagination*, 209: "Under the spell of the Wanderer's living voice, the Pastor's wife can convince herself that she sees and feels as he does; but without that living voice even she has her doubts." In a sense, then, it is the living voice that provokes those doubts even as it allays them.

30. E. de Selincourt, ed., *"The Prelude" or Growth of a Poet's Mind*, 2d ed. rev., Helen Darbishire (Oxford: Clarendon Press, 1959), 581. It is interesting to remember—particularly in light of the self-contesting nature of this gesture—a similar incident in Book IX of *The Prelude*, in which the "Poet" realizes that he is not part of the French Revolution. Sitting amid the ruins of the Bastille, he recalls having "gathered up a stone, / And pocketed the relick in the guise of an enthusiast; yet, in honest truth, / Though not without strong incumbencies, / And glad—could living man be otherwise?—/ I looked for something which I could not find, / Affecting more emotion than I felt" (65–71). For a different reading of the two ram scenes, in which the *The Excursion* version is deemed inferior for its verbose religiosity, see Stephen J. Spector, "Wordsworth's Mirror Imagery and the Picturesque Tradition," *ELH*, 44 (1977): 100.

31. James Engell and W. Jackson Bate, eds., *Biographia Literaria*, no. 7 of *The Collected Works of Samuel Taylor Coleridge* (Princeton, NJ: Princeton University Press, 1983), vol. 2, 126. It is fitting, moreover, that Coleridge's complaint about "*accidentality*" as "contravening the essence of [Wordsworth's] poetry" is made with particular reference to *The Excursion*, whose descriptive passages could be better rendered "by half a dozen strokes of [a draftsman's] pencil, or the painter with as many touches of his brush"

(126–27). Coleridge is undoubtedly to right to seize upon this aspect of *The Excursion,* but what is even more relevant is his unwitting exposition of the threat—or, if you prefer, the counter-intentionality—that "accidentality" belies.

Sincerity and Selfhood in
Early Wordsworth

The custom of assuming that Wordsworth was a "poet of sincerity" and that sincerity was among the principal features of his romanticism began, not surprisingly, with Wordsworth himself. In the Preface of 1802 Wordsworth justified the poet's need to be faithful to himself by defining that need as a fidelity to his audience. Yet it is clear from the Preface that these needs are only provisionally synonymous or, to use Coleridge's term, "desynonymous." Speaking of the poet's ability to "conjur[e] up in himself passions, which . . . do more nearly resemble the passions produced [in the reader] by real events," Wordsworth in effect discriminates between what the poet feels and what "other men are accustomed to feel themselves." The poet enjoys a "greater readiness and power in expressing . . . those thoughts and feelings which, by his own choice, or from the structure of his own mind, arise in him without immediate external excitement."[1] A difference in degree—a "greater promptness to think and feel"—in fact becomes by degrees a difference in kind: the poet shows a "greater promptness to think and feel *without immediate external excitement*" (my emphasis [*Literary Criticism* 54]). Although Wordsworth is quick to add that these feelings are still the "general passions and thoughts and feelings of men" (*Literary Criticism* 54), no amount of qualification can cover his sudden distinction between the particular, individual poet and his collective, dependent readership.

   That this transparent separation from the reader has remained unquestioned for nearly two centuries is itself an interesting critical issue. For in addition to showing the complicity between Wordsworth the critic and Wordsworth criticism, it illustrates posterity's need to promote what even Wordsworth knew better than to say outright: there *is* a difference between the poetic stance on the one hand and a representative, or sincere, position on the other.[2] Why this difference has been promoted for as long as it has may be best explained by its effects, which are surprisingly unambiguous. By enshrining Wordsworth as a poet of sincerity, modern criticism has avoided the more vexing problem of dealing with two Wordsworths: a poet like "other men," and a poet sufficiently "greater" than other men to be unlike them.[3] Criticism has not yet considered the possibility that sincerity and selfhood may be contingently linked in Wordsworth, that differences in degree imply differences in kind. Nor has criticism shown clearly enough how these latter differences of kind are a response to still other imperatives of which differences of degree are already an important measure. When Wordsworth defines the "Poet" as a "man speaking to men" (*Literary Criticism* 48), is he arguing simply for a concord between his status as a poet and his status as a man? Or is it more that the character of the poet, vacillating between exemplary and representative status, requires an audience—an "Other"—in whose image he is somehow defined? Do the poet and his audience share a fundamental affinity? Or is their affinity only one of relation?

My aim in this chapter will be to address these questions in certain of Wordsworth's earlier poems, up to and including "Tintern Abbey," in order to show that sincerity in Wordsworth was both sporadic and by its nature short-lived. Sincerity, I will demonstrate, was an accidental stage during which Wordsworth became a poetical self—a product of his writing—prelusive to becoming a romantic self with a more unique, less traceable identity. More than anything, the ideal where in being true to himself he was being true to all men enabled Wordsworth to serve himself with the general assistance of an audience. The imperatives, indeed, which led first to a *relationship* between the "man speaking" and the "men" he was addressing led inevitably to a relationship based on difference, making sincerity, in the end, a virtual condition of its dissolution.[4]

My reading of Wordsworth draws on two fashions of literary history: a conventional or humanistic literary history which holds that romantic poetry succeeds in representing a self by disengagement from what Lamb, again, termed the "past century"; and a poststructural or "new" literary history which contends that the "self" in romantic poetry is largely a fiction mystified by the very language with which the Romantics kept faith with the past. That there was a movement in English literature we can call "romantic," occurring at a particular interval with a discrete agenda, there is little doubt—just as there is little doubt that Wordsworth eventually wrote of a self in whose authenticity he utterly believed. At the same time, however, there is much to suggest that this self was wholly written as, and was the product of, an interchange with a hypothetical reader. In being the "strong poet" Harold Bloom describes, the writer whose unique place in literary history remained a function of his equally unique identity as a practicing poet, Wordsworth (as even Bloom allows) had first to identify with *something* of which he then became a reflex.[5] As a poet, Wordsworth would not always accommodate this peculiarly deconstructive anatomy. Nevertheless, it is possible (following the Preface of 1802) to trace the conditions of self-representation, beginning with the obligations to society, to the differences in kind, or obligations to the self, that eventually developed.

If in 1797–98 Wordsworth has no greater purpose than to write, only by being "a man speaking to men" is he able eventually to fashion a stance toward the world. His self-fashioning thus seems a reaction to two different, if related, imperatives—the commitment to individual expression that Trilling calls "authenticity" (and historians have variously termed "sensibility"), and to the "uniformitarian" imperative which held that all men were fundamentally the same.[6] Unable as an expressive subject to be anything but that (in the manner, say, of either *An Evening Walk* or *Descriptive Sketches*), Wordsworth proceeds to do the next best thing; he becomes like all men by making his audience into a version of the subject. This involves more than simply creating an audience in the subject's image or creating the taste, as Wordsworth would later say, by which the poet can be enjoyed. It entails, more dynamically, the reciprocal creation of a reader in the image of what the poet himself *becomes* in the act of reading. The "implied reader" described by Wolfgang Iser in his various studies is for Wordsworth, then, an *inferred* reader whose identity, while dictated by the poet's, also preexists his. An implied reader, in the formulation of Iser and others, is created by the author, and is authorized by him; the inferred reader, in a more symbolic function, is always there and is a model to whom the author need also conform.[7] Thus, the reader is at times a figure whom the poet sanctions in two ways: the reader is his listener and, in the reader's capacity as Other, the prototype for the "man speaking."

By way of clarifying my position further, a comparison with Charles Rzepka's recent treatment of otherness and identity in Wordsworth (*The Self as Mind* 1–99) is most helpful. Citing Wordsworth's well-documented tendency to solipsism, originating in the early loss of both parents, Rzepka argues that Wordsworth's concomitant need of an "Other" (in the Lacanian sense) chiefly to confirm his identity as an embodied person is both impetus for and the scene of his major poetry. Here, in what are often poems of "encounter" ("Resolution and Independence," "Tintern Abbey," the "Discharged Soldier" episode, etc.), Wordsworth invariably enlists an Other as a way to self-authentication. Sometimes Wordsworth will incorporate the Other only to "preempt" the latter's "responses to his presence"; at other times he will "appropriate the Other in his own scenario"; and finally, Wordsworth will sometimes "characterize the Other in such a way as to assure himself he is recognized properly" (71).

Few will dispute the validity of the self-Other interaction as Rzepka describes it, either in Lacanian terms or, as he demonstrates, in the post-Kantianism by which the Romantics elaborated the *cogito* of Descartes and Locke. What is more problematic about his interpretation is its conflation (or confusion) of Wordsworth's "constitutional" and "professional" dispositions (51). If Wordsworth were constitutionally in need of an Other—and there is no reason to doubt this—then he was able *as a poet* to satisfy that need immediately. Writing, regardless of how private and discrete, was writing to a reader—to an Other, real or imagined—making poetry a solution to the very problem Rzepka describes. Rzepka runs something of a risk in making poetry conform to a historically provable disposition when, as the very act of writing shows, poetry involves a reconstitution of "constitution" sufficient to indicate the influence of literature on life.

In Wordsworth's case this influence may be described as twofold: as a way to "get even" with circumstances that left him in need of recognition by some authority, and as a means, consequently, by which the poet is left vulnerable to the agency of getting even. This latter agency, to borrow Rzepka's formulation, is reflected in the way the poet becomes that "Other"—or authority—whose recognition the act of writing ensures. To be a *man* speaking to *men* involves not only the creation of an audience by act of speaking; it involves, as Wordsworth's earlier poems confirm, the creation of a "Poet" by creation of an Other in whose image the poetical self (as distinct from the "constitutional self") is simultaneously fashioned.

The twinning of poet and reader, pursuant to an identity which the poet will claim, is especially apparent in "Simon Lee, the Old Huntsman, with an incident in which he was concerned."[8] Unlike the later version of the poem, which is at once coyer and more authoritative in its exposition, the initial version of "Simon Lee" is

clearly an attack on the social conditions leading to Simon's abandonment. Thus, it comes as something of a surprise for the reader
to discover that he or she has been participant in the very order
attacked. Far from remaining an enlightened respondent—or an
implied reader compelled to share the poem's concern—the reader
of "Simon Lee," as the speaker eventually describes him or her, is a
"gentle reader" (75) and thus implicated in the social order the
poem criticizes. The doggerel manner of the opening stanza, which
implies no reason to take the poem or its subject seriously, is only a
prelude to the irony of the succeeding stanza, which gives the
reader every reason to reverse that initial impression:

> A long blue livery-coat has he,
> That's fair behind, and fair before;
> Yet, meet him where you will, you see
> At once that he is poor.
> Full five and twenty years he lived
> A running huntsman merry;
> And, though he has but one eye left,
> His cheek is like a cherry. (9–16)

The highly rhetorical emphasis on perception and on the (partially
blinded) object of readerly perception ("you see / At once that he
is poor") has the double effect of enlightening the reader and, in the
aftermath of the innocuous first stanza, of diplomatically admonishing the reader for having to be enlightened.

But this, it turns out, is only preliminary to a more severe
catechism. After recounting the details of the old huntsman's deracination, whose criticism of the social order is inescapably clear
and virtually incontestable, the speaker turns once more to the
reader and credits him or her, rather sarcastically, with having
waited patiently in the expectation that the speaker, like Simon, will
fulfill *his* designated role as minstrel:

> O reader! had you in your mind
> Such stores as silent thought can bring,
> O gentle reader! you would find
> A tale in every thing.
> What more I have to say is short,
> I hope you'll kindly take it;
> It is no tale; but should you think,
> Perhaps a tale you'll make it. (73–80)

The peculiarly "savage irony" of this rebuke (in Heather Glen's description) has the effect of almost daring a "reading" of what will follow. Unlike the poem's second stanza, whose ironization of the first was retroactive, the ironization of what has followed subsequently wages contest now with a very palpable and sympathetic radicalism.[9]

The poem's concluding anecdote, which recalls Simon's tearful gratitude for the speaker's performance of a simple task, is important, then, for two reasons: for its challenge to the reader, whose radical reading or interpretation has been put in question; and for the speaker's interpretation, which is offered, by way of closure, *in propria persona*:

> —I've heard of hearts unkind, kind deeds
> With coldness still returning.
> Alas! the gratitude of men
> Has oftener left me mourning. (101–04)

If these final lines do, in fact, provide a less mediated access to the "poet," it is not by excoriating a social system that makes one man dependent on another's largesse; rather, it is in their imitation of the reader, whose "tale," in effect, has already replaced the previously ironic ballad. The concluding lines, which appear only to express a radical sentiment shorn of all irony, reveal, at the same time, an identity born of the ironization of irony. And this is clarified by the preceding anecdote, the "reading" of which now precedes and thereby glosses the speaker's reading.

On the one hand, of course, the tale, like the preceding poem, is about the speaker's concern and the (comparative) generosity elicited by his concern. Yet the tale is also preeminently about the teller, whose service to Simon is recounted so as to expose the former's callousness. It is not enough for the speaker to remember how "vainly" Simon had laboured at removing a root; instead, he must counterpoint the futility of this endeavor (which he allowed to continue for too long) to the heroic (and "vain") disposition of his "proffer'd aid" (92):

> I struck, and with a single blow
> The tangled root I sever'd,
> At which the poor old man so long
> And vainly had endeavour'd. (93–96)

That the speaker's feat achieves a certain representational felicity by rhyming with Simon's failure, reveals, in ways that only *the reader* can appreciate, how the speaker's art recapitulates the dominant order in its putatively gracious treatment of Simon. Consequently, the ensuing and concluding lines, where the speaker offers his summary observations on the "coldness" of "kind deeds," are both belated—in repeating what has already been read—and yet proleptic by representation of a "new," morally circumspect consciousness independent of the artistic apparatus.

The presence of an implied reader, therefore, who earlier imitates the speaker as a concerned citizen, is not nearly as important for Wordsworth's purposes as the presence of an inferred reader, whom the poet or more properly the "poetical self" ultimately imitates. The inferred reader, to be sure, is created by the poetry. But the peculiar inferability of this reader—specifically, the ability both to anticipate and follow the poetical self in reading against the speaker's tale—necessarily figures the reader's autonomy. Although the reader remains subject to coercion in "Simon Lee," the reader nevertheless subjects the "poet" to his or her influence—to an *identity* which, as the latter's influence on the reader concurrently shows, the poet is increasingly assimilating.

Similar exchanges occur in both "The Thorn" and "We Are Seven." In the former, the "poet" reverts to the persona of a gossipy guide whose refusal to draw conclusions places this responsibility with the reader. The speaker of "The Thorn" is less a distinct fiction than a provisional mask for a personality that cannot escape expression. But personality is masked so sufficiently in "The Thorn" that it is the reader, and not the "poet," who first takes the expressive risks in surmising what happened to Martha Ray. Indeed, it is so impossible to read "The Thorn" without making these surmises that the question is not whether the reader is being coerced, but why is the reader being manipulated by a heart in hiding? The answer is that coercion and concealment are interdependent. Coercing the reader not only gives the "poet" a way to express his own personality indirectly; it is a way ultimately for him to imitate a figure in whose image both he and the reader are effectively created.

An almost identical escape to personality or to poetical selfhood transpires in "We Are Seven," where the reader must actually join the poet in hiding. As in previous poems the speaker of "We Are Seven" is a subterfuge, who has been directed in this instance to contest the belief of a "little Cottage Girl" in the immortality of her dead siblings. In the course of their exchange, however, the reader—who is positioned initially as a detached observer—finds himself or herself less in alignment with the young girl whose plight merits sympathy, and in greater proximity to the material-istic speaker:

> "But they are dead; those two are dead!
> "Their spirits are in heaven!"
> 'Twas throwing words away; for still
> The little Maid would have her will,
> And said, "Nay, we are seven!" (65–69)

In giving the little girl the last word, Wordsworth also wrests it from her by allowing the reader's response, in effect, to supersede it. Resuming the speaker's part, the reader is exposed to an intelli-gence about himself or herself which differs from the intelligence in "Simon Lee" in that it is textual (i.e., provoked by the text) rather than explicitly inscribed. Moreover, it resembles the intelligence of "Simon Lee" in the way the reader is disabused by the poem of former beliefs—specifically the belief in providence. It is impor-tant, then, that this awareness or disabusal not be a condition of the poem proper, but that it transcend inscription in implying a greater authority whose example the reader imitates. For unlike the implied reader, who emerges as a function of the text, the inferred reader represents a model here to which the implied reader and poet mutually conform.

Coerced in these lyrical ballads into imitating some other exam-ple, the reader is also imitable, commensurate with the identity he or she foreshadows. The most alluring of Wordsworth's traps turns out not to be the one he creates for his reader; it is the identity that develops from making the reader into a second self. The synon-ymity with his audience that Wordsworth sought yielded almost immediately to a reflexivity by which the poet could do no more and no less than resemble his reader. Thus "uniformitarianism," the belief that the poet and his audience were fundamentally alike, remained the sanction paradoxically by which Wordsworth was driven to refute it. Only by imitating an inferred reader, that is, was Wordsworth also removed from his audience *to* an identity in which difference—not similarity—would remain paramount.

* * *

To recognize the paradoxical way this deferral works, we need only examine *The Ruined Cottage*, which inhibits identity by resisting the

uniformitarian imperative.[10] In the version of this poem subsequently published as Book I of *The Excursion,* the meaning of this
deferment—the similarities linking the otherwise disparate figures
of the Poet, the Wanderer and Margaret, and the ostensibly opposed doctrines of Calvinism, pantheism and humanism—is (as we
have noted) disclosed. In the earlier versions, Wordsworth is led by
the imperatives of his vocation into contradictions which, failing to
be resolved, can only anticipate the use to which they are later put.
For failure now to serve himself as he was able in "Simon Lee,"
Wordsworth serves neither the speaker nor his audience in *The
Ruined Cottage*—all of which may explain why a poem often acknowledged as perhaps the finest of the poet's early achievements
was denied a place in *Lyrical Ballads.* In ultimately making the
speaker of *The Ruined Cottage* exemplary, Wordsworth makes his
example impossible to follow. As a result, the role of representative
"man" devolves to Margaret, the poem's narrative subject, who is as
removed from her narrator, Armytage the pedlar, as the speaker is
finally removed from the inferred reader and, by turns, an inferable identity.

This is not initially the case. In the well-known introduction added to the poem in 1798, the consolidation of "Poet" and poet into a
poetical self is typically abetted by the way the reader is implicated in
"their" partnership of loss. Here, the Poet-narrator does not state
that his walk across the "bare wide Common" (19) was difficult in the
summer heat; he confesses it, effectively securing the reader's sympathy. While the mention of the "dreaming man" (14) in this introductory section suggests at least two ways of looking at the world,
the act of reading supplies only one way of seeing. When the
speaker confides at last that his "lot" differs from that of "[the
dreamer] who on the soft cool moss / Extends his careless limbs"
(10–11), the propriety of this confidence cannot be attributed
simply to the speaker's "greater promptness to think and feel . . .
the general passions and thoughts . . . of [other] men." It is in fact
the other way around: "other men" have been empowered in
reading to think the particular thoughts and feel the particular
passions of the "man speaking." The unattributed description of
"embattled" nature (6) does not gain a subject until *after* the description of the dreamer, who "[w]ith side-long eye looks out upon the
scene . . . [m]ore soft and distant" (16–18). In other words, even
before the Wordsworthian speaker claims the enmity that afflicts
the world as his own perception in his own poem, the reader is
already mocked by the dreamer for failing to see things otherwise,

for having accepted as real a fallen state wherein strife, not ease, is the order of being. The effect of the Poet's admission that his "lot" (18) also differs from the dreamer's is less a revelation for the reader than a vindication: a sense of having found—in the very speaker of the poem—a kindred spirit.

This interchange, whereby the reader is made a prototype for the poetical self, corresponds to the pattern of much of Wordsworth's early poetry. Why was it prefixed to *The Ruined Cottage?* Did Wordsworth wish to focus on the reader for the purpose of ministering next in the guise of Armytage, who narrates the story of Margaret? Or is it that Wordsworth wished to draw attention to the poetical self (with assistance from the reader) so as to avoid confusion with Armytage, who in earlier drafts had all but usurped the Poet's role? Wordsworth seems to be doing both things; and characteristically these agenda are opposed. By distinguishing himself from his reader at this juncture in the poem—that is, after the introduction—the Poet merely cancels the "other lot" to which he has previously laid claim. Thus, it is the Poet, more than the poem's reader, who is ministered to by Armytage, for it is the Poet who, by aligning himself with an inferred, differentiated reader in the introduction, effectively forfeits the right to be anything but that differentiated self. By joining the *implied* reader, then, as he does subsequently (or as he had done in the initial draft) in becoming a merely silent respondent to the Pedlar's narrative, the Poet eschews the *inferred* reader's assistance in sustaining an identity. And this makes the Poet, more than the reader, acutely vulnerable to the narrator who follows.

Most critics would argue that the opposite has taken place: that Armytage generally prevents the Poet from disclosing anything further that might jeopardize his affinity with the implied reader— whose part, it is assumed, the Poet takes throughout.[11] But this does not explain why Wordsworth added the introduction after all. If it was the poet's intention to transform the reader or to affect the reader's orientation toward life, then this is not really served by forcing the reader to follow what, after the introduction, is an increasingly inscrutable example. It is likely that Wordsworth was doing something different by the introduction, using it to show what the remainder of *The Ruined Cottage* is *not:* an occasion that will allow him either to sustain an identity or to be representative.

In the same way that the Poet is initially representative in recreating himself in the image of other "men," so Armytage is exemplary in recreating a self—Margaret—to whom he in turn is a counterpoise. The subject of the Pedlar's story is by default the subject of the poem—if only because, unlike the Poet, Margaret remains unaffected by the Pedlar in art as in life. If Margaret is vulnerable to anyone, it is to herself: like the Poet in the introduction, she is shown to have been her own worst enemy. This is why Armytage's "wiser mind," which rejects "foolishness of grief" (118–19), nevertheless enables the reader to share Margaret's "impotence of grief" (500). For what Armytage's "story" of Margaret recalls is the universal sympathy that had existed earlier between what, in aftermath, are *three* distinct participants: the character of the Poet, the reader, and the poetical self. It is not that there is no sympathy in *The Ruined Cottage*. It is that such sympathy as the reader experiences in the end protests its disruption, which begins with the Pedlar and with the relinquishment simultaneously of the speaker's inferable identity. So long as Margaret remains the chief repository of "other"-ness in *The Ruined Cottage*, Armytage remains her representer, and the Poet their silent witness, the link between the Poet and Margaret (though implied) is more tentative by far than that between Margaret and the reader.

The tenuousness of the Poet's link to Margaret is confirmed at the conclusion when the implied links dissolve and the reader must ponder the Poet's remarkable metamorphosis into the old man's "fellow-travelle[r]" (41). Having learned apparently to "read / The forms of things with [milder interest]" (510–11, 502), the Poet derives comfort at last from the phenomena that earlier oppressed him: from "sorrow and despair, / From ruin and from change, and all the grief / The passing shews of being leave behind" (520–22). These, asserts Armytage, are an "idle dream" (523) and the Poet's parting perception shows that he concurs:

> By this the sun declining shot
> A slant and mellow radiance which began
> To fall upon us where beneath the trees
> We sate on that low bench, and now we felt,
> Admonished thus, the sweet hour coming on.
> A linnet warbled from those lofty elms,
> A thrush sang loud, and other melodies,
> At distance heard, peopled the milder air. (526–33)

While "we" refers to the Poet and the Pedlar, it also recalls the dreaming man in the revised opening, who also saw things "more soft and distant" and whose "careless" ease is here repeated. The only participant, therefore, not explicitly of this society (which even "people[s] the . . . air") is the reader. And it is for the reader that "we" has been employed.

Has the Poet actually discovered something in his interval of silence? Or has he, as his silence signifies, become someone else? The answer, as usual, lies with the reader, toward whom the conclusion of *The Ruined Cottage* is directed with its veiled threat of social expulsion. If, in the poem's opening paragraph, the reader is confronted with his or her fallen nature, then the threat of social expulsion (which we normally associate with comedy) is consistent now with the restoration of calm in the poem. The only problem is that *this* has already happened to Margaret, whose consignment to the grave is quite literally a precondition for peace: "She sleeps in the calm earth," observes Armytage, "and peace is here" (512). An additional expulsion would likely undermine this "peace" especially since such "balance," as Northrop Frye theorizes, must come "from the audience's side."[12] That the reader is thus threatened or otherwise instructed in how to avoid expulsion remains a problem— rather than a means to inclusion. For while the Poet is initially isolated as that "other" figure whom the reader represents, the Poet is still more "other" as the reader's "representative": his concluding reflections are inappropriate both to his experience in *The Ruined Cottage* and to the experience of reading it. In characteristic accord with Margaret, then, who is in the "calm earth," the self conceived in the revised introduction of *The Ruined Cottage* is laid to rest in the "body" of the poem.

* * *

The two poems in the 1798 *Lyrical Ballads* that are most clearly poems of sincerity are "Lines left upon a Seat in a Yew-tree" and "Lines written a few miles above Tintern Abbey": a status indicated not only in the way they virtually enclose the 1798 volume, but also in the way they make the occasion of their reading, their very textuality, the occasion for achieving a provisional union between the "man speaking" and those who, in listening, are written upon and transformed into a society of selves.

The first of these, the "Yew-tree" lines, follows the trajectory of "Simon Lee" by literally creating a self in public. Like the actual "lines," which are "left" in search of a reader, Wordsworth's first offering in *Lyrical Ballads* is typically in search of an author too, both of whom are "found" in the act of reading. Following his accustomed strategy of displacement or disappearance, the speaker asserts control by adopting the mask of a sententious epitaphical

guide, whose persona is then stripped away. Yet unlike "Simon
Lee," where the poet himself dissolves the mask, the persona in
"Lines" dissolves only by readerly consent. This dissolution,
whereby the speaker becomes that subject of whom he speaks,
marks a revelation on the reader's part, whose part the speaker only
then assumes.[13]

It would be difficult to imagine a more disorienting beginning.
Restraining the reader in an apparent gesture of solicitude ("—Nay,
Traveller! rest"), the speaker proceeds to divest the natural scene of
all beauty in the very act of praising it:

> what if here
> No sparkling rivulet spread the verdant herb;
> What if these barren boughs the bee not loves;
> Yet, if the wind breathe soft, the curling waves,
> That break against the shore, shall lull thy mind
> By one soft impulse saved from vacancy. (2–7)

The rhetorical questions do not describe the landscape. They diminish it. And because the reader is charged with answering them,
the diminution is essentially his or her response. Nor is the question-
er's identity clear: these could well be "lines left" by the recluse and
proof of his incorrigible nature; or they could be questions posed or
ventriloquized by the speaker. But whatever their origin, the lack of
definitive punctuation immediately implicates their reader as an
autonomous subject, as maker of his or her own wasteland rather
than a respondent dependent on another's vision.

As if to emphasize this charge, an ellipsis follows, after which the
nothing that is not there gives way to a wholly different subject and
stance. The stance, from which vantage the narrative subject is
introduced, joins sympathy and judgment, but in a way that pro-
longs the reader's autonomy. Where paradise lost is initially reenacted as a readerly epiphany, the account of the narrative subject's loss of paradise, although more conventionally mimetic, is
dependent still on a sympathetic imagination.

Following this account, however, are a series of more arbitrary
judgments: the subject's selfhood and solitude are acts of will and
morally accountable, and his individuation is somehow aberrant.
Where initially the reader is coopted or controlled by the text, he or
she is now a resisting reader. For reading, with its peculiar "fate" (to
borrow Hartman's notion), has already impressed the reader with
other judgments—facts about process, isolation and autonomy—to
which the reader is incontrovertibly privy.

And so it will be for the speaker, but only when he exercises the readerly or sympathetic prerogative, relinquishing the mantle of prophet for that of poet:

> —Stranger! these gloomy boughs
> Had charms for him; and here he loved to sit,
> His only visitants a straggling sheep,
> The stone-chat, or the glancing sand-piper. (21–24)

Just as the speaker's astringency comes as something of a shock, so his exclamatory "stranger" is equally disarming, following (as it does) a passage that has recalled the reader to that very fact: to an affinity with the other "stranger" to whom the apostrophe also refers. Equally disarming is the recollection that follows, which reconstructs the narrative subject's "morbid pleasure" (28): a "pleasure" that, as the speaker remembers it, modulates to melancholy, then to ecstasy, and from ecstasy to even deeper despair. And yet, what most "disturb[s]" the subject, we are told, is not his gyrations of spirit, but the conviction that "others" apparently have "felt / What he must never feel" (39–40). This belief is disputed by the evidence of these same lines that others *do* feel what the subject ironically assumes they "must" not. Moreover, because it is the reader who is charged with admitting this counter-testimony, the very estrangement he disproves necessarily places him in the company of other estranged spirits, not the least of whom is the man speaking. This point is subtly reiterated by the speaker's assumption that the reader may actually behold the landscape as he—the speaker—is beholding it ("how lovely 'tis / Thou seest" [31– 32]). For in sympathizing with the poem's subject as he or she has done, the reader has already (and quite literally) followed the *speaker's* example in imagining or seeing what cannot be seen.

The "Yew-tree" lines may be more direct in their claim than *The Ruined Cottage,* but they are scarcely less demanding. Like the reader of the latter, the reader of this poem must manage at the close not only to see what he or she "cannot see," but also to recover an identity that is in fact not there. The reader's only advantage will be in not having been betrayed by a false (or hypothetical) sense of insecurity. Unlike the reader of *The Ruined Cottage,* whose betrayal is inevitable, the reader of "Lines" has been systematically schooled in himself as reader: in how to trust the spoken and not necessarily the man speaking:

If Thou be one whose heart the holy forms
Of young imagination have kept pure,
Stranger! henceforth be warned; and know, that pride,
Howe'er disguised in its own majesty,
Is littleness; that he, who feels contempt
For any living thing, hath faculties
Which he has never used; that thought with him
Is in its infancy. The man, whose eye
Is ever on himself, doth look on one,
The least of nature's works, one who might move
The wise man to that scorn which wisdom holds
Unlawful, ever. O, be wiser, thou!
Instructed that true knowledge leads to love,
True dignity abides with him alone
Who, in the silent hour of inward thought,
Can still suspect, and still revere himself
In lowliness of heart. (44–60)

In trusting *this teller* certain problems are immediately present. Do these "lines" manifest inward thought, or chronicle an otherwise "silent" suspicion? Or do they, as the conclusion also indicates, merely caution, or "war[n]" how not to live? The reader must decide; he or she must make sense of a conclusion more suited to a sermon, save that it is so irrational, so contradictory. Innocence is no sooner assumed than negated ("Stranger!"); sympathy masquerades as judgment (and vice versa); and there is genuine confusion in tone—whether the speaker is speaking at or to the reader.

That for all their posturing the concluding lines are oddly personal raises another possibility. Perhaps the speaker is in dialogue with himself, "lost" as Rossetti termed it "on both sides." Unthinkable in the beginning with its various injunctions to the reader, the prospect of a dialogue of one (as opposed to a dramatic monologue) seems increasingly likely. There are further suggestions: "The man," for example, who looks "ever on himself" (51–52) also looks "on one" who judged "the least of Nature's works" would likely move the man to "scorn" (52–54). This is true as well of the analogous "wise man" (54) whose "wisdom" does not always prevent him from failing to show it. That both men, like the wise man, are one and the same, may be confirmed by removing the dependent clauses: "The man whose eye / Is ever on himself doth look on one . . . ever." With the supporting analogy or without it, the implications are clear enough. In looking "on one," "one who own'd / No common soul" (12–13), the speaker's "eye is ever on himself" at once scornfully *and* reverentially. And this is really no surprise—unless of course, by trusting the teller only, the reader may have thought himself the only auditor.

But for the attentive, inferred reader—now in some sense an implied reader—things are more disturbing than surprising. "Stranger" to the proceedings for perhaps the first time, it is up to the reader simply to take his or her place among the "lost" (40), or in this case the living-dead. Undoubtedly that "process of creativity" where, having been denied "the whole story," reading involves "working things out for [one]self," the reading of "Lines" shows at the same time that the poem has "go[ne] too far" (in Iser's words) in stimulating the reading process. In lieu of simply encouraging the reader to resist its narrator, "Lines" makes this resistance a condition of authority to which the reader, more than the speaker now, has access.[14]

In recognizing, therefore, that the speaker and his subject are one divided self, the reader ultimately shows why—why, that is, he who "piled these stones" did *not* "di[e]" (43). Putting his or her estrangement to interpretative use, the reader will next put interpretation—with assistance from the speaker—in the service of identity or "love." Attributing purity and innocence to his auditor, the speaker does so mainly to remind the reader that these attributions are inaccurate. He begins the conclusion with a provisory allusion to the reader's purity, followed by an imperative reiterating the latter's estrangement. No matter how alien the speaker of the conclusion appears, his estrangement is not unique, but dictated, like the reader's, by a "visionary vie[w]" (41) of paradise which neither he nor the reader can hope to realize. Lost on both sides, in the present as well as to the past, the "man speaking" must, like the reader, mediate between opposing selves, for in his loss of innocence there is identity and a kind of sustenance; there is food on which "fancy" or desire "feed[s]" (41).

We may wonder, certainly, whether such identification is truly possible, whether any reader can be pressed into such service. What is clear, however, is that without readerly consent the poem founders. The key to the poem's conclusion is its utter fatuity: its self-satisfied invective against subjectivism, its conceited strictures against pride, its quite mystified claim to a higher innocence everywhere denied. If truth, "true knowledge" of oneself, leads to "love" in the "Yew-tree" lines, it does so only by allowing oneself to be read and to be suspected: for the reader there are tears—perceptible sadnesses—amid truths that, independent of the speaker's confidence, lie too deep for tears. The forced "dignity," the defensive "lowliness," the contraries of self-love and self-loathing—in short, all of the things dramatized—are, in reading, personalized. They are in the reader who brings "love" and a sense of identity to the "Yew-tree" lines and by reading them (and him or herself) reconciles two selves whose opposition the speaker cannot otherwise resolve.

In creating an audience in this way, a reader charged with "loving" a self whose identity is thereby confirmed, Wordsworth enlists the evidence of love to prove that the beloved is in fact no fiction. Rather than deconstructing himself, Wordsworth has done almost the opposite; he has created the reader as a prelude to joining him or her in their joint-construction.[15] If the act of reading is commensurate with selfhood in "Lines left upon a Seat in a Yew-tree," then selfhood is equally a matter of being read or, as the case may be, of being loved. Literary history, from the Preface on, asserts a less complicated process: to be a "man speaking to men" all Wordsworth had to be was himself or, as he observes somewhat cryptically, the "Poet." It is clear that in "Lines" this is not immediately the case; indeed, the "man speaking" must be extrapolated from those listening even as they are also forced to imitate him.

With this in mind, we can better understand the narrative linking Wordsworth's first and last lyrical ballads. That is, while "Lines *left* upon a Seat in a Yew-tree" remains (following its title) the most anonymous or readerly of the 1798 *Lyrical Ballads*, "Lines *written* a few miles above Tintern Abbey" remains (as its title implies) the most personal and writerly. Reversing the movement of the "Yew-tree" lines, "Tintern Abbey" contracts around the speaker in order to expand outward to the reader, by-passing the speaker's "friend"—the listener in the poem—whose difference reveals a lack of identity, and worse, a deficiency of love.

"Tintern Abbey" is neither a grand affirmation, nor in failing as such, testimony to skepticism's greater triumph.[16] What the poem demonstrates is the existence of a poetical self, and with it, a society of selves to whom the poet can be true simply by speaking. Disinclined to hide from his audience, Wordsworth moves instead to full expression in this poem, whose alleged "balance" of negative and positive forces is grounded in a still larger synthesis.[17] Despite the emphasis that criticism is frequently inclined to give either to one or to the other, self-reliance is inseparable from despair in "Tintern Abbey." This makes the exemplary Dorothy, the embodiment of unself-consciousness or hope, a scapegoat whose exclusion is as much a measure of sincerity—of the identity of poet and reader—as of the antipathy that identity ultimately warrants.

To fathom the "great darkness" of "Tintern Abbey," as Keats discovered, requires little more than a willingness to read its "dark passages." From the opening lines, where irreversible change is conveyed paradoxically by repetition, by the recognition that although the past repeats itself it is different this time, the speaker displays a remarkable ingenuousness that only rhetoric renders disingenuous. A reader disposed to look for darkness has no trouble finding it. We can begin with the several "agains," whose sheer number subverts their meaning, coinciding with an alienation more varied and profound. Very clearly, change in "Tintern Abbey" begets forgetfulness, a detachment from one's previous identity. On on the one hand, "[f]ive years have passed" (1), taking their normal toll on the speaker's powers of recollection (which may explain why memory appears unconscious and sensational as opposed to rational). On the other hand, "pleasure" (32), "kindness" and "love" (36) are all "unremembered" (32, 35), forgotten as if by conscious will. Even worse, they may have never existed. The poem's first thirty-five or so lines emphasize the way things are, not the way they were, with active verbs—"hear," "behold," "impress," "repose," "see," "run," "sits"—enhancing this present-ness. Part of this present, too, is the presence of "thoughts of more deep seclusion" (7) themselves engaging numerous allusions to solitude, isolation and loneliness: the "dwellers in the houseless woods" (21), the "Hermit sit[ting] alone" (23), the speaker "in lonely rooms . . .'mid the din / Of towns and cities" (26–27). Separated from a previously familiar world by an interval of quantitative growth, the speaker can no more unlive those five years (which, experienced, seem more like fifteen) than he is able to bridge the "long [absence]" (23) suffered in their tenure. Hence, the ability of the past—the remembered past—to affect the present is itself a memory, much as the speaker's sense of the present is preconditioned less by the distant past than by another past—"unremembered" after "five long [years]"—and thus, tautologically, by itself. The return to the Wye is more spatial than temporal.

Still, by pitting one repetition against the other—landscape against timescape, eye against "I"—Wordsworth presents the reader with a choice or, more accurately, with a test that persists through the poem. Wish fulfillment, aligned with regression, opposes understanding, which for the reader and speaker involves submission to the here and now, to the "still, sad music of humanity" (92). Consequently, when the speaker states of his unremembered feelings: "Nor less, I trust, / To them I may have owed another gift" (36–37), the act of reading is almost identical to that of utterance. In each, an ultimate confrontation with a life of diminishing returns is neither avoided nor pursued but postponed. The reader knows very well that the negative syntax and that "may" and "trust" all signify doubt; yet it is difficult at this juncture for the reader to consider this without feeling he or she is being unfair, both to the speaker and to him or herself.

Nor is Wordsworth at all reluctant to appeal to this sense of fair play. Nearly every passage in "Tintern Abbey" proves an exercise in readerly ethics, although ethics are hardly what the poem is about. What the poem tests is the reader's ability to remain an adult, to resist the regression toward harmony and order to which the speaker continually feigns capitulation. There is, for example, the well-known disclaimer, "If this / Be but a vain belief" (50–51)—"this" being the "other" gift of unremembered feelings, "that serene and blessed mood" (42), whose existence the poem qualifies prior to describing it. How is the reader to read such a statement? As an assertion to the contrary as the rhetoric encourages? Or as a surrender to the speaker's and reader's worst fears? The answer, I think, is clear and, unlike the speaker's condition, not even a matter of "sad perplexity" (61). It has been evident, rather, from the first that while the "time [of youth] is past, / And all its aching joys . . . [a]nd all its dizzy raptures [are now no more]," "other gifts" have *not* "followed" except as useful fictions (84–88). Belief only half conceals doubt, just as the numerous negatives— "These forms of beauty have not been to me" (24); "no trivial influence" (33); "Nor less . . . I may have owed another gift" (36–37); "Not for this / Faint I" (86–87)—are the inevitable tokens of this transvaluation.

Nevertheless, propositions such as these serve an important function; they hold matters in abeyance long enough for the reader to be his or her own poet. So long as "Tintern Abbey" can be read in two ways and so long as belief remains conditional ("for such loss, I would believe, / Abundant recompense" [88–89]), and so long as each "therefore" remains a transparent attempt at syllogistic sleight of hand ("Therefore I am still / A lover of the meadows and the woods" [103–04]), wish fulfillment remains a resistible impulse: a benign, not undesirable form of imaginative play. As David Simpson notes, the various "conditionals and back-up explanations inscribe into the poem an impression of tentative or partial conviction" (*Wordsworth's Historical Imagination* 110). But when the speaker moves finally to address his dramatic auditor and to view himself as he imagines this "dearest Friend" (116) does, he forces the issue, provoking the same dislocation in the reader that he has reached in himself.

To "catch / The language of [his] former heart" in his sister's "voice" (117–18), as the speaker contends he has, is also a way to relinquish it and to own up to the present: "Nature," he now asserts, "never did betray / The heart that loved her" (123–24). He is correct, for it is "the heart" that betrays itself; its language—always "of [the] former heart"—is extremely catching, a linguistic contagion that has already spread in the act of reading. This is why the introduction of the sister into the poem is so very crucial. Vying with the reader for the speaker's "friend"-ship as she vies with the speaker for his identity, the sister is ironically a dissociative force, who returns both the poet and the reader to the present: to a "dreary" world bounded by a forgotten past and an uncertain future. To take her to heart would necessitate a change in identity, or involve a shift in emphasis from wish to fulfillment.

And neither of these is possible. Both the poet and the reader must in their own ways reject Dorothy for the sake of something worse, which turns out, in any case, to be their (that is, the poet's and the reader's) friendship:

> Therefore let the moon
> Shine on thee in thy solitary walk;
> And let the misty mountain winds be free
> To blow against thee: and in after years,
> When these wild ecstasies shall be matured
> Into a sober pleasure, when thy mind
> Shall be a mansion for all lovely forms,
> Thy memory be as a dwelling-place
> For all sweet sounds and harmonies; Oh! then,
> If solitude, or fear, or pain, or grief,
> Should be thy portion, with what healing thoughts
> Of tender joy wilt thou remember me,
> And these my exhortations! Nor, perchance,
> If I should be, where I no more can hear
> Thy voice, nor catch from thy wild eyes these gleams
> Of past existence, wilt thou then forget
> That on the banks of this delightful stream

We stood together; and that I, so long
A worshipper of Nature, hither came,
Unwearied in that service: rather say
With warmer love, oh! with far deeper zeal
Of holier love. (135–56)

For all their passion, these final clarifications, each more dramatic than the preceding, are curiously out of character for one who, as he claims, is dependent upon his "friend" for glimmers of past existence. So, too, the images of Dorothy wracked by nature, solitude, fear, pain and grief are hardly consistent with her embodiment of "what I was once" (121). These inconsistencies are not inconsistencies *per se;* they are inconsistencies in perspective, which in turn create a niche for the reader.[18] In envisioning his friend as a version of himself, the poet emphasizes this projection (or appropriation of Dorothy) by immediately representing himself as his friend, presumably, will perceive him.

Thus, what seems an intensely private moment in "Tintern Abbey" is, in this shifting, a very public one: a bid for representative status based on the mutual differentiation of the "man" and the "*men*" to whom he is speaking. It remains only for the "men" to resist a resolution which opposes the differentiation on which sincerity finally depends:

Nor wilt thou then forget,
That after many wanderings, many years
Of absence, these steep woods and lofty cliffs,
And this green pastoral landscape, were to me
More dear, both for themselves, and for thy sake!
(156–60)

Even so, and the familiar "thou" notwithstanding, this final exhortation provides yet more dramatic proof of the differences between the speaker and his auditor that unite him with his audience. Removing himself from the proceedings, the speaker reaches closure by allowing his friend to remember what neither he nor his reader can. Of the various things which describe the "dear[ness]" of the landscape, none involves the speaker directly: neither the landscape nor the sister, now or in the future. A ventriloquist, rather, who implicitly opposes what he ventriloquizes (note how even the sister's memory is qualified by negatives), Wordsworth's speaker reveals by mutual exclusion how years of absence have made forgetfulness— unmemory—a more potent faculty than memory can hope to be.

Wordsworth never duplicated the achievement of "Tintern Abbey," nor has a century of interpretation mediated the poem's power to disconcert. If anything, most readings of "Tintern Abbey" continue to illustrate the vast differences between interpretation as we customarily practice it and the "good interpretation" that, in Paul de Man's description, is forever mindful of "the steady fluctuation of [the literary] entity away from and toward its own mode of being."[19] Reconstructive in their aim, conventional interpretations of "Tintern Abbey" tend both to create meaning and to ensure that it is stable. Whether this meaning originates in Wordsworthian quietism and its presumed love of nature, or in a formal or historical approach concerned chiefly with poetic argument, or in a biographical approach which lays stress on the efficacious reunion with Dorothy, or, more recently, in the new historical approach which criticizes Wordsworth for necessarily ignoring painful, social reality, the readings of "Tintern Abbey" invariably enlist ambiguity in the service of clarity.[20]

The act of reading "Tintern Abbey" is a different matter. Undermining its reader as well as itself, "Tintern Abbey" not only creates an audience on whom nothing is lost; it creates an audience for whom everything is lost. Important for the differentiation it signifies, this loss, or sense of loss, is just as important for the differentiation it exerts, by which the reader is finally his own "poet" for want of one to imitate. And yet this becoming, so painstaking in its deliberation, is only temporary. The hard-won orientation, in fact, almost immediately yields a way to another orientation in contrast to the reader who has become (following the poet) the representative man. This new identity, which burgeons for Wordsworth in the poetry of 1802, is no less a deferral, no less a reaction to certain imperatives. It will mark, in fact, the culmination of Wordsworth's "romanticism" which, like the "poetry of sincerity," would be short-lived.

NOTES

1. *Literary Criticism of William Wordsworth*, ed. Paul M. Zall (Lincoln: University of Nebraska Press, 1966), 49. Because W. J. B. Owen and Jane Worthington Smyser do not print the 1802 Preface in their edition, but instead print the 1800 Preface and the revised version of the Preface (incorporating the changes made in 1802) that ultimately appeared in 1850, I use Zall's edition of the Preface rather than the version in *The Prose Works of William Wordsworth* (3 vols. [Oxford: Clarendon Press, 1974]). My choice of the 1802 Preface as a key to the peculiar difficulty of Wordsworthian sincerity, finds its justification in the fact that by 1802 (as I

demonstrate) Wordsworth was in a better position to recognize both the lineaments and consequences of the ideal he first anatomized in 1800. And, indeed, the sections of the Preface that I find most crucial, including the definition of the Poet as "a man speaking to men," appeared initially in 1802.

2. A notable exception is David Ferry who in *The Limits of Mortality* stresses Wordsworth's contempt for common man. Yet Ferry is concerned chiefly with Wordsworth's subjects and not explicitly with his direct treatment of the reader.

3. Typical in this regard is Brian Wilkie, "Wordsworth and the Tradition of the Avant-Garde" (*JEGP*, 72 [1973]: 194–222), who uses the idea of the avant-garde to explain the vacillation in the poet's manifesto "between relaxing assurances that poetry is nothing special and warnings that it is a supremely exalted thing" (211).

4. A different—though altogether relevant—view of Wordsworth's interchange with community is advanced by David Simpson in *Wordsworth and the Figurings of the Real* (London: Macmillan, 1982). According to Simpson, Wordsworth's notably subjective or authoritarian stance, which he frequently refigures or transforms, actually represents a Kantian effort at consensus or at representing a universal experience. Wordsworth's figurative attributions, then, are not gestures of power but ways of "alerting the mind to that part of itself which is most valuable. . . . [J]oys shared are more important than those unshared, [and] it is the strictly mental component in the experience of joy which matters most, and may most properly be assumed to be universal" (48–49). Without contesting the universalizing tendencies of many of Wordsworth's poems, I would argue nevertheless that Wordsworth's efforts at consensus are, in his major poetry, increasingly disingenuous at best—that for every endorsement of community in some represented act of mind, there is (as I show in succeeding chapters) an additional endorsement of the poet's individuality in the *representative* nature of those mental activities.

5. For Bloom's theory of influence, particularly as it helps forge the poet's identity, see *The Anxiety of Influence* (New York: Oxford University Press, 1972). Aligned with his paradoxical (if nevertheless Freudian) sense of the strong poet's individuation, is Bloom's humanistic view of romanticism as essentially Promethean, a view most fully articulated in *The Visionary Company*. For a related view, albeit one more suspicious of the humanistic inviolability of poetic identity, see Brisman, *Romantic Origins*.

6. My definition of sincerity owes much to Lionel Trilling (*Sincerity and Authenticity* [Cambridge, MA: Harvard University Press, 1972]), who with assistance from both Arnold and Shakespeare nevertheless grounds his view in Wordsworth, particularly in the notion of the poet as "a man speaking to men." Although Trilling's view of sincerity is fairly generalized—"a most arduous effort . . . of supreme importance in the moral life . . . of Western culture for some four hundred years" (6)—it is nevertheless consumed by the question of audience. Here, the moral end of

"avoiding falsehood to others" is not only a "public end," but is also tanta-mount to being "truly true to oneself" (9). Only by being true to oneself can one—according to the principle of sincerity—"avoi[d] being false to any man" (5). The view of sincerity as union of public and private is not entirely shared by David Perkins, who in *Wordsworth and the Poetry of Sincerity* (Cambridge, MA: Harvard University Press, 1964) set out to define "what Wordsworth meant by sincerity" beyond the fact that a "poet must deeply feel the emotion he expresses as he creates the poem" (3). Sincerity, in Perkins' view, is more akin to Trilling's notion of authenticity: "personal rather than typical, intimate rather than public, spontaneous or natural rather than heightened and planned" (13). Wordsworth's audience, then, is not "the reader" but a coterie: "his family and friends plus a few enthusiasts in the reading public" (159). Because he defines sincerity as essentially personal, Perkins is able to regard sincerity as the informing feature of Wordsworth's "major" poetry as against the "later poetry" (227–69). But since, as I see it, sincerity is audience-bound, it is pertinent only to a discussion of *Lyrical Ballads,* during which the compact of poet and reader was forged as a prelude to being broken. A view of sincerity similar to Perkins' is shared by Donald Davie ("On Sincerity from Wordsworth to Ginsburg," *Encounter,* 31 [1968]: 61–66) for whom sincerity is a "confessional" mode, although not in a rhetorical or Augustinian sense. For a discussion of "uniformitarianism," see M. H. Abrams, *The Mirror and the Lamp* (New York: Norton, 1958), 103–07. See also Stephen Prickett, *Coleridge and Wordsworth: The Poetry of Growth* (Cambridge: Cambridge University Press, 1970), 147–74, for a more detailed view of the "fundamentally egalitarian" sense of the poet as "differ[ing]" not in kind, but merely in degree from that which makes us human." Contemporary discussion of "uniformitarianism" begins with A. O. Lovejoy ("The Parallel of Deism and Classicism," in *Essays in the History of Ideas* [Baltimore: The Johns Hopkins University Press, 1948]), who cites the term in reference to a system which, as Abrams observes, informs Wordsworth's critical theory through the "early years of the nineteenth century" (105).

7. It is important to emphasize the difference between an "implied reader" who, in Iser's conception, is empowered by a stronger authority who "prestuctur[es]" a "potential meaning" for the reader (*The Implied Reader,* xii), and a reader such as Wordsworth creates, who precedes and otherwise imitates the "prestructuring" function. The notion of an implied reader gives primacy to an authorial self which, at this stage, is more properly a readerly self in Wordsworth.

8. For a fuller reading of "Simon Lee" along similar lines, see Andrew L. Griffin, "Wordsworth and the Problem of Imaginative Story: The Case of 'Simon Lee,'" *PMLA,* 92 (1977): 392–409. See also Simpson, *Wordsworth's Historical Imagination,* 149–59, who notes both the interaction of poet and reader and the necessarily unstable identity to which it is corollary: "'Simon Lee' does not clearly and openly transcribe a subject in a state of historical and biographical crisis. Not only does it continue to foreground

the questions raised by the 'objective' dimension, the old man's decay and excessive gratitude; it also displaces the production of meaning onto the alerted reader" (159). References to "Simon Lee" and the other lyrical ballads are, unless otherwise cited, to the original printed versions of 1798 and 1800 in *Lyrical Ballads*, ed. R. L. Brett and A. R. Jones (London: Methuen, 1968).

9. According to Heather Glen (*Vision and Disenchantment: Blake's "Songs" and Wordsworth's "Lyrical Ballads"* [Cambridge: Cambridge University Press, 1983]), in "Simon Lee" and the poems of 1798 in general "Wordsworth is clearly playing upon his readers' simplifying schemata, refusing to present this expected subject-matter in easily digestible form, and demanding that they take a much more active attitude towards it" (44). However, what is striking about "Simon Lee," particularly the 1798 version, is that there is nothing easily digestible about the poem's subject, which is treated ironically from the very beginning. Glen is certainly correct about the peculiarly active relationship of reader and text in these poems, but this relationship, it seems to me, is additionally complicated by a peculiarly mutable poetic authority to which the reader has almost equal access.

10. References to *The Ruined Cottage* are to the version of the poem in MS. D in *"The Ruined Cottage" and "The Pedlar"*. Although this version of the poem was not transcribed until 1799, it derives in large part from the text of 1797 in MS. B (1798), save that it lacks the biographical information about Armytage, which was added in 1798 (along with the introduction) and was later expanded in *The Pedlar*. For further discussion of the various texts of *The Ruined Cottage* and their dating, see Butler's introduction to *"The Ruined Cottage and "The Pedlar"*, 3–35. In establishing the order and chronology of Wordsworth's compositions (at least through 1815), I follow Mark Reed, *Wordsworth: The Chronology of the Early Years*, 1770–1799 (Cambridge, MA: Harvard University Press, 1967) and *Wordsworth: The Chronology of the Middle Years*. For the dating of *The Ruined Cottage* and its progress into other variants, see *Early Years*, 27–28, 337–39, and *Middle Years*, 665–66.

11. For a generally pantheistic interpretation of *The Ruined Cottage*, see Jonathan Wordsworth, *The Music of Humanity*, 3–153, who argues for the universal sympathy linking the reader with the poem's other participants. See also Hertz, "Wordsworth and the Tears of Adam," and Parker, " 'Finer Distance': The Narrative Art of Wordsworth's 'The Wanderer,' " both of whom bring this "standard" reading to bear upon the later text of the poem in Book I of *The Excursion*. Sheats (*The Making of Wordsworth's Poetry*, 137–51) also argues that *The Ruined Cottage* "braces and supports the observing mind, allowing the contemplation of painful objects without loss of control" (137–38). In contrast, Hartman notes the poem's "reflexive (and modern) emphasis," resulting in "a spectrum bounded at one side by the apocalyptic imagination and at the other by an alien nature" (*Wordsworth's Poetry*, 139–40).

12. *Anatomy of Criticism* (New York: Atheneum, 1969), 164– 65.

13. See Mary Jacobus' reading in *Tradition and Experiment in Wordsworth's "Lyrical Ballads" [1798]* (Oxford: Clarendon Press, 1976), 24–37. According to Jacobus, the "Yew-tree" lines are "in some sense . . . a self-portrait of the poet who had put his faith in the Revolution, in a Godwinian millennium, or simply in his own intellectual power" and had subsequently "retired" prior to the "realization that withdrawal is no answer" (32). Hartman's treatment of the poem ("Wordsworth, Inscriptions, and Romantic Nature Poetry," *Beyond Formalism* [New Haven, CT: Yale University Press, 1970], 206–29) is concerned less with the poem as a self-projection than with its pivotal position in both generic and literary history.

14. *The Implied Reader,* 275. Reassessing Iser and other reader-response critics, Peter J. Rabinowitz ("Truth in Fiction: A Reexamination of Audiences," *Critical Inquiry,* 4 [1977]: 121–41) divides Iser's one reader into four readers the last of whom—"the ideal narrative audience"—more closely resembles the reader in "Lines." The initial distinction between the poem's narrator and its authorial self forces a resistance of the narrator, and this resistance (following the speaker's own resistance) is tantamount to poetic authority rather than to a condition, as Iser would have it, of the reader's becoming an ideal audience. More than an authorial audience, the reader of "Lines" has become an authorial self.

15. Clearly related is Sheats' observation that "Wordsworth sought [in *Lyrical Ballads*] to bind poet and audience together in a community of Christian charity" (*The Making of Wordsworth's Poetry,* 220).

16. Of the numerous such interpretations of "Tintern Abbey," see: Sheats (*The Making of Wordsworth's Poetry,* 205– 45), a detailed reading that illustrates the way the poem substantiates a correspondence between mind and nature; Onorato (*The Character of the Poet,* 29–87), a psychoanalytic approach which shows how the poem rehearses the process of individuation and ego formation; and Albert J. Gérard ("Dark Passages: Wordsworth's *Tintern Abbey,*" in *English Romantic Poetry* [Berkeley: University of California Press, 1968], 89–117), who observes "Wordsworth's stern determination— while contemplating his greatest loss—not to give himself up to the annihilating power of his sad perplexity. . . . [but] to seek the meaning which his experience, past and present, holds for the future" (115). Hartman, somewhat reluctantly, also adopts a quietistic view of the poem: "Wordsworth, though sensing his mortality—that nature can no longer renew his genial spirits—continues to go out of himself and toward nature. His sight gradually expands into communion" (*Wordsworth's Poetry,* 27). Finally, for a reading that parallels my own in stressing "Wordsworth's willingness [in "Tintern Abbey"] to show the pressure of questions within the designs of affirmation," see Wolfson, *The Questioning Presence,* 60–70.

17. Sheats, *The Making of Wordsworth's Poetry,* 244. See also Gérard, "Dark Passages."

18. David Simpson writes of this passage that "the expressed possibility that life might not hold happy prospects for Dorothy, and for William, works to heighten the urgency of the personal bond between them, and also

to call it into question" (*Wordsworth's Historical Imagination*, 111). I agree with Simpson that there is an "urgency of personal bond" here. But I would argue that this bond—a personal bond with the reader—is necessarily forged (and thus necessarily coexists with) the "questioning" of the speaker's attachment to his sister.

19. "Literary History and Literary Modernity," in *Blindness and Insight*, 2d ed. rev. (Minneapolis: University of Minnesota Press, 1983), 163–65. In *On Deconstruction: Theory and Criticism After Structuralism* (Ithaca, NY: Cornell University Press, 1982), Jonathan Culler observes more broadly how the focus on "readers and reading" in recent criticism is a critique of intentionality, revealing how interpretation often rewrites and legitimizes what is not readable (31–83).

20. For the "new historical" reading of "Tintern Abbey," which underscores the contrast between the social realities of the abbey itself as a refuge for the homeless (the vagrant dwellers) and the pastoral orderliness of Wordsworth's obfuscatory, postrevolutionary, vision, see especially Levinson, *Wordsworth's Great Period Poems*, 14–57. See also McGann, *The Romantic Ideology*, 85–88. In noting the way the poem erases "1793 and the turmoil of the French Revolution," McGann concludes that "Dorothy is, of course, the reader's surrogate" (88). The need to interpret, in this instance, masks a crucial—less stable—dynamic, whereby Dorothy (as I have argued) is cast out so that the poet and reader may become surrogates of one another.

FOUR

Allegories of Reading, 1798–1799

The more tangible achievement of the 1798 *Lyrical Ballads,* as Wordsworth later described it, was their creation of the "taste by which [they could] be enjoyed."[1] But it was the less tangible, if more enduring, measure of the poems' "original[ity]" to have managed this tastemaking by agency of an inferred reader, or *figure* for the poet, which may be also taken as an allegory of self-expression.[2] By "allegory," I am speaking not only of a parallel narrative or text— the reader reading—that "says one thing and means another."[3] I am referring also to the structure born of that text: to a structure of identity requiring an "other" whom the poet resembles, yet from whom, following their resemblance, the poet is simultaneously re- moved. Identity, in short, is achieved by marking difference. This sense of allegory has certain affinities with the destabilizing allegory in which the romantic self, according to de Man and others, is made vulnerable in its very representation. But my use of the term refers more to a mode of displacement—to a structure of differentiation by which the self, as we have seen, is defined ultimately by what it is not.[4] I do not disagree with de Man's view that romantic selfhood is forever linked to an "intentional" or symbolic structure which Wordsworth's poetry alternately covers and uncovers.[5] I am inter- ested, rather, in the way Wordsworth is brought to a similar aware- ness by assimilating this structure as a prelude to discarding it.

The chief consequence of this double movement, then, which is the eventual relinquishment of identity or poetical selfhood, owes entirely to the genesis of identity in Wordsworth. Identity, after all, is forged early on by likeness with another figure. Even at its incep- tion, therefore, identity is a matter of forfeiture, of being like an- other as a measure of one's individuality. But it is also the case that, as a measure of one's individuality, this forfeiture must be forgotten or disavowed. In "Tintern Abbey" the identity of poet and reader leads almost immediately to a disaffiliation, which is marked by the speaker's disappearance in the final lines. Following the differentiation to which the reader, in imitation of the speaker, has been made subject in the course of the poem, their disaffiliation at the close discloses how identity, by its very constitution, is more properly *a way to identity*. The identity that the speaker and reader share in "Tintern Abbey" confirms only that the speaker is like someone or something else, not that the "something else"—in this case the reader—is like the speaker.

Such asymmetry and open-endedness are even more characteristic of the poems that follow immediately in Volume II of *Lyrical Ballads* (1800). In these, the allegorical figures whose otherness properly reflects poetic identity invariably resemble the speaker on the basis of a mutual difference: so that in replacing the inferred reader with a figure such as Matthew, with whom the speaker can only sympathize, Wordsworth stands poised, like the speaker of "Tintern Abbey," between what he "was once" and what he has become in aftermath. This more discrete identity (or "difference to me") gradually situates the speaker between two figures: between a figure of the reader and some other figure from whom the reader is distinct. For it is the case that affection or "love" (as the treatment of the sister in "Tintern Abbey" shows) comes inevitably to disaffection in Wordsworth. The very self with whom the speaker "would" identify is, in light of the latter's new affinities and new identity, the very self from whom the speaker is now different.[6]

This "difference" succeeds for a time in obscuring the intentional structure that (as Wordsworth describes it in "A Poet's Epitaph") is the "[poet's] house." By the poems of 1802, Wordsworth suspends this apparatus of allegorical differences. The configuration whereby the poetical self is aligned with one figure as opposed to another gradually narrows to the point where this self becomes a figure for itself or, in Richard Onorato's phrase, the "character of the Poet." This refiguration, as *The Prelude* subsequently demonstrates, imposes more than the burden of simply being different. It requires a mythology of the self *as Other*—the "sense of God"— that, beginning with the poetry of sincerity, has been kept in abeyance.

Thus, although allegory is undoubtedly instrumental in exposing what de Man calls the "pseudo-dialectic between subject and object," for Wordsworth it is more immediately a means by which he reaches that "passing moment" where, to cite de Man again, "sympathy" is "an intersubjective, interpersonal relationship that, in the last analysis, is a relationship of the subject toward itself" ("The Rhetoric of Temporality" 183, 188, 180). This sense of allegory, which de Man terms the "rhetoric of temporality," clearly mitigates the tendencies of both the Romantics and their admirers to privilege the self in its ability to escape its "temporal destiny" ("The Rhetoric of Temporality" 190). But what it necessarily occludes, in Wordsworth at least, is another aspect of allegory, involving both affinities and disaffections with other figures. Far from returning him to some temporal condition, these affinities and disaffections are the means (for a time) by which Wordsworth intimates an immortality. My view, then, must also be distinguished from that of Morris Golden, for whom the self in Wordsworth is both "individual" and "archetype," both real and the stuff of literature. The ability to create and to observe one's selfhood by seemingly independent sanctions is, as I see it, an interdependent function: the self's observability is a condition, not a consequence, of its archetypal status. It is this interdependence, in fact, that underlies Wordsworth's poetic identity.[7]

Ultimately, as we have seen in *The Excursion*, Wordsworth will anticipate de Man in revealing that the self is, in large measure, a mystification or, to use Golden's term, an "archetype." Yet here, the means for this demystification are not the de Manian allegory which continually eliminates the "possibility of an identity or identification" ("The Rhetoric of Temporality" 191); they are the "hierarchizing" tendencies of allegory by which identity in Wordsworth's case has been a representation of authority and, to reiterate the term employed both Timothy Bahti and Joel Fineman, always part of a "structure."[8] Hence, it devolves to the "consciousness between two selves" (that de Man, to distinguish it from allegory, calls "irony")[9]—between a self sufficiently implicated in an "allegorical structure" and one sufficiently "conscious" of its implication—to turn allegory to more deconstructive purposes. The identity that allegory fosters, which is pitched from the first toward an identification with the Other (eventually "God"), is gradually replaced by a more reflexive consciousness through which Wordsworth accepts his temporal destiny and, as *The Excursion* finally shows, his place in the community of men.[10] As most readers are aware, this return also takes the form of a more "orthodox" orientation, wherein permanence and authority are assigned to "God, who is our home." Yet what is not often appreciated is how ironic and allegorical both this assignment is: that without God or a "sense of God," there would be no authority, nor an identity, for the poet to resign to Him.[11] It is not that Wordsworth becomes an orthodox Christian in his later phase. Rather, his Christianity so cancels the authority it supersedes as to cancel as well the authority it ostensibly promotes.

The allegorical movement from self as other to the "Other" *as self* can be seen as early as "Tintern Abbey," whose reader is manipulated as a measure of the difference toward which he and the speaker have grown respectively. Unlike the previous poems, where the reader is often a model for the man speaking, the speaker in "Tintern Abbey" prefigures his reader in the act of reading. What similarity there exists is, in the end again, a matter of dissimilitude, of a difference from which the "poet" is distinct in turn.

Thus, despite a growing detachment from the reader, the reader's reading, so to speak, is quite vital to the development of Wordsworth's poetry. And indeed, the series of poems written after "Tintern Abbey," beginning with "Nutting" and continuing in both the "Lucy" and the second group of "Matthew" poems (where the speaker actually assumes the role of auditor), are allegories of reading in just this sense: they are poems that imagine reading as a different (if universal) activity, and poetic identity as the obverse of that difference. Contrary to the customary view of the Lucy poems as allegories about the poet's relationship with someone (possibly his sister), these poems continue the more symbolic (or hierarchizing) mode of allegorization that, as recently as "Tintern Abbey," demanded the marginalization of the sister in deference to a more discrete, more representative auditor. To the extent that the Lucy poems are about Dorothy, it is because she is now a figure— Lucy—whose death considerably alters the prefiguration "Dorothy" was earlier instrumental in sustaining.[12] So long as "Dorothy" was different from the speaker, or, as the case had been, undifferentiated from nature, she underscored the relative (and comparable) uniqueness of both reader and poet. Yet without "Dorothy," or her "living" difference, it is increasingly up to the reader to perform her differentiating function. The reader's function at this stage is really twofold: the reader is both a figure *of* differentiation (as he or she was previously), yet one whose increasingly anterior difference also does the work of differentiating the poet from him or her.

This shift in the poet's stance toward both Dorothy and the reader is already evident in "Nutting," which in resembling "Tintern Abbey" manages to rewrite the earlier poem without diminishing the selfhood toward which both works are pitched.[13] Beginning, in fact, where the earlier poem leaves off—at a point of individuation underscored this time through a recollection of a boyhood

trespass—the speaker of "Nutting" tells his recollection directly to
the reader, or in a manner that keeps the reader from being aware,
until the poem's last lines, that he or she is not also the poem's
dramatic listener, the "dearest Maiden." Consequently, the account
of the trespass—the boy's violation of a bower of trees that previously lacked any "ungracious sign / Of devastation" (17–18)—
makes it difficult for the reader to identify with the man speaking,
since unlike his or her counterpart in "Tintern Abbey," the reader is
a listener to the man speaking and nothing more:

> Then up I rose,
> And dragg'd to earth both branch and bough, with crash
> And merciless ravage: and the shady nook
> Of hazels, and green and mossy bower
> Deform'd and sullied, patiently gave up
> Their quiet being. (42–47)

The reader's status as mere reader is evident in the way the speaker
merely speaks. By making Nature more "human" than the young
boy himself, Wordsworth reveals how the speaker's crime was really
against civilization, against an authority that held sway over the
boy and normally restrained him. Having overcome this "being,"
however, the speaker is equally overcome by a feeling of omnipo-
tence, by a "rich[ness] beyond the wealth of kings" (50). Hence, the
remorse he also remembers feeling, the "wealth" that authority
usually garners in compensation for its violation, is not guilt in the
conventional sense, but the pain rather of beholding one's handi-
work and further testimony to the boy's power.

All of this, of course, the reader—a member of civilization—has
had to absorb in unmediated fashion. But the greater obligation still
will be for the reader to concede that the speaker cannot, or should
not, abdicate his rule. At the very moment that the reader might
think that he or she is confessor to this narrative, empowered in
some way to reduce the speaker to a version of him or herself, the
speaker turns abruptly to an auditor in the poem, whose presence
has thus far been suppressed, and offers a most arbitrary de-
duction:

> Then, dearest Maiden! move along these shades
> In gentleness of heart with gentle hand
> Touch,—for there is a Spirit in the woods. (53–55)

Although this injunction coincides with the speaker's paternalistic posture, it is also self-exculpatory, allowing the speaker to attribute his earlier action to a natural-supernaturalism that he violated as much as obeyed. Enjoining the listener to submit to the very restraints he had earlier rejected (and, in rejecting, has since appropriated), the speaker also implies that his opposition to restraint was not, like his present action, entirely an act of will. Like the maiden who is being told what to do, the speaker has, in retrospect, been the beneficiary of guidance as well, since it is the result of his boyhood action that he is in a position to confess it without the service of a confessor. At variance, obviously, from the dramatic listener, the speaker is even more displaced from the reader, whose absolution amounts to an acceptance of the speaker as a more exalted version of the listener and reader both.

The extent to which "Nutting" marks a reversal of "Tintern Abbey" is the very extent to which Wordsworth has actually proceeded from that poem, revealing how in a space of less than six months, he has entered the very hierarchy he was earlier compelled, both as a boy and later as a poet of sincerity, to mitigate. The speaker's admission of wrongdoing, of having been representative, is surely a confession; but as a confession it manages to displace the reader-confessor with a dramatic auditor, and to displace that auditor, in turn, by a speaker who is quite literally his own best listener. In the manner of traditional confession, as Frank McConnell details, the "plot" of the speaker's past in "Nutting" remains an ordained narrative, which resembles the text of selfhood in "Tintern Abbey" only in the requirements it continues to place on the reader. For without the poet's mediation, the dramatic listener to whom the speaker is mediator of grace, there is no way for the reader to play his or her mediatory role between the exemplary narrator and the "acceptance" of the latter's "semidivine status."[14]

Although the sudden interposition of the maiden at the close of "Nutting" has the effect of relegating the reader to secondary status, this removal has actually been anticipated by the maiden's absence. In declining to play the reader of "Nutting" against this dramatized listener as he had done in "Tintern Abbey," Wordsworth eliminates both figures so as to make way for their interlocutor.

This disalignment is equally evident in the Lucy poems composed at approximately the same time. Here, in a similar triangle, the speaker's uniqueness depends upon his privileged, and mutually exclusive, relationships with the deceased Lucy and living reader. In "Strange fits of passion," for example, the speaker confirms this uniqueness by conceiving a more representative function for his reader, whose "reading," in turn, reveals a difference that now distinguishes the two. This reader—the "person" to whom the speaker confides (or to whom, as the Preface states, "the Poet [will] bring his feelings near")— is imagined as necessarily incapable of understanding the estrangement the speaker is confiding. Thus, it is both vital and ironic that the poem *begins* in a familiar, conversational vein. "Strange fits of passion I have known," the speaker declares,

> And I will dare to tell
> But in the lover's ear alone,
> What once to me befel. (1–4)

The "lover' "s identity is already problematic before we read the "But," and that word aggravates the issue, even as it raises questions about the speaker's disposition to his listener. "But" appears to mean "save" or "only," designating "the lover" as the implied, presumably kindred auditor, who has replaced the beloved or loved object as the recipient of the speaker's passion. Yet the word also suggests that the reader has achieved this intimacy by default: there is no one else to whom to communicate these passions. Further, there is the altogether curious "I will dare to tell," which simultaneously indicates the speaker's determination to express himself and his reluctance to do so—in which case "telling" becomes the reader's responsibility (something the "lover" is "dared" to essay) in the absence of an ability to respond sympathetically. This shift in responsibility accounts also for the apparent redundancy in "But . . . alone"; it is the *speaker's* "alone"-ness, conceivably, that makes the reader his sole audience.

Thus, even as the reader is enlisted as the speaker's intimate, such intimacy is immediately troubled by the poem's work in casting the reader as either a surrogate or secondary teller. This resistance to intimacy with the listener is particularly evident in the way the poem is told: telling and reading are increasingly unrelated (or related only in that reading has become another kind of telling). Similarly, the aims of readerly desire or consciousness (where Lucy's absence is a prelude to reunion) are increasingly unrelated to poetic consciousness (which knows her absence is irrevocable):

> When she I lov'd, was strong and gay
> Fresh like a rose in June
> I to her cottage bent my way,
> Beneath the evening moon.

Upon the moon I fix'd my eye,
All over the wide lea;
My horse trudg'd on, and we drew nigh
Those paths so dear to me.

And now we reach'd the orchard plot,
And, as we climb'd the hill,
Towards the roof of Lucy's cot
The moon descended still. (5–16)

Among the suggestions in these quatrains, none—not even the
countermovement to Lucy's strength in the downward trajectory of
the descending moon—is more important than the suggestion that
the "love[r] . . . alone" into whose "ear" the narrative is being told is
none other than the speaker himself. He is the interlocutor who,
like his counterpart in "Nutting," gradually displaces all others. The
displacement of Lucy is obvious enough, and reiterated in the way
various objects—the rose, the cottage, the plot, the roof—virtually
rush to occupy the breach created by her absence.

The reader's displacement is a subtler affair. In continuing to
accompany the speaker in the illusion that he is a kindred lover and
auditor, the reader discovers only that he is another version of the
"horse," whose path habitually leads to Lucy. Admitted to the poem
as the speaker's confidante, the reader, it turns out, gains this confidence in fantasy, just as the anticipated union with Lucy serves to
distinguish this "lover's" narrative from the fit of "the love[r] . . .
alone."[15]

Accordingly, as the speaker proceeds in time, the memory of
what happened "once" usurps the readerly text:

What fond and wayward thoughts will slide
Into a Lover's head—
"O mercy!" to myself I cried,
"If Lucy should be dead!" (25–28)

The "fond and wayward thoughts" reject the reader from the linear
narrative of desire and consummation, which he thought he was
being told, and so emphasize what the speaker in another of the
Lucy poems calls "the difference to me." This difference, then, not
only distinguishes the reader from the "lover" who cried solely "to
myself"; it also separates the reader from the "poet," whose narrative of separation is, in contrast to the reader's hoped-for narrative
of union, subsequently proven.[16]

That "Strange fits of passion" means to have this retroactive effect, that it demonstrably desynonymizes the "man speaking" and the "men" who are still his audience, becomes even clearer when we examine an earlier version of the poem composed shortly after "Tintern Abbey" in the fall of 1798. In a manner similar to that of "Tintern Abbey," the earlier "Strange fits" begins in anecdotal fashion ("Once, when my love was strong and gay") and closes with a recollection of having recounted the entire episode to Lucy herself:

> I told her this; her laughter light
>   Is ringing in my ears;
> And when I think upon that night
>   My eyes are dim with tears.
>   (*Letters, 1787–1805* 237–38)

If narrative or readerly time usurps lyric or poetic time in the early draft, then it is the case too that nature usurps rather than proves the speaker's fantasy: Lucy perishes not by act of will or by imagination, but by forces beyond the speaker's control. It is the reader, as much as the speaker, who measures his thought (or fear) of Lucy's death against her laughter—who is made aware in the duration of the poem of the grim *if accidental* correspondence of mind and nature. And like Dorothy in "Tintern Abbey," it is the living, laughing Lucy, who is vital to this synonymization, whose work in demystifying poetic imagination is reenacted by the way reading proves equally vulnerable to contingency or fate. In the published version, the privilege earlier wrested from the speaker is returned to him at the expense of both Lucy and the reader. Now, with Lucy's absence, the imagination requiring her presence is discredited in deference to the poetic imagination, which forsees or fitfully fears her death—both as the figure who earlier united the poet and the reader and, more immediately, as a revelation confirmed.[17]

Nor is it always the premonition of death that distinguishes the speaker of the Lucy poems from their reader. In "She dwelt among th' untrodden ways," it is the memory of Lucy and the knowledge of her death that differentiates the speaker from other men, to whom no such memories are vouchsafed:

> She *liv'd* unknown, and few could know
>   When Lucy ceas'd to be;
> But she is in her Grave, and Oh!
>   The difference to me. (9–12)

If Lucy, as the speaker suggests, had "*liv'd* unknown," it should go without saying that "few could know / When [she] ceas'd to be." Yet the speaker indulges this redundancy because it is the knowledge of Lucy's death, the capacity to have known the living "unknown" (as the poem's emphasis suggests), rather than a loneliness in the wake of Lucy's passing, that properly dictates the speaker's "difference."[18] Similarly, the provisional innocence in "A slumber did my spirit seal" is less a refutation of this knowledge than a refiguration of the "difference" to which that knowledge refers:

> A slumber did my spirit seal,
>   I had no human fears:
> She seem'd a thing that could not feel
>   The touch of earthly years,
>
> No motion has she now, no force
>   She neither hears nor sees
> Roll'd round in earth's diurnal course
>   With rocks and stones and trees! (1–8)

That the speaker "had no human fears" places the onus of fearing on the reader, whose "humanity" is implicitly contrasted to the fearless, nonhuman examples of the poem. But it is impossible, even with this contrast, for the reader to confuse the two examples: Lucy's integration or "thing"-ness is so different from both the speaker and the reader as almost to parody the speaker's slumber. By refusing, in any case, to articulate this discrimination—which allows the reader the prerogative of "reading" the irony in Lucy's difference—the speaker ensures his own difference from the human, readerly condition to which Lucy too is opposed. His spirit is "sealed," or authenticated, as much by slumber (or imagination) as by the poem, or the readerly acuity from which his dreaming, both earlier and "now" (5), is similarly set apart. Hartman is surely right to describe the poem as "meditative beyond irony"; for without irony, which only the reader in this case actualizes, there is no passage to meditation—no sealing of the spirit—for which irony is merely a precondition.[19]

Since it is the speaker's "difference" from the reader, rather than the speaker's ignorance or knowledge, to which his slumber refers, it is not at all contradictory that the reader's slumber might similarly be employed to expose the speaker's "solitude." This is the situation in "Lucy Gray", which, though often excluded from the group, is

sufficiently "separative" in its effect to warrant discussion with the
other Lucy poems. In "Lucy Gray" it is the reader's fear that both
separates and preconditions *his* slumbers in innocent faith. In a
variation, then, on the previous poem, Lucy's death in nature is so
utterly demystified that the reader must remystify it as a necessary
alternative to the "human" condition. The very pantheism, in fact,
just parodied in "A slumber did my spirit seal" is promoted by the
reader under the pain of death. No longer the privileged knowledge of the speaker, Lucy's death is suddenly common·knowledge, a
"human fear" which the reader, among others, now shares:

> Then downward from the steep hill's edge
> They track'd the footmarks small;
> And through the broken hawthorn-hedge,
> And by the long stone-wall. . . .
>
> They follow'd from the snowy bank
> Those footmarks, one by one,
> Into the middle of the plank;
> And further there were none. (45–56)

That these lines are for the reader's "ear alone" is reinforced as
much by their anecdotal tone as by the very melodrama that renders
Lucy's death a return—in the act of reading—of the repressed.

Problematic, too, are the ensuing intimations of her immortality.
Such speculations provide the speaker with a way out by giving him
an excuse not to be engaged in kind:

> Yet some maintain that to this day
> She is a living Child,
> That you may see sweet Lucy Gray
> Upon the lonesome Wild.
>
> O'er rough and smooth she trips along,
> And never looks behind;
> And sings a solitary song
> That whistles in the wind. (57–64)

If the reader cannot imagine Lucy's apotheosis, then the speaker
provides assistance, encouraging a suspension of disbelief. The
traces of Lucy that end in nothing inscribe what the reader already
knows and fears, and so create a need in the act of reading that the
mystification of nothing into being satisfies.

But whether the speaker is satisfied in kind, whether he endorses the belief that makes the apotheosis possible, is another matter. Couched in vaguely accusatory language, the "some" who "maintain that . . . [Lucy] is a living Child," who argue against all material evidence that she is not dead, turn out to be "you"—the audience—rather than "the man" addressing them. It is the reader, not the poet, who seals the speaker's spirit in writing over what, according to the poem, is no longer—from the reader's vantage—even readable.[20]

* * *

In foregrounding the reader's role, the Wordsworthian speaker does not imitate the reader or become the "self" prefigured by him or her, as he had done in earlier poems. Instead, he rejects the reader in moving from a situation where the self is forever mediated by a hermeneutic relationship to a less mediated representation requiring that the speaker's only relationship be to himself. But it is consistent with the allegorical disposition of this movement, by which the speaker must stand *in relation* to himself, that in displacing the reader as secondary, the "poet" is displaced pursuant to his primacy. The narcissistic completeness by which the speaker of the Lucy poems is consistently his own best auditor not only marginalizes the reader as necessarily different; it makes that marginality a reflection simultaneously of the poet's "difference." Less a token of his disaffection with the idea of apotheosis, the speaker's removal of himself from the concluding lines of "Lucy Gray" is more realistically a defection that, like his deferral to the sister at the end of "Tintern Abbey," uncovers a structure of differentiation reciprocally signified by the reader. Thus, it is the paradox of such poetry that to be self-enclosed it has also to be allegorical, since without allegory there is literally no other-ness, no alterity, for the Wordsworthian speaker to assimilate.

One clear instance of the way the foregrounded or increasingly marginal reader marks a passage between the speaker and his poetic identity is "A Poet's Epitaph." Here, the speaker characteristically rejects a host of possible readers—the "Statesman," the "Lawyer," the "Doctor," and so on—before settling on the only possible respondent:

He is retired as noontide dew,
Or fountain in a noonday grove;
And you must love him, ere to you
He will seem worthy of your love. . . .

But he is weak, both man and boy,
Hath been an idler in the land;
Contented if he might enjoy
The things which others understand.

—Come hither in thy hour of strength,
Come, weak as is a breaking wave!
Here stretch thy body at full length;
Or build thy house upon this grave.—(41–60)

As in the Lucy poems, where the speaker's address to the reader is concurrent with, rather than tantamount to, speaking to himself, the speaker addresses someone here who, until the penultimate stanza, presumably belongs to one of the categories mandating his or her rejection. Worse, the reader is being asked to set all this aside and to accept on faith this version of the "poet" ("And you must love him, ere to you / He will seem worthy of your love") as a better version and person than the reader.

That the poem has, at this putatively inclusive juncture, shifted suddenly to the figure of the poet is more than an instance of bad manners. It is a movement *from the speaker,* whose difference—in virtual imitation of the reader's—has essentially provoked the shift. In light of what has already transpired, the "you" of the final stanzas is not (as in "Lucy Gray") simply the reader, who in one guise or another has already been discarded. It is the speaker himself, who is looking backwards—hypothetically—from a position when he will have become the dead poet. More, surely, than the hackneyed description of the "poetic" frame of mind or the progress of the poet's soul, it is this circularity that mandates the epitaphical apparatus. That is, by doubling as the deceased poet the speaker is sufficiently removed from his living self for their narcissistic separation ("I" and "You," "Man and Boy") to be healed by separation from the reader. In the final stanza, the displacement of all readers with the exception of the man speaking, confirmed by the exclusionary shift from "you" to "thy," transforms the poem into an epitaph (and the epitaph into a poem) by bridging the space between one poet and another.

The extent to which poetic identity forces a distinction now between the reader's reading and the "poet"'s ability to read or "understand" himself is demonstrated more clearly yet in the second group of "Matthew" poems, written at virtually the same time as the Lucy poems. While the speaker wishes to be aligned with Matthew in these works—with the figure who most clearly represents a "difference" characteristic of the poetical self—he is thrown back upon his previous identity as a reader. Earlier, in the poems up to and including "Tintern Abbey," that inferrble identity was simultaneously the "poet" 's so that understanding or reading was really tantamount to expression or meaning. Now, in the aftermath of this accord, the reader's anterior (if still necessary) function is signaled in the poet's mediation between potential identities and in the separation of reading and understanding. Oscillating between the reader and Matthew, the speaker of the Matthew poems ultimately identifies with a new figure—the old schoolmaster—and by understanding him, displaces the previous agent of understanding, the inferred reader. For, as the poem subsequently titled "Matthew" shows, to understand Matthew is not to read Matthew as the reader will, but rather to imagine him in ways that are almost incomprehensible to the reader. The "text" of this poem remains a text of Wordsworth's double-life as a poetical self. It reveals that poetic vision would be impossible were Matthew not inscrutable to the reader and, hence, a fit object of the "poet" 's sympathy.

Like "A Poet's Epitaph," the commemoration to Matthew, "If Nature, for a favorite Child," is also an epitaph that commences by naming an audience whose exclusiveness fails nevertheless to include *another* reader, the poem's speaker. No matter how privileged the audience may be, or how childlike, its suitability lies in its lack of understanding. This is proven by the description of Matthew that eventually follows:

> Poor Matthew, all his frolics o'er,
> Is silent as a standing pool,
> Far from the chimney's merry roar,
> And murmur of the village school.

> The sighs which Matthew heav'd were sighs
> Of one tir'd out with fun and madness;
> The tears which came to Matthew's eyes
> Were tears of light, the oil of gladness. (21–28)

The "tears," which the reader will undoubtedly construe as Matthew's own, may be conceived at another level as belonging to the gladsome children, whom Matthew regards in fact or, more likely, in his mind's eye. The second reading, then, which is barely a reading at all, has the effect of aligning someone—call him the "poet"—with someone else—call him "Matthew"—in contradistinction to a sentimental speaker and a (now) misconstruing reader. The realignment of the speaker, by which he proceeds from one reader to another, is managed less by act of sentiment or "common sympathy" (16) than by imagination, which is some other function because the "misreading" is actually more plausible.

It is only afterwards that the reader's reading is put in question, that we are exposed by the speaker to a revisioned Matthew:

> Yet sometimes when the secret cup
> Of still and serious thought went round
> It seem'd as if he drank it up,
> He felt with spirit so profound.
>
> —Thou soul of God's best earthly mould,
> Thou happy soul, and can it be
> That these two words of glittering gold
> Are all that must remain of thee? (29–36)

The disjunction of the penultimate stanza, where somberness replaces Matthew's "gladness," is reversed in the conclusion where Matthew is again a "happy soul." However, as the speaker's own disjunction (or identity) depends on a readerly need for Matthew's happiness (and upon the readings and misunderstandings which engender that desire), it devolves to the reader to help forge the identification of speaker and subject. The Matthew the speaker would imitate, who comes to represent the "poet," is not the "happy" Matthew with whom the poem concludes. It is the impenetrable Matthew in whose somber, solitary image both poem and poet "remain." Like the stanza describing Matthew's tears (and, earlier, the close of "Lucy Gray"), the poem's final stanza essentially distinguishes two different sympathies: one poetic and the other readerly. To the extent that Matthew is of "God's best earthly mould," he is of course special. Yet his "difference" in this instance owes to his having become a "soul." It owes to a mystification in death that only the speaker, among all readers, recognizes as such and to whom, in consequence, Matthew's "earthly" difference devolves.

Accordingly, the final question of Matthew—"Are [these words] all that remain of thee?"—is rhetorical in two distinct ways: its literal answer is "yes," but insofar as the implied response from the speaker's quarter is "no," it justifies his inclusion in the concluding and exclusionary "thee." The inscription of Matthew's name on the commemorative tablet are the words, to be sure, to which the speaker is referring. But the words that "remain" are also, following "A Poet's Epitaph," those of the poem itself, which as the headnote observes, was placed "opposite" Matthew's name by the "Author" himself. Similar to "A Poet's Epitaph," which is by and about the same person, the subject here turns out to be less a remembered Matthew than an imagined Matthew, and aligned in that process with the poem's real signified—the man speaking. Even as the reader perpetuates Matthew in reading or through a veil of mystification, the "poet," by perpetuating "Matthew" in "words," departs his role as the speaker kindred with his audience. But to depart it, the speaker must first speak to that audience in such fashion that the misunderstanding due the reader opposes the more discrete understanding of yet another reader *and speaker* to whom Matthew's difference falls.[21]

The "sympathy," by which poetical character resists "common" or readerly sympathy is dramatized more effectively in "The Two April Mornings," which moves from misunderstanding as the obverse of understanding to an understanding that links the speaker and Matthew. Anne Kostelanetz [Mellor] has observed how the repetition of the "April morning . . . in Matthew's own experience . . . is being repeated again by the narrator in his memory." This structural irony, according to Kostelanetz, enables Wordsworth to "wor[k] against the authority of Matthew's statements," chiefly through his speaker's demonstration of "the joyous repetitions of nature."[22] Kostelanetz is clearly right to note the repetition of Matthew in the poem's speaker. But she overlooks the effects of Matthew's repetition on the speaker's relationship with *his* auditor—the poem's reader—which the assimilation of Matthew, so to speak, attenuates. The precariousness of the speaker's relationship to the reader, in fact, is evident in the poem's "incorrect" title. As Kostelanetz shows, the poem is ultimately about a third April morning. This third morning, as we shall see, resembles the first two in distinguishing one way of seeing from another. But where "the two April mornings" (both the mornings and the poem thus titled) serve to distinguish Matthew from both the speaker and the poem's reader, the third April morning distinguishes the speaker from the reader as well. One hermeneutic circle breaks in deference to another from which the reader is consequently excluded.

"The Two April Mornings" begins by distinguishing its ostensible subject, Matthew, from both the speaker and the reader who are thus akin. Because the speaker's outing with Matthew (which he here recalls), immediately reminds Matthew of a similar morning many years earlier, the distinction between the two men, whose orientations are subsequently different, is also figured by the reader, whose reality for all practical purposes is identical to the speaker's. It is the poem, furthermore, that works this figuration. That is, in the very way the speaker has transformed his past into a remembered *present*, which is the poem, he also follows the trajectory of renewal in making that present, the poetic or hermeneutic present, an interval to which all time leads.

Matthew is of course different, and just as the speaker moves forward, subordinating his past to the here and now, so Matthew is observed to have moved backward, deliberately departing the remembered present by memory, oddly, of a similar present. It was then paradoxically that Matthew's disengagement from all subsequent renewal (and union) began. For it was on a similar April morning "full thirty years" ago that Matthew came suddenly upon his daughter's grave and experienced the following encounter:

> And, turning from her grave, I met,
> Beside the church-yard Yew
> A blooming Girl, whose hair was wet
> With points of morning dew.
>
> A basket on her head she bare,
> Her brow was smooth and white,
> To see a Child so very fair,
> It was a pure delight! (41–48)

At this point, there is little that distinguishes the poem's reader from the speaker: both remain ensnared in the present by a narrative of apparent wish fulfillment.

Yet unlike the previous poem, where such wishes are fulfilled in the act of reading, here hope is turned against the reader. We discover that such wishes not only are impossible to realize but are no longer shared:

> There came from me a sigh of pain
> Which I could ill confine;
> I look'd at her, and look'd again;
> —And did not wish her mine. (53–56)

Matthew's "wish," as he aptly calls it, follows a negative way, illustrating that for him hope is really desire. Recognizing what he wants in an immediate, readerly way, Matthew similarly realizes that his own needs are altogether different. That he does "not wish" the girl his own, hardly means that he has lost the ability to wish. It means that his wishes are more consistent with material reality—with the girl *not* his daughter—whom Matthew does "not wish" to resist. But resist Matthew does. He knows better perhaps than to make claims upon the world, but this does not prevent Matthew from preferring a world elsewhere. Whatever he accepts of the material world is enabled, paradoxically, by another world (and girl) for which the present (e.g. spring) provides no objective correlatives, and where imagination must supply its own objects. "Nine summers," he recalls of this world,

> had she scarcely seen,
> The pride of all the vale;
> And then she sang!—she would have been
> A very nightingale. (33–36)

Weighing the reality of the "blooming girl" (or blooming nature) against the speculation that his own daughter "would have been / A very nightingale," Matthew seizes upon the latter. In this he contrasts sharply with the reader who has already chosen the former. The speaker's response is, in contrast, more complex. The extremities he has exposed as intermediary and auditor— namely, to trust the world as the reader will be inclined, or to trust oneself as Matthew does—are ones between which he cannot steer a simple course. Nevertheless, in making a choice, he chooses in a way that incorporates the choice *not made:*

> Matthew is in his grave, yet now
> Methinks I see him stand,
> As at that moment, with a bough
> Of wilding in his hand. (57–60)

In trusting desire by envisioning the deceased, the speaker ultimately follows Matthew. He resigns faith in the material world and in a poetic present, where, as it is already shown, requital is impossible. The reader will likely be disappointed by this recapitulation of Matthew's imaginative departures from the present, especially given his previous affinity with the speaker. But the poem as a whole remains (much like the Lucy poems) an introduction to both the reader's *and* the speaker's worlds: to the present and to a world elsewhere, which are cast in mutual relief. What is "seen" in the end by the speaker—Matthew on the very day he encountered the "blooming girl"—is, and always has been, inaccessible to the reader. Thus, only in conjunction with the reader is the speaker's sudden loss of faith in "blooming" reality apparent. In distinguishing himself from the reader, who is left ultimately to his own devices (as he was similarly discharged with the Statesman, the Moralist and the Doctor in "A Poet's Epitaph"), the speaker makes his uniqueness correlative to his auditor's. And this is also true of the reader's adversariness, which is as much a resistance to what the poem asserts as a counter-resistance to what the poem denies: a skepticism about the poem's skepticism that, amid this doubling, the speaker partly shares.

The speaker's image of Matthew does more than confirm his kinship with Matthew; its status as an object seen simultaneously resists that kinship by showing imagination to be of the reader's party. "What," the final stanza also demands of the reader, "were you expecting Matthew to do or the 'blooming girl' to be?" Since the girl is not Matthew's daughter, there is no way for him to recapture the past "at that moment" any more than the poet can recapture him at this "moment." At the exact moment, then, that he is ostensibly privileging himself as a version of the beheld (that is, Matthew), the speaker discredits himself by exposing his equivalence to his beholder.

Nor is this the only time their equivalence has been an issue. Two stanzas earlier, the speaker is similarly admonished by Matthew himself. At this juncture, having brought Matthew's recollection to its crisis, a number of options were available. First, the speaker might have intervened, either in fact or more likely in his capacity as narrator. And Matthew might have paused, if only in deference to his auditor. Yet their agreement in the poem—Matthew's to continue uninterrupted and the speaker's to remain silent— underscores the self-enclosed, "sealed" character from which the speaker is removed yet evidently sympathetic with. Not only, in other words, does the speaker of "The Two April Mornings" come to identify with Matthew whose "difference" he ultimately assimilates; he has, in an archaeology of this "difference" (and like his counterparts in either "Matthew" or "A Poet's Epitaph"), managed also to become his best and worst readers simultaneously. He is both a reader of Matthew through whom a new identity emerges, yet a naïf to whose status in the end a former self is consigned. By silence first, and only later by imitation, the speaker gives testimony on this third April morning to the common sympathy from which his uncommon sympathy issues. His stance owes as much "now" to his vision of Matthew as to envisioning himself seeing Matthew. It owes to his ability to see himself "as at that moment"—a moment alternately here and elsewhere—when reading and speaking are synonymous yet different.

Less conclusive, though equally determined to discriminate among sympathies, "The Fountain" recounts a "conversation" between the speaker (who again assumes the auditor's role) and Matthew. Unlike the previous "Matthew" poems, where reading is allegorized by way of demonstration, "The Fountain" is strictly an allegory. Where previously the Matthew speaker is "both Man and Boy"—a figure to whom Matthew provisionally refers—he remains, as a figure of the reader, youthful to the point of caricature. Thus, unlike those of the other Matthew poems, where the speaker is given the last word, the "conversation" in "The Fountain" ends properly with the "poet" Matthew, who firmly rejects his "reader" 's bid for kinship.[23]

"The Fountain" begins *in medias res* during an exchange in which the speaker and Matthew have "talk'd with open heart, and tongue / Affectionate and true" (1–2). That this conversation is not remembered, save in the most impressionistic of terms, is an important detail made more important by the speaker's subsequent proposal that he and Matthew sing "some old Border-song" (11) or "[t]hat half-mad thing of witty rhymes" (15) Matthew had himself composed. In response to these entreaties (and indeed to the songs themselves, whose liminal disposition makes them literally unsharable), Matthew is silent. He is silent, moreover, not out of any animus toward the speaker but in deference to a more immediate exchange in which he must answer to himself.

Unable, however, to pursue *that* conversation, as he had in "The Two April Mornings," Matthew responds to the speaker by justifying his inability to reply to either of them. If time, as Matthew implies, has served to separate him from himself, it has served, more crucially, to separate Matthew as "Man" from the very "Boy" to whom *in time* he is nevertheless obligated:

My days, my Friend, are almost gone,
My life has been approv'd,
And many love me, but by none
Am I enough belov'd." (53–56)

At this point, significantly, the speaker interrupts, expressing his determination to "be a son" (62) to Matthew. Yet the very fact of this interruption demonstrates how, as a measure of his inability to "love" Matthew enough, the speaker misreads "approval." Approval, which refers to the sanction or approbation of the "many" who "love" Matthew, makes this obviously insufficient love typical of the filial love that Matthew's "approval"—the test or ordeal of his "life"—makes it impossible for him to reciprocate.

Matthew's reply to the speaker's suggestion, then, recapitulating his response to the "blooming girl" in "The Two April Mornings," is "Alas! that cannot be" (64). His decision finally to sing "those witty rhymes / About the crazy old church-clock / And the bewilder'd chimes" (70–72) is thus not an accession to the speaker, who suggested that they sing together, but rather a response to a need of Matthew's own that supplants one "conversation" with another. Nor is it insignificant that Matthew's song is reported sung but remains in the experience of the poem unheard. In separating self-expression from its apprehension, this detail serves to distinguish one kind of poetry from another. Replacing the initial, unrecoverable, conversation between the poet and Matthew, the song abides as another unrecoverable conversation— one for which there can be, in effect, no auditor. It is the speaker's inability to love Matthew "enough"—enough, that is, to share his authority as a singer, or to maintain his role as kindred conversant—that makes him, according to both Wordsworth or Matthew, unworthy of being privileged or "approv'd." And for Matthew, it is the inability to converse, to be understood by "none" save himself, that accounts for his current approval and, paradoxical as it may sound, his ability finally to sing. Compelled in the end to sing his song—a "thing," not surprisingly, about mutability and bewilderment—Matthew sings to an audience all his own, albeit one in which the "reader" is still implicated.

NOTES

1. "Essay, Supplementary to the Preface," *Prose Works*, vol. 3, 80. In arguing for his poems' originality, Wordsworth follows Coleridge's lead in making originality the character of the 1798 poems. Yet this is only sometimes the judgment of posterity. Following Robert Mayo ("The Contemporaneity of the Lyrical Ballads," *PMLA*, 69 [1954]: 486–522), who, in detailing their "contemporaneous features," endeavored to show how the *Ballads* were not such a 'complete change' as some writers would have us believe" (486), critics such as Stephen M. Parrish have been obliged either to defend the "originality" or "art" of the *Lyrical Ballads* (*The Art of the "Lyrical*

Ballads" [Cambridge, MA: Harvard University Press, 1973) or, like Charles
Ryskamp ("Wordsworth's 'Lyrical Ballads' in Their Time," in *From Sensibility to Romanticism,* 357–72), to show how, in their peculiar "movement of
mind," the ballads may still be distinguished from the popular poetry of the
day. At all events, the originality that has been a matter of controversy in the
1798 poems is universally conceded in the poems that follow.

2. A related, if fundamentally different, view has recently been advanced by Don H. Bialostosky (*Making Tales: The Poetics of Wordsworth's
Narrative Experiments* [Chicago: University of Chicago Press, 1984]). Drawing directly upon Bakhtin, Bialostosky argues for a "poetics of speech" in
Wordsworth in which the intelligibility of words must be seen not simply "in
[words] themselves or even in relation to their speaker alone but in relation
to a situation in response to which the speaker speaks" (39–40). This
conception of an "inner listener," much championed by Bakhtinians, not
only has the general effect of privileging fiction or narrative over more
subjective or self-enclosed forms of expression such as the lyric; it effectively revises the nature of both identity and originality by replacing otherness, in which they are ultimately grounded, with the sameness or dialogism
which at some level can be said to subsume otherness. Nevertheless *Lyrical
Ballads* and the poetry after replace this sense of "community" with a sense
of originality or difference which dialogism, in retrospect, can be said
therefore to foster.

3. Angus Fletcher, *Allegory: The Theory of a Symbolic Mode* (Ithaca, NY:
Cornell University Press, 1964), 2.

4. See, in a related argument, Timothy Bahti's analysis of "becoming"
in Book I of *The Prelude* ("Wordsworth's Rhetorical Theft," in *Romanticism
and Language,* ed. Arden Reed [Ithaca, NY: Cornell University Press, 1984],
86–124). According to Bahti, there is a necessary relationship between
certain acts of appropriation—for example the stolen boat—and the self
thereby "produced." For in appropriating the boat, the Wordsworthian
self becomes "structurally dependent"— "appropriated, so to speak, into
[a] figural structure, itself a structure of allegory, wherein a thing both is
itself and also signifies or figures something else, an insubstantial state and
meaning" (88–89).

5. Among the writings of de Man's that pursue this argument with
reference to Wordsworth are: "The Rhetoric of Temporality" (in *Interpretation: Theory and Practice,* ed. Charles S. Singleton [Baltimore: The Johns
Hopkins University Press, 1969], 173–209), "Intentional Structure of the
Romantic Image," and "Autobiography as De-facement" (*MLN,* 94 [1979]:
919–30).

6. In many ways, of course, I am recapitulating the judgment earlier
advanced by David Ferry in *The Limits of Mortality* on the "enmity" for man
that Wordsworth mistook for love. Where I diverge from Ferry is in my
attempt, with benefit of hindsight, to show that this is not simply a paradox
that the poet might have overcome, but a condition of his poetry and of the
self therein, whose paradoxes reveal the mythology or archetype on which
identity is founded.

7. *The Self Observed: Swift, Johnson, Wordsworth* (Baltimore: The Johns Hopkins University Press, 1972), 100–37.

8. Bahti, 88. For a treatment of allegory that contests this de Manian or deconstructive sense of allegory as indeterminate or destabilizing, see Fineman, "The Allegorical Structure of Desire," in *Allegory and Representation,* ed. Stephen Greenblatt (Baltimore: The Johns Hopkins University Press, 1981), 26–60. Using, like Bahti, a psychoanalytic paradigm, Fineman nevertheless argues for the "hierarchized sexuality" in allegory (39), which "initiates and continually revivifies its own desire, a desire born of its own structurality" (44). Similarly, Angus Fletcher notes that despite the "conflict of authorities [at the heart of any allegory]," the "mode is hierarchical in essence" (*Allegory,* 22).

9. "The Rhetoric of Temporality," 191–209. Drawing on Baudelaire's *De l'essence du rire,* de Man defines irony in precisely the way it exists allegorically in *The Excursion* and, as we will also see, in *The Prelude:* as "a relationship, within consciousness, between two selves, yet . . . not an intersubjective relationship" (195).

10. This point is made in a somewhat different manner by Eugene L. Stelzig in "Mutability, Ageing, and Permanence in Wordsworth's Later Poetry," *SEL,* 19 (1979): 623–44. Although noting the non-subjective disposition of the later poetry, Stelzig still regards its expressions of mutability as "more detached and conventionally rhetorical, . . . frequently colored by a Christian-stoic attitude" (624). I would argue, to the contrary, that this stoicism can only be viewed against the backdrop of Wordsworth's earlier subjectivism, making it a detachment, in effect, from the very "detachment" to which it more immediately represents a response.

11. In some ways, then, this final ironic turn in Wordsworth follows "the paradigm of 'Romantic Irony'" as Anne K. Mellor describes it in *English Romantic Irony* (Cambridge, MA: Harvard University Press, 1980), 3–30. Where it departs from Mellor's paradigm is in its anti-humanist dimension. That is, in "consciously deconstruct[ing the] mystifications of the self," Wordsworth is necessarily *removed* from the "greater creative power" or authority to which, as Mellor maintains, the romantic ironist is thereby privy (5).

12. Of the various studies to consider the Lucy poems as a unit, the most representative in their attempts to deal with Lucy's figurative status are: Geoffrey Durrant (*Wordsworth and the Great System* [London: Cambridge University Press, 1970], 135–74), in which "the completed cycle of [Lucy's] life" resembles "the cyclical pattern of the earth and the planets" (155); Spencer Hall ("Wordsworth's 'Lucy' Poems: Context and Meaning," *SIR,* 10 [1971]: 159–75), who sees them as Wordsworth's attempt to come to terms with "humanness" in a more objective, less personalized, way; and Richard Matlak ("Wordsworth's Lucy Poems in Psychobiographical Context," *PMLA,* 93 [1978]: 46–65), where the poems are seen against the backdrop of the poet's "vocational anxiety" and his relationship with Dorothy, whose proximity was "probably stifling and inhibitive" and had therefore to be managed. In all of these, however, the connection between

the figure of Lucy and the figurative "friend" of "Tintern Abbey" (composed just six months earlier) goes unexamined.

13. In an interesting study that examines the initial drafts of "Nutting" in Dove Cottage MS. 16 ("Wordsworth's Lucy of 'Nutting,' " *SIR,* 18 [1979]: 287–98), Douglass H. Thomson observes that the initial identification of the dramatic auditor as both "Lucy" and "My beloved Friend!" further identifies "her" with Dorothy in "Tintern Abbey" as a "direct embodiment of Wordsworth's own sense of past experience" (294). This, submits Thomson, is why "Lucy" is effectively admonished for crimes she did not commit. Nevertheless, as Thomson also shows, the final version of "Nutting" based, like the initial draft, on the "pre-existing conclusion" differs from the initial draft in its refusal to admit the speaker's guilt. Hence, the speaker's "protestation 'I am guiltless here' " (296) in the manuscript version serves to highlight what is more subtly encoded in the final version: namely, the speaker's passage from the representative, guilty condition of "Tintern Abbey" to the more exemplary, guiltless condition, in which (as in the Lucy poems) the speaker remains different from "Lucy" and the reader both.

14. *The Confessional Imagination: A Reading of Wordsworth's "Prelude"* (Baltimore: The Johns Hopkins University Press, 1974), 44. In noting the parallel between "Nutting" and the episode of the pear tree in St. Augustine's *Confessions,* McConnell inadvertently resolves the paradox in "Nutting" where, according to David Ferry, the "Nutting" speaker both desires nature's "virginity" and desires to destroy it (*The Limits of Mortality,* 22–27). By admitting to this paradox in his own language, the "confessant" implicitly distinguishes it (and the condition it represents) from the "salvation" which his ability to construct such a "narrative" now intimates (*The Confessional Imagination,* 6–10).

15. Frances Ferguson has also noted the "renunciatory movement" by which the Lucy poems "establis[h] the poet-speaker . . . as an increasingly solitary voice" ("The Lucy Poems: Wordsworth's Quest For a Poetic Object," *ELH,* 40 [1973]: 536, reprinted as chapter 6 of *Wordsworth: Language as Counter-Spirit*). Yet for Ferguson this solitary "accession to knowledge" (543) is in the end a "renunciation of the poet's claims to knowledge" (547)—rather than (as I see it) an "accession" or greater solitude that only the renounced reader will read as a renunciation. Another reading of the Lucy poems that stresses their movement from "past to present" and "from error to self-knowledge" is Peter Manning's ("Wordsworth and Gray's Sonnet on the Death of West," *SEL,* 22 [1982]: 505–18). Using the paradigm of mourning and the "psychic murder" that mourning is believed by psychoanalysts to entail, Manning shows how the reaction to Lucy's death, especially in "A slumber did my spirit seal," marks a "deeply felt 'difference' to the speaker himself," and systematically marks the passage "from the dead beloved to the continuing self" (510–11). To be sure, these poems are about death, but they are about a death, characteristically, whose intensely personal relevance is sharply underlined by the way the reader is simultaneously prevented from participating not only in the speaker's grief, but

also in the memory of Lucy. The "psychic murder," then, that the poems document is attendant, as I see it, upon an even more aggressive stance to the reader.

16. Both Richard Matlak ("Wordsworth's Lucy Poems in Psychobiographical Context") and John Price ("Wordsworth's Lucy," *American Imago*, 31 [1974]: 360–77) stress the "radical" (Matlak, 51) wish fulfillment in "Strange fits" "that Lucy die." For Matlak, this fantasy is at base an anxiety about vocation, where for Price it is less "a disguised wish-fulfillment" than an anxiety on the poet's part "regarding sexuality in general" (373).

17. Hall and Matlak comment on the effect of the deleted final stanza. For Hall, the stanza sentimentalizes "what is a markedly unsentimental poem" and deflects "attention from the poem's central theme"—which is "human loss" (166). For Matlak, the "lover's reaction in 'Strange Fits' is separative," distinguishing the speaker's premonition from the actual cause of death (53). By contrast, William P. Dawson ("The Perceptual Bond in 'Strange Fits of Passion,'" *TWC*, 13 [1982]: 96–97), who also views the "rejection of [the] stanza" as separative, stresses how the "final version of the poem shifts the emphasis away from considerations of the ironic truth of the rider's thought and toward an examination of perception and thought itself."

18. In a stylistic analysis, Roger L. Slakey demonstrates how the "full force of the poem . . . presses down on the speaker himself"—"that the experience of the poem is his, and his alone" ("At Zero: A Reading of Wordsworth's 'She Dwelt Among the Untrodden Ways,'" *SEL*, 12 [1972]: 636–37). Hall, too, observes how "the famous second stanza" underscores the "cleavage between human lover and nature" (166).

19. *Wordsworth's Poetry*, 159. By contrast, E. D. Hirsch—in attempting to mediate between Bateson's view of the poem as celebrating immortality and Cleanth Brooks' bitterly ironic reading—concludes that the two readings are irreconcilable, eliminating thereby the possibility that Hartman judiciously provides (*Validity in Interpretation* [New Haven, CT: Yale University Press, 1967], 227–30). Finally, J. Hillis Miller ("On Edge: The Crossways of Contemporary Criticism," in *Romanticism and Contemporary Criticism*, ed. Morris Eaves and Michael Fischer [Ithaca, NY: Cornell University Press, 1986], 96–126) shows in more specifically deconstructive ways how "A Slumber" discredits the fantasy by "dramatiz[ing] the impossibility of fulfilling [it]." For Miller, the poem "demonstrates that [the fantasy] can only be fulfilled in fantasy, that is, in a structure of words in which 'thing' can mean both 'person' and 'object,' in which one can have both stanzas at once, and can, like Lucy, be both alive and dead, or in which the poet can be both the dead-alive girl and at the same time the perpetually wakeful survivor" (107). The poem's trajectory, as I view it, is effectively toward what Miller might deem an "impossibility," but it is an impossibility made possible by the poem's rather cultivated skepticism.

20. Hall verges on this point when he observes parenthetically that "the scepticism potentially present in 'Yet some maintain' is not . . . actualized

in the poem" (170). That potentiality, I would argue, is precisely what *is there*—and must remain potential so as to separate the speaker from the hermeneutic that allays skepticism.

21. Ferguson observes how the "ambiguous address to Matthew" underscores the "futility" of supplementing the "authority of the gilt words on the tablet" with the poet's own words (*Wordsworth: Language as Counter-Spirit*, 85–88). As I see it, however, this "ambiguity" of the address does not register futility but merely removes the speaker from the stigma of inadequacy.

22. "Wordsworth's 'Conversations': A Reading of 'The Two April Mornings' and 'The Fountain,'" *ELH*, 33 (1966): 43–52.

23. Kostelanetz observes, on the contrary, how the narrator and Matthew are "'related' . . . above all as poets" (52). While this is true, it is a relation based also on the difference that continually prohibits the speaker from "really" being, as Kostelanetz would have it, "a 'son' to [Matthew]."

"By our own spirits are we deified": Allegories of Writing and the Advent of Genius, 1800–1802

Perhaps the most expedient way to accommodate the problems posed by Wordsworth's earlier poetry, especially in *Lyrical Ballads,* is simply to consent, as Steven Knapp reluctantly has, to "the fact of allegorization."[1] In consenting to allegory's facticity, so to speak, we admit a referent or direction to Wordsworth's poetry without submitting to the rigors and frustrations of also following it. To the reader who will not consent, but who must follow or otherwise decode Wordsworth's allegory, the various deferrals we have previously outlined—which by introversion or appropriation scarcely seem deferrals—are bound to cause frustration. This will be true for the deconstructive critic as well. Although the instabilities of Wordsworthian allegory are undoubtedly more felicitous to this reader, the authoritative dispensation under which allegory operates in the earlier poetry is likely to prove just as disconcerting.

Knapp's consent, therefore, both recognizes the futility of reading Wordsworth's allegory and, paradoxical as it may sound, the utility of Wordsworthian allegory as the mode on which the "self" has come exclusively to rely. Indeed, despite his efforts to account for the "quasi-allegorical . . . figures" in Wordsworth, who replace the "formal personifications of the eighteenth century," Knapp finds himself trapped between the "ostensibly natural" disposition of these figures and the "preternatural self-enclosure" that also mitigates their ability to "inhabit the same narrative or discursive space as the poet himself" (98–102). Knapp's response to this entrapment, again, is to concede that there is something relentlessly allegorical in these configurations. And in this, Knapp reveals a way of mediating (along with Wordsworth) between two contradictory extremes: the hierarchizing tendencies of allegory (and of the identity sustained thereby), and allegory's tendency to construct *as it deconstructs* "the difference" that both rightfully and arbitrarily devolves "to me." Most crucial to Knapp's perplexity is not, as he describes it, "the fact of allegorization as such" (106); what is crucial, rather, is the relational disposition of Wordsworth's figures, who are now objects of sympathy commensurate with the poet's difference. What most perplexes Knapp is the way various figures of sympathy are necessarily inherent to, yet necessarily at variance with, the poet's identity.

Following those early poems, then, that engage the reader in a poetics of sincerity, an overlay of sympathy exists even in the works that call subsequently for the reader's exclusion. The problem, even for so judicious a reader as Knapp, lies in taking sympathy and naturalization at face value—rather than in conjunction with the "preternatural" figuration on which understanding and sympathy are increasingly based. If Wordsworth's earlier efforts are defined by a sympathy with an inferred reader—who prefigures the "poet" or "man to come"—then the poems that immediately follow are defined by their sympathy with another figure—Matthew, or the buried "poet," or even Lucy's "lover"—with whom the speaker may be aligned only by abandoning his reader. This latter poetics of sympathy breaks with the reader by choosing to elaborate a figure of sympathy beyond him.

This transformation, and the hermeneutic reversal in which it immediately issues, is important as much for the change it reflects as for the transformation it undoes. In making sympathy part of an ever-exclusive idealization or, as we have seen, "[un]common sympathy," Wordsworth makes the fact of sympathy, like the self-enclosure in which it issues, a "fact of allegorization." A result of the *apparatus* of self-expression, of the "discrepancy" (as Knapp calls it) on which identity depends, the exclusionary poems of 1799 recall the inclusionary works of 1798 in that neither are fundamentally acts of sympathy. Both are acts of self-enclosure, albeit ones requiring a conception of the self—either a "man" of whom the speaker is an extrapolation, or a "man," like Matthew, whom the speaker would imitate—as a condition of the spirit's sealing. That this conception remains one of other-ness, informed by a "sublime" or "hierarchical" figuration on which the notion of identity remains grounded, is not yet a problem. Indeed, such information is more a means by which poetry, in acts of sympathy, verges on an ever-burgeoning authority.[2]

Thus, just as the poems written after "Tintern Abbey" allegorize reading as a way to distinguish this activity from the authority of writing, so the poems following these "allegories of reading" allegorize the authority of writing in order to distinguish writing from reading. This movement is less tautological than it sounds. What the allegories of writing elaborate in their various representations of poetic authority is the poetics of otherness only disclosed in the allegories of reading. No longer an object of identification or prototype for the "man speaking," Wordsworth's reader is increasingly testimony in these latter allegories against both the existence *and* the preexistence of the earlier configuration. The typology whereby the speaker was a type, and the reader his antetype, gives way in 1800 to a new typology, which includes the reader, or a figure of the reader, in a continually subordinate capacity.

Yet subordination only emphasizes the contingency of the poet's otherness. In sympathizing with the figures of authority, against whom various "readers" are now set, Wordsworth does not so much refigure his poetics of sincerity; he reenacts them by distinguishing Michael or Leonard (in "The Brothers") as surrogates for himself as poet. As long, that is, as the machinery for sympathy remains intact, allowing Wordsworth's speaker to identify with the authority of Michael, Leonard or even the Waterfall in "The Waterfall and the Eglantine," allegory is protected as allegory from what it also exposes: that poetic identity is forever part of a larger, pervasive structure.[3] Thus, it is hardly a coincidence that the figures with whom the speaker sympathizes in recognition of his identity as poet, and whose uniqueness remains a prerequisite for the poet's sympathy, have figures of their own—"secondary" figures for the reader—to help signify their difference. The possibility of an escape from allegory's structure, especially as a measure of one's authority, is ever more remote in Wordsworth.

The difficulty of such an escape is particularly evident with the suspension of allegory in the lyrics composed in 1802. By 1802, Wordsworth not only achieves the authority indicative of poetic "genius"; he manages an internalization of the allegorical structure which also eschews the protection of "allegorization as such." The claims to genius clearly elevate the "man speaking" among the "men" he would represent, and who previously are his representatives. Yet such claims simultaneously make the "poet" answerable *as an authority* of which he is merely a refiguration. The effects of eschewing allegory's protection are registered in two significant ways, then: in the still larger "discrepancy" of selfhood that Wordsworth immediately calls "genius," and in the internal discrepancy or "insubstantiality" by which the self proves unequal to its alleged sublimity.[4]

This system of differences on which the mystification and eventual demystification of the poetical self depend—that stands poised between the authority it promotes and the authority it withholds—is already evident in "Hart-Leap Well," which, coincidentally, is the first entry in the second volume of *Lyrical Ballads* (1800). Divided into two parts, the first of which—the story of the hart's death at the urging of Sir Walter—is "understood" in the "second" part, the poem remains an allegory of both writing and reading. Further, like the speaker/listener of the "Matthew" poems (composed approximately a year earlier), the speaker here is sufficiently implicated in both allegories to move in two directions at once: backward, toward a recognition of the origins of a poetical self, and forward, to a reconstitution of them. A sentimentalist, at one level, who seeks to excoriate the hart's killer for failing to be a good pantheist, the speaker is also the poetic authority who never quite recognizes his mistake in dissociating Sir Walter's life from the one life within us and abroad. "One lesson, Shepherd, let us two divide," he enjoins the Shepherd (and implicitly the reader who has previously heard the account of the hart's death), "[n]ever to blend our pleasure or our pride / With sorrow of the meanest thing that feels" (177–80).

This view, according to the speaker, is also nature's view and one of several such views preferred by him throughout the poem. Approaching the site where, as he subsequently learns, the hart died in a desperate effort to avoid capture, the speaker is immediately struck by the desolation of the scene. He attributes this first to nature and afterwards to a natural-supernaturalism:

> The trees were grey, with neither arms nor head;
> Half-wasted the square mound of tawny green;
> So that you just might say, as then I said,
> "Here in old time the hand of man has been."
>
> I look'd upon the hills both far and near;
> More doleful place did never eye survey;
> It seem'd as if the spring-time came not here,
> And Nature here were willing to decay. (109–16)

The irony of this recognition, as the pathetic fallacy of Nature's will makes clear, is that the wasteland—whether by accident, intention, or distortion of memory—results from a human action. Previously (as we learn in the first part), this same waste issued from another human action: having pursued and triumphed over the stag, Sir Walter resolves to commemorate the hart's last, giant leap with a monument. That nature has since subverted this commemoration, reducing the knight's "Pleasure-house" (169) to an infamous ruin, hardly diminishes his status as prime mover.

To the contrary, it is the speaker's argument that is diminished, for from the vantage of the poem it remains a commentary on his need to argue against the facts. Although the speaker is clearly out to disparage Sir Walter, the poem nevertheless confirms the knight's power, as it does the speaker's, over the external world. It is not that the human is greater than the natural in "Hart-Leap Well"; it is that there is no longer any point in privileging one over the other. This is shown in the perseverance of two "Hart-Leap wells"—both the poem and the monument it recalls. And it is evident in the perpetual character of the hunt, to which *both* Walter's commemoration and the tale recording the insubstantiality of his commemoration refer. No matter how the speaker contrives to dissociate these events, the monument's decay turns out to be the work of the very forces that first provoked Walter "restless as a veering wind" (17). Human action—either Walter's or the speaker's—is a correlative to either natural or (in Hartman's description) "preternatural" action.[5]

This doubling of Walter and the speaker is not acknowledged by either the speaker or the Shepherd, each of whom reads events wrongly. The speaker errs in humanizing or domesticating nature; the Shepherd, who initially recounts Walter's story to the "poet," errs in naturalizing man. Thus, Part II of the poem, which is given over to their dialogue, becomes a shared allegory of reading, making Part I, in which the Shepherd's tale has been rendered poetically by a single speaker, a representation of writing. The common sympathy of Part II—what the speaker in Part I terms his "second rhyme" (95)—remakes the first section into a register of uncommon sympathy: Part I is a *poem* now or primary rhyme whose omniscient, already privileged voice is further privileged. Reciprocally, the speaker's retrospective designation of the primary rhyme as a "former rhyme" (122) in Part II further dissociates it (and its author) from his reading against Walter in the latter section. Indeed, the very existence of a first part makes this "reading" in Part II plodding and familiar as befits the "second[ary]" status of common sympathy. In mediating, therefore, between the moralistic readings of the shepherd and the previously inscribed (and reinscribed) aggressiveness of Sir Walter, the speaker (like his counterpart in the Matthew poems) actually admits a hierarchy by which the respective functions of reading and writing are at once deferred and set at greater remove.

Still more ruthlessly, the generally overlooked "The Waterfall and the Eglantine," composed at the same time as "Hart-Leap Well," discredits both reading and the "self," of whom the reader was earlier a reflection, simply on the basis of their anteriority. Unlike the equally contemporaneous "poems on the naming of places," where reading is subordinated to, or otherwise subsumed in, the act of naming, the curious eclogue about a tree and a torrent actually justifies that subordination. The majority of the naming poems, which form the penultimate section of Volume II—"It was an April Morning," "To Johanna" and "A Narrow Girdle of Rough Stones and Crags"—are alike in the way they force a respondent (either "Emma" to whom the "dell" in the first poem is dedicated, or the Vicar and Johanna to whom "To Johanna" is simultaneously addressed, or the implied reader who, along with the speaker's remembered companions, renders the "rash-judgement" for which the third poem is expiation) to take a backseat to the inscribing, "naming" authority.

But before these poems and their various acts of exclusion, "The Waterfall and the Eglantine" discovers a mandate for the inclusion of poems on naming in Wordsworth's volume. The exchange dramatized in "The Waterfall" is not merely one of dominion or subsumption, but rather an interchange that has *become* that: a symbiosis that presently allows one element, the Waterfall, to gain primacy over the other. Lacking the assertiveness of the poems on naming, "The Waterfall and the Eglantine," much like the eclogues of Virgil and Spenser, is consumed instead by a peculiar stoicism; in lieu of asserting himself, the speaker speaks instead of a self's assertion. Following "Hart-Leap Well," whose speaker alternately behaves as both reader and writer as a way of distinguishing these roles (and himself), the eclogue initially removes the speaker from these respective functions to dramatize their interchange: the roles of writer and reader are assigned respectively to the "Waterfall" and the "Eglantine." And the Waterfall, as if to activate that dispensation, has the first (and, one is tempted to say, by now familiar) word:

"Begone, thou fond presumptuous Elf,
Exclaim'd a thundering Voice,

Nor dare to thrust thy foolish self
Between me and my choice! (1–4)

In charging the briar with having presumptuously interposed its
"self" between him and his "choice," the Waterfall does two things:
he imitates the counterpart from whom he wishes, in consequence,
to be different; and he *projects,* as both testimony to that difference
and to the identity in which he has nurtured the other, his own,
increasingly aggressive posture:

"Dost thou presume my course to block?
Off, off! or, puny Thing!
I'll hurl thee headlong with the rock
To which thy fibres cling." (11–14)

The underside to nurturing one's audience, no doubt, is the conviction that the listener can be un-nurtured or destroyed. This belief,
however, owes as much to the Waterfall's autonomy as to an earlier
accord on which his present state depends. While the Waterfall may
have nurtured the Eglantine, he could not have become a cascade
(an unreflecting body of water) without a counterpart to cast him in
more impressive relief.

As we have seen, it is symptomatic of Wordsworth in 1799 that
having inherited it, he seeks to undo this figurative legacy. Having
created a self in the image of the reader, he is compelled to dissociate the reader from the image created. The movement, consequently, toward a more autonomous self in the eclogue—or from
water that once reflected to water that opposes—is a movement also
toward the annihilation of a "self," whose liquidation becomes both
proof and consequence of its difference. In part, this tautological
dissociation is masked by a sense that the initial auditor, the Eglantine, is comparatively weak or inferior. Yet as the Eglantine's reply
suggests, this is (from the Waterfall's perspective) a misreading of
the reader, whose passivity remains a function of "reading" rather
than a sign of complicity:

"Ah!" said the Briar, "Blame me not!
Why should we dwell in strife?
We who in this, our natal spot,
Once liv'd a happy life!
You stirr'd me on my rocky bed—
What pleasure thro' my veins you spread!

> The Summer long from day to day
> My leaves you freshen'd and bedew'd;
> Nor was it common gratitude
> That did your cares repay. (21–30)

Appealing first to the privilege of responding in which a "life"—
indeed a mutual life—was effectively conceived ("*our* natal spot"),
and only afterwards to the stream's indulgence of that privilege, the
briar continues by invoking the continuity of past and present.
Their relationship has been reciprocal *and* "[un]common," involving exchanges of help, and more important, of "voice" ("when you /
Had little . . . or none"[39–40]). His sense of betrayal quickening,
the Eglantine charges the Waterfall with pride, infidelity and, finally, with having forgotten their past and future synergism:

> Ah! would you think, ev'n yet how blest
> Together we might be!
> Though of both leaf and flower bereft,
> Some ornaments to me are left—
>
> Rich store of scarlet hips is mine,
> With which I in my humble way
> Would deck you many a Winter's day,
> A happy Eglantine!" (43–50)

At this point the dialogue breaks off as the poem yields to an
omniscient narrator:

> What more he said, I cannot tell.
> The stream came thundering down the dell
> And gallop'd loud and fast;
> I listen'd, nor aught else could hear,
> The Briar quak'd and much I fear,
> Those accents were his last. (51–56)

That "I" (repeated three times) and the flood are each isolated at the
poem's close not only implies a relationship between the speaker,
whose voice is "last" and loudest, and the Waterfall, who is previously this way. It also follows the allegory in differentiating the
speaker from his prototype—all of which returns him ironically,
with the Waterfall and the Eglantine, to prototypical status.

The "I," in other words, may be willing to represent the Waterfall's actions, but he is quite reluctant to acknowledge them as representative and thus to bear responsibility for their consequences. And this reticence is no more surprising than it is unique. Beyond silencing the briar, the Waterfall's actions anticipate the "I" 's in the way they establish the Waterfall as similarly silent and no longer, as it were, a "man speaking to men." It is therefore left to some other authority, to an omniscient allegorist *distinct* from the formerly omniscient speaker, to expose the latter's disingenuousness by demonstrating how the speaker's inability to "tell" necessarily equates with the Waterfall's actions in allowing unbridled, self-assertion its own justification. What prevails in the peculiar sympathy and symmetry of Wordsworth's allegory amounts finally to a series of deferrals: a "self" as much projected in the events it "tells" as it is fashioned by a refusal to "tell" what its tale or narrative—what the poem provocatively terms its "choice"— dictates instead.

And yet, for all its reflexivity, "The Waterfall and the Eglantine" is in the end self-enabling, uniting the will as world with the will as representation. No matter how we read the allegory, whether as testimony to the Waterfall's primacy, or to the primacy of those forces that make up a "thundering" stream, everything in the poem up to and including the seemingly endless sequence of deferral, is subsumed within a larger, retrospective "self" to which all selves lead.

With "The Brothers," in fact, which preceded "The Waterfall and the Eglantine" by six months, Wordsworth's allegory anticipates T. S. Eliot's famous observations on the "process of depersonalization" whereby "only those [poets] who have personality and emotions know what it means to want to escape from those things" ("Tradition" 53, 58). It hardly requires saying that Wordsworth's aim was utterly different from Eliot's, for his goal in 1799 was to escape *to* personality. But it is difficult in any case to read either "The Brothers" or the eclogue without seeing something of the painful "knowledge" of which Eliot would later speak, both in his essay and in "Gerontion" where forgetfulness, albeit necessary, is impossible. The double desire that one encounters in "The Brothers"—that prevents "Leonard," the returning "brother," from returning, thereby making him "want" to return—is a desire by which Leonard maintains his autonomy through the claims and impositions of past brotherhood.[6] Thus, like "The Waterfall and the Eglantine," "The Brothers" is an exercise in "self"-criticism becoming, through the machinery of sympathy (and allegory) once more, an act of self-

justification. It is a poem by and about a resigned self, whose understanding (like the "I"'s at the end of "The Waterfall") reveals his
power and powerlessness at once, or the "choice" by which he is
effectively chosen.

Wordsworth ostensibly lodges authority with two other figures in
"The Brothers," the parish priest and the actual speaker; but their
authority is leagued with ignorance, and in the narrator's case, with
a decidedly common understanding of things. The voice speaking
to men in "The Brothers" is choric, pathetic or readerly in disposition and opposed to the poetical self. And this is reflected in the way
that Leonard Ewbank, the departed brother remembered by the
speaker, is contradicted by the dramatic persona designated as
"Leonard." Moreover, in "setting up" his narrator in this fashion, the "poet" of "The Brothers" opposes the speaker's friend,
"the homely Priest of Ennerdale" (16), whose initial surmise that
"Leonard" is not one of them is no less common in its understanding
of the situation than the narrator's counterassertion that the
"Stranger" before "him," "Leonard," was "well known to [the Priest]
in former days" (36–37):

> And now at length,
> From perils manifold, with some small wealth
> Acquir'd by traffic in the Indian Isles,
> To his paternal home he is return'd,
> With a determin'd purpose to resume
> The life which he liv'd there, both for the sake
> Of many darling pleasures, and the love
> Which to an only brother he has borne
> In all his hardships . . . . (63–71)

A necessary corrective to the Priest's judgment, the narrator's
knowledge requires a corrective of its own. It is all very well that
"Leonard" is not, as the Priest would have him, a "moping son of
Idleness" (11) or a frustrated urbanite "who needs must leave the
path / Of the world's business, to go wild alone" (103–04); but this
should not be taken to mean that his apparent reintegration into the
"paternal" system, or even his excitement in returning home, are
verities that negate his estrangement. "[H]is heart," as even the
narrator concedes, "[f]ail'd in him" as he "approach'd his home"
(75–76), and the sight of "another grave" (88) beside those of his
parents has the immediate effect of placing "Leonard" at still further remove.

Indeed his survey of the graveyard discloses "[s]trange . . . alteration on every side," after which the familiar landscape and "the eternal hills, themselves" appear "chang'd" (95–97). This is followed by an encounter with the Priest, whom "Leonard "recogniz[es] . . . at once" (115), yet to whom, in accordance with the general transformation, he remains anonymous. Their exchange, which like the majority of the poem is cast in dramatic form (further effacing the narrator's authority), remains charged with dramatic irony. But what it dramatizes even more is the extent of "Leonard"'s estrangement: "Leonard" must remain unknown or otherwise opposed to family, community, and significantly, to an overarching patriarchy (or extended "patern[ity]") that seeks to dominate him.

In what did "Leonard"'s estrangement originate? The answer has to do with the referent of his "story," the poetical self, who characteristically is the only self capable of understanding "Leonard." Like the poet of the 1798 *Lyrical Ballads,* "Leonard" became an estranged, individuated self "chiefly for his brother's sake" (312). Convinced that he left his paternal home and brother James with no self-benefit in view, "Leonard" is convinced equally that no such benefits were received. These convictions, however, are mostly self-exculpatory. While "Leonard"'s sense of difference comes most dramatically with the news of James' death, such intelligence is already a foregone conclusion—a wish fulfillment—that "Leonard" cannot accept as such and leaves to the Priest to communicate:

> . . . we all conjectur'd
> That, as the day was warm, he had lain down
> Upon the grass, and, waiting for his comrades
> He there had fallen asleep, that in his sleep
> He to the margin of the precipice
> Had walked, and from the summit had fallen head-long,
> And so no doubt he perish'd. (409–15)

In one sense, this represented death re-presents *Leonard's* death, the passing of the "brother" known and formerly obligated to community, whose disappearance is also a form of waking. In a more immediate sense, James' death makes clear the representational need to have his brother return as a condition of common sympathy or understanding. For if James is to Leonard as the reader is to the poet (the reader being either the "brother" who earlier supplants Dorothy, or that "lover" who would supplant Lucy), then Leonard's return would be a reassertion of brotherhood and a denial of James' death and a desirable end in the act of reading.

Yet, as "The Brothers" is no more a poem to the reader than a poem from the Priest or its ostensible narrator, it is Wordsworth's purpose, in finally sympathizing with "Leonard," to ensure that the reader will be disappointed. This way, Wordsworth rewrites the past by showing that sympathy, like understanding, is circumscribed by uncommon sympathy (or by the death of understanding) in the very way that brotherhood is sublated in the very identity that distinguishes "Leonard" from Leonard Ewbank. "Leonard" 's "turn" to the churchyard (following his heart's failure) is surely a gesture toward community; but it is immediately superseded by his turning from community, suggesting that it was for his own "sake" chiefly that "Leonard" went to sea. Moreover, the "turn" shows, in conjunction with the foreknowledge that provokes it, that leaving was tantamount to staying, that it was a selfish, reflex action by which Leonard internalized and appropriated the very authority he both embodies and, in the dramatic configuration, opposes.

Such contradictions with respect to selfhood—specifically, that the authority of the individual is never more than an imitation of authority—will have serious implications for Wordsworth's poetry, and in not many years Wordsworth will confront them. In the meantime, selfhood and estrangement are as much opposed to brotherhood as they depend, in canceling it, on its continued function. This is true both of "Leonard," whose individuation is preconditioned by thoughts of James and of James' death, and, in a different way, of the poem's narrator, whose various turns toward *his* brother, the poem's reader, make him a poet of sincerity fallen from the role of poet. As an agent of "common sympathy," of the wish in this case for Leonard's return as brother, the narrator little appreciates the significance of "Leonard" 's various references to himself in the third person. These references are for the narrator ironic, emphasizing the painful proximity of their referent to the character speaking—and, at the level of common sympathy, understandably poignant.

However for the "poet," possessed of uncommon sympathy, such references have a far different significance. To be "Leonard" the dramatic persona, they reveal, is not to be Leonard Ewbank but *to have been him* and, by implication, both his brother's brother and their "father's" son:

PRIEST
—Poor Leonard! when we parted,
He took me by the hand and said to me,
If ever the day came when he was rich,
He would return, and on his Father's Land
He would grow old among us.

LEONARD
If that day
Should come, 'twould needs be a glad day for him;
He would himself, no doubt, be happy then
As any that should meet him—(328–36)

At points in "The Brothers" such as this the question of textual authority, of what is being told by whom, becomes paramount. The exchange is no longer simply a dramatic one; it has become a larger, allegorical gesture. As there is nothing in the poem to indicate that "Leonard" has not grown rich, much less that he has in consequences of his riches grown "happy," it is virtually asserted in the poem that "Leonard" is not Leonard. Thus, the very fact that the man speaking to the Priest and the one spoken of share the same signifier, that "Leonard" is at best his "father's" son, not only suspends the Priest's happiness; it suggests, even worse, that only on the "day" of his interment can "Leonard" achieve the happiness that his "return" presumably holds in store.[7] For every impulse of "Leonard"'s to return, to take his rightful place "on his Father's Land," there is a greater need to shun his father and a "happy" death, either by reneging on an earlier vow (made typically to a surrogate father, the Priest), or by actively subverting the Priest's hold on him in consciously differentiating this day from "that day." Anonymity thus becomes an assertion of personality, enabling "Leonard," like the equally removed "poet" he represents, to control his "father" in ways that he could not have managed as a fathered and brothered person and, to the extent he is *named* "Leonard," may never manage entirely.

It is with respect to "Leonard"'s equivocal independence—his reversal of the family hierarchy by appropriation of "paternity" thus abolishing fraternity—that James' death is crucial. In addition to being surmised by "Leonard," James' death was actually precipitated by his brother's departure. In the spirit of their shared paternity from which "Leonard" currently begs severance, the death (actually the "fall") of one brother is virtually contingent upon the apparent good will that earlier compelled Leonard to be *"always* by [James'] side" and "[do] so many offices about him" (343–44, emphasis added). No matter which way he "turns," it seems, whether toward James or away, "Leonard" is turning both ways by paternal dispensation. Hardly ironic, then, in the way the narrator interprets them, the results of Leonard's departure are perfectly in keeping with the paternalistic—now autonomous—spirit in which the departure was undertaken. This is demonstrated figuratively in James' fall and materially in the fact of "Leonard"'s survival. It is impossible, indeed, to differentiate Leonard's fear of James's death (i.e., his desire for his brother's welfare) from his wish for James' death, which marks the death in turn of Leonard Ewbank and the birth of the individuated "Leonard."

Not surprisingly, it devolves to common sympathy in the poem, to the past (and present) brotherhood uniting narrator and reader, to mask this confusion by allowing a false (if still poignant) distinction between selfishness and selfhood. "Leonard"'s final gesture, his letter to the Priest confessing his identity, remains within the limits of common understanding a recuperation of a previously autonomous gesture of failing to identify oneself and a "return" perhaps to a state where brotherhood represents one's identity. Yet from the standpoint of the allegory, and the uncommon sympathy for which it proves a basis, it is also true that by declaring his identity in this way, namely at a distance, "Leonard" makes clear the incompatibility of brotherhood and selfhood—if only in that one has been subsumed by the other. A distinction must be made in "The Brothers" between brotherhood, which is unrestored, and the forces that earlier made James and Leonard brothers, which are very much intact.

These forces, as "Leonard"'s final gesture confirms, are the very authority, "now" the very selfhood, toward which brotherhood and its opposing self—both Leonard Ewbank and "Leonard"— continually "turn." While "Leonard"'s eventual return to sea merely resists the Priest in imitation of his earlier resistance (both dramatized and before), it shows at the same time that for failure to return home, to be both brother and son, "Leonard" became something else "and is *now* / A Seaman, a grey headed Mariner" (448–49, emphasis added). The present is given priority in "The Brothers" (along with the *poem*) on the grounds that "Leonard" is no more his brother's brother. And the past, which is alternately demystified in the poem along with the narrator's narrative, warrants demystification on the grounds of its anteriority, and for admitting the sympathy of too many. Only "now," in other words, will "Leonard" disclose his identity, for only "now" is he someone who repels sympathy.

Inured to little else beyond the fact that "Leonard" is in exile and able thence to return as a communicating self, "The Brothers" is less resigned than "The Waterfall and the Eglantine" to the "poet"'s need to renounce his former obligation to society. While "choice" in "The Waterfall" comes simultaneously as a torrent, it is impeded in "The Brothers" by the stigma of relinquishing one obligation in deference to a new obligation. It is not that the situation is any different in the two allegories; it is only that the will to exile is more humanized in "The Brothers" and more complex. And yet, it is no coincidence that only through a death are "Leonard"'s wishes realized, his premonitions fulfilled—just as it is no accident that without Leonard's absence there can be no letter to the Priest confirming "Leonard"'s presence. Unlike the poet's omniscience in "The Waterfall," which relegates even the allegorical speaker to antetypical status, "Leonard"'s final expression of *personality* grounds the entire representation in "The Brothers": both the narrative, which engenders sympathy for Leonard Ewbank, and the allegory, where "Leonard"'s authority (indeed his identity with the poet) issues in a more exclusive sympathy. Leonard's letter actually preserves the distinction, then, between story and allegory (to ensure common understanding) but also differs from the eclogue by collapsing the distinction between the poet (now formerly the narrator) and his signifier ("now / A Seaman, a grey headed Mariner"), who is formerly James' brother. Without sympathy, either from the Priest to whom "Leonard" writes a letter in the guise of Leonard Ewbank, or from the reader to whom the poet speaks in the guise of the narrator, there can be no uncommon sympathy: neither estrangement for the poet nor the memory of his integration of which writing and difference are the inevitable result.

The paradox of being obligated to the reader and opposed to the reader following that obligation, is reflected in the almost protean character of "Leonard"'s guilt. If he cannot but feel guilty for having failed James, "Leonard"'s guilt is virtually indistinguishable from what empowers him to depart his home on two occasions—or later empowers the Waterfall into a thundering stream. The obligations to the briar and to James are in each case obligations to "self." And this is equally the case in "Michael," where the patriarch (Michael) displaces his son—to whom he is similarly obligated—as the signifier of autonomy and selfhood.[8] No longer strictly contraries, self and society are opposed by virtue of what they share, which in "The Brothers" owes immediately (and dramatically) to a "father" whom the "brothers" share, yet whose authority one of them dramatically resists in the course of asserting his own. For "Leonard" obligation to self turns out to be *that*—an obligation no different finally from either filial devotion or the guilt of having forsaken that devotion. While pressed, therefore, in the service of its deconstruction, selfhood is sufficiently *constructed* in "The Brothers" to make "Leonard"'s "letter to the Priest" (444), over the circumstances of its composition, the Alpha and Omega of the poem.

When Wordsworth attempts, then, in the Preface of 1800 to describe his compositions to date, the results are remarkably equivocal. This equivocation begins with the very nature of the Preface, which makes belated the very "representative[ness]" by which "Poet" and "Reader" have "discover[ed]"—in verse—"what is really important to men" (*Prose Works,* I 126). Likewise, the failure to differentiate between the Neoclassic issues of metre, sense and the submission to law, and the more "modern" injunctions for spontaneity, for simple diction—in short, for the entire machinery of common exchange that would lead eventually to the definition of the poet as a man speaking to men—makes Wordsworth's defense of his poetry in the Preface too much a defense, too much an accommodation to presumably hostile tastes. This waffling, of course, has been a problem for historians as early as Coleridge, and has required in most instances siding with one or the other: either tradition (in deference to history and convention) or, more frequently, the claim for new-ness, which readers invariably apply to the poetry in order to distinguish the features of "romanticism."

Nevertheless, what criticism almost never concedes is that the Preface *as a preface* is little concerned with becoming the manifesto it could have been. Instead the common view of things inherent in Wordsworth's claims to representativeness, as well as in the moderation to which poetry must additionally conform, serves to adumbrate a more extraordinary orientation. Wordsworth's attack on the urbanized sensibility which "produces a craving for extraordinary incident," is an attack, to be sure, on a certain kind of popular writing (*Prose Works,* I 128). But there is no mistaking that the commonalty to which poetry is "ideally" bound by the Preface also creates a need for the extraordinary, for some *other* orientation, that Wordsworth is not about to disclose. In remarking at the outset that the reception of the 1798 poems had far exceeded his expectations, Wordsworth implicitly contrasts the "more than common pleasure" they were intended to produce with the common pleasure they actually produced (*Prose Works*, I 118). As in the Preface as a whole, what was once more-than-common has become a register (in aftermath) of common sympathy and thus prefatory to the uncommon status to which the poet is exclusively heir.

This same trajectory is retraced in the beginning of "Michael, A Pastoral Poem," where the understanding once common to both poet and reader is characteristically given prefatory status. In the introductory address to the poem's reader, what is at first direct and unaffected becomes progressively indirect and oblique, illustrating the tension between common sympathy and what, by agency of both allegory and its hierarchizing tendency, has become uncommon sympathy:

> If from the public way you turn your steps
> Up the tumultuous brook of Green-head Gill,
> You will suppose that with an upright path
> Your feet must struggle; in such bold ascent
> The pastoral Mountains front you, face to face.
> But courage! for beside that boisterous Brook
> The mountains have all open'd out themselves,
> And made a hidden valley of their own. (1–8)

If the speaker is imitating the reader in a gesture of mutual understanding, he is also instructing the reader in the greater difficulty of imitating a self who has already "[turned] from the public way." It is not clear yet how irrevocable a "turn" this is, and this uncertainty persists throughout much of "Michael," during which the man speaking (indeed the one now "speaking to men") retreats to the narrative mode.

In the meantime there is mention of an "object which you might pass by, / Might see and notice not" (15–16), after which the speaker turns from the reader to speak about himself and of a "Tale" concerning the object that as "a boy,"

> Careless of books, yet having felt the power
> Of Nature, by the gentle agency
> Of natural objects led me on to feel
> For passions that were not my own, and think
> At random and imperfectly indeed
> On man; the heart of man, and human life. (27–33)

The "passions". . . not [yet]" the speaker's "own" are related to an act of sympathy in this passage, which despite masquerading as common sympathy, is as discrete in its peculiar affection as the "man" speaking is from the perfectible "boy" he was once. This is shown in the accompanying shift from "you" to "I," as well as in the readerly default that initiates these shifts, emphasizing the speaker's particular affinity and perfection. Rather than defend his exclusive position, the speaker defers this responsibility to two figures: one for whom he feels an affinity and another, who not recognizing the object, fails to recognize a marker *already ignored* by Michael's wayward son Luke. It is Luke, or someone like him, in whose image the reader is initially cast: a *figure* who, in bearing the onus of commonness and imperfection, enables the speaker to remove himself *with* Michael to the "Tale" proper and the poetic function of telling it.

Increasingly a foregone conclusion, the poet's uniqueness, like his counterpart's in "The Brothers," need no longer be negotiated.[9] All that is required is that it be justified or "approved," which is achieved momentarily by reference to a story that refers, in turn (as we shall see), to the distinction between the poet and his "public." Likewise, it is only after this reference by prolepsis that the reader is enjoined not to imitate the speaker but to assent instead to a secondary role where, despite the latter's turning from him, the reader will endeavor to become the poet's "second self" (39). This charge to imitate the poet turns out, of course, to be nothing less than an obligation: a resolution that recognizes the differences between the common self, whom Luke already imitates, and the uncommon or poetical self, whose object of sympathy is Michael. Should it be the case that the reader wants to be a poet, it is more immediately the case that the reader accept a hierarchy where, despite his or her expectation, a "history" must be told the reader for his or her own "sake":

> Therefore, . . . I will relate [a history]
> For the delight of a few natural hearts,
> And with yet fonder feeling, for the sake
> Of youthful Poets, who among these Hills
> Will be my second self when I am gone. (34–39)

Whether the "poet" is anticipating Michael here, or simply revealing what, in conjunction with Michael, he has already become, is less important than the fact that without a son or "second self" there is no way for the poet to "[stand] single" in the vicissitudes of his vocation. "This was a work for us," Michael will later tell Luke of the partially constructed sheep-fold, "and now, my Son, / It is a work for me" (395–96).

What Michael never realizes of course is that the distinction is a false one: work for a second self, following the poet-reader relationship (or the brotherhood of James and Leonard), is always work for a primary self. Nor does Michael realize what the poet himself is equally unwilling to acknowledge: the covenant here of father and son, or between first and second selves, has been contracted in the understanding that it is already broken or belated. Thus, the nominal responsibility of breaking it devolves not to the maker/breaker, but to a secondary figure—James or Luke or the reader—who is really quite innocent. Whatever Luke does, in fact, benefits Michael in some way.[10] If Luke stays, or if he returns, Michael enjoys the status of a father who labors for two. If Luke departs, Michael not only stands to keep his paternal land but enjoys the prospect of working for himself:

> —I will begin again
> With many tasks that were resign'd to thee;
> Up to the heights, and in among the storms,
> Will I without thee go again, and do
> All works which I was wont to do alone,
> Before I knew thy face. (402–07)

It is important to emphasize that Michael's solitude (indeed, the height to which he must ascend) is retroactive, that without Luke there is no way that life, before or after him, can be described in these terms. "Before" Luke, there is no history to repeat itself, no work for Michael to reappropriate and do "alone"—just as after Luke, the failure to complete the sheep-fold can be attributed to Luke's failure "to do [his] part" in their joint-labor.

Gestures such as these emphasize the predestiny and inevitability of Michael's independence. And this is equally true of Luke's failure, which is no more a failure, again, than was the reader's in the poem's introduction. In both cases, an agreement was contracted in anticipation of being broken, allowing the covenant-maker to distinguish "you" from "me." Where the son or second self allegedly violates the covenant, the father or primary self (or, in "Leonard" 's case, the surviving brother) is left with responsibility of *not completing it* by turning from the public way. What appears bad faith one one level is merely an assertion of faith, or covenant with oneself, consistent with the broken covenant, whose maker and breaker—

before "he" knew Luke's face (and the difference attendant upon that knowledge)—had taken that face to be his own. But now, in rejecting that face by forcing it to take leave of the poem (and by appropriating Luke's various "tasks"), Michael does unto Luke what the poet had earlier done to Dorothy, who is also a version of "what I was once." The difference is that in breaking the covenant with a "second self," the poet, unlike Michael, is left with two ruined covenants as a prelude to the completed covenant on which a poet's "house" is finally built. Unlike "Tintern Abbey," there is no difference in "Michael" between the reader-past and the reader-present, both of whom are positioned in such a way that the failure of each to fulfill what in the course of the poem becomes an obligation to the "man speaking" is used to illustrate the speaker's difference from them. It is this identity, furthermore, that mandates the reader's rejection, leaguing him or her with that son (or earlier that sister) no longer waiting to be born.

In "Michael," to mark the arrival of this second self and of the primary self who knows its face, the reader must suffer with Luke a language that is as much the poet's as the father's to whom it is directly ascribed:

>   —Heaven bless thee, Boy!
> Thy heart these two weeks has been beating fast
> With many hopes—it should be so—yes—yes—
> I knew that thou could'st never have a wish
> To leave me, Luke, thou hast been bound to me
> Only by links of love, when thou art gone,
> What will be left to us!—But, I forget
> My purposes. Lay now the corner-stone,
> As I requested, and hereafter, Luke,
> When thou art gone away, should evil men
> Be thy companions, let this Sheep-fold be
> Thy anchor and thy shield; amid all fear
> And all temptation, let it be to thee
> An emblem of the life thy Fathers liv'd,
> Who, being innocent, did for that cause
> Bestir them in good deeds. (407–422)

The "link" between various authorities, between God the father ("Heaven"), the "Fathers" and the father speaking, is seconded in this passage by the geometric disjunction of father and son.[11] No longer is the auditor a younger version of the speaker prevented by youth from imitating Michael's example. Like the poem's reader, who must passively accept this speech within a speech, Luke must accept or otherwise ignore the fact that paternity, like poetical authority, is an ontological distinction and, in effect, an article of faith. Ignoring it, as Luke does, is represented in "Michael" as a failure to keep faith, and so mystifies its "author" as both father and defender of the faith. More important, it mystifies Michael for not being Luke—and, more immediately, for not being the reader, who has also failed to understand the covenant marker. Where Luke has had only Michael's example to follow, the reader has had, in addition to Michael, the example of the poet and the cautionary example of Luke himself. This considerably enhances both the reader's imperfection and the "perfection" to which the speaker and Michael are, in contrast, privy.[12]

Thus, although paternity depends upon a son and auditor, Wordsworth has transformed paternity, and the authority it signifies, into a more immaculate conception still, forsaking the very figures—Dorothy, the reader, and their conflation Luke/Lucy— who in contrast to the man speaking must travel the "public way." The relationship that the young speaker would maintain with Matthew, that the Eglantine would maintain with the Waterfall, that even James, through his spokesman the Priest, would maintain with "Leonard," is no longer the relationship that Luke maintains with Michael or that the reader of "Michael" maintains with its "poet." That relationship "cannot be," because (as Matthew's earlier reply suggests) it calls for a uniqueness, a capacity for understanding, that only "Fathers" removed from their sons can enjoy. What Luke and the reader represent, by contrast, is the representativeness or common understanding that both justifies Michael's uniqueness and accounts simultaneously for the speaker's aloofness—notably, his endorsement of Michael's failure to "lif[t] up a single stone" (475). The sheep-fold, the figure for the poetry of sincerity, has been abandoned by the poet because it had to be: because such abandonment involves both sympathy with Michael and antipathy to a reader who can be nothing but a "second self" even when the poet—his father—is "gone."

This movement away from the reader in "Michael," toward the authority by which reading is rendered secondary, also entails a movement toward the reader as that "second self" on whom a hierarchy is founded. Many of the poems in the second volume of *Lyrical Ballads* expose this interchange. But where "difference" in these is increasingly deemed necessary after the fact, "Michael" presents difference as necessary before the fact, and so emphasizes the destiny or "choice" for which the poetical self has been chosen. The failure of the "Tale" to justify the poem's introduction, to be anything but a supplement to the poet's claim to primacy, uncovers what is masked by the illusion that the poem and the poet do justify each other: the destiny or "choice" that supersedes justification. Far from originating in one's progeny (or in the ability to beget a second self), authority in "Michael" is linked now to an already begotten son, whose perennially secondary status prevents him from ever having been "father of the man."

Thus, the various contradictions, beginning with its subtitle, that seem to inform this "pastoral poem," are not always contradictions. Lodged in the idea of "pastoral," after all, is the authority by which Michael himself is justifiably incapable of keeping the covenant— and in contrast to whom Luke, with virtually no justification, becomes the prodigal charged with breaking it. Likewise, the dependency on a "second self" is transformed over the course of "Michael" from a dependency on Luke (invested with saving his paternal land) to an independence from Luke for whose "sake," as we see in both the covenant scene and the poem's introduction, the "father" merely feigns dependency. Reverting from the very first to some predesignated or chosen state, which typically predates the "knowledge" of Luke's face, "Michael" essentially explains why the poet, as Wordsworth subsequently writes, must travel "among unknown men." Like the covenant already broken, such travel is a condition of un-knowing, of taking leave of the poetical charge that called earlier for an identity with other "men."

Marked increasingly by a process of "un-knowing" the "men" with whom he was previously associated, Wordsworth's course is both a birth and a forgetting, which his allegories (however enabling) have in some sense resisted. "[W]hen thou art gone," Michael implores Luke in a moment of uncharacteristic candor, "[w]hat will be left to us" (412–13). Coming as this does at the very close of *Lyrical Ballads, With Other Poems,* Michael's complaint retraces the development by which identity has remained a "fact of allegorization." Remembering the union that earlier begets identity, Michael's question (and the recourse to "us") concurrently confirms Michael's sympathy with someone not his son—and the "being" contingent on it. What is "left to us," to answer Michael's own question, is a self who, in the absence of the figure to whom he was previously linked, no longer remembers any counterpart save himself. Left is no longer a ruin—a testimony to departed wholeness—

but rather a synecdoche of a ruin, whose contraction implicitly negates union. What "stands single" at the end of *Lyrical Ballads* is less an abandoned covenant than a covenant completed by abandonment: a covenant that argues that the relationship between "first" and "second" selves is no longer sequential—not a function of "becoming" a "poet"—but is, in fact, hierarchical and unchanging.

* * *

The two years following "Michael," which saw virtually no new compositions by Wordsworth, were more articulate, more indicative of the breach between the man speaking and his audience, than the brief hiatus in the winter of 1798, which had separated "Tintern Abbey" from the Lucy poems and from "Nutting." The earlier silence, by the poet's insistence, was involuntary and provoked by a stomach ailment. "As I have no books," Wordsworth complained to Coleridge in December of 1798,

> I have been obliged to write in self-defence. I should have written five times as much as I have done but that I am prevented by an uneasiness at my stomach and side, with a dull pain about my heart. I have used the word pain, but uneasiness and heat are words which more accurately express my feeling. At all events it renders writing unpleasant.
>
> (*Letters, 1787–1805* 236)

The concern here with the actual cause or disposition of the poet's reticence, ranging from "uneasiness" to "pain" to "heat" to "it," points to a certain undecidability of "feeling"—of sensations or feelings in place of emotions or feelings—equally characteristic of Wordsworth's allegories, which manage by a similar strategy to render writing a "self-defence." The feelings that allegedly prevent Wordsworth from writing "five times as much as [he] had done" are, by his own demonstration, surrogates for other feelings, not the least of which may involve the peculiar dependency of writing on reading. Although the poet claims, in the absence of books, to have been forced to write, the fact remains that *without* books—or reading—"self"-expression remains difficult at best.

By no means am I suggesting that Wordsworth did not have a stomach problem (whose symptoms sound suspiciously like those of heartburn) or that he would not have preferred to have been reading in the winter of 1798 instead of writing. I suggest only that the silence around which these other phenomena cluster, no less than the poet's "words" themselves, may well indicate a shift toward a more exclusive (if still allegorized) position yet to be negotiated. In the aftermath of the 1800 *Lyrical Ballads,* by contrast, there is no mediation or uncertainty, but merely the observation (amid inactivity) that "Nutting" was one of only two works to "show the greatest genius of any poems in the second volume."[13] Regardless of whether Wordsworth is correct in this assessment, his conviction of his own "genius" marks an important development, for it is grounded, whether as judgment or idea, in an identity sufficiently stable to dispense with the apparatus of difference—or "defence"—on which the poet's house was earlier built.

Nor is the choice of "Nutting" as a document sufficiently unencumbered to "show . . . greatest genius" a bad one. More than any poem in the second volume, "Nutting" represents a "self " independent of the other figures with whom the self might be associated. In the superiority bolstered by guilt, and in the ability to confess and absolve himself simultaneously, the speaker of "Nutting" anticipates, in one way or another, subsequent allegorized selves—the Waterfall, "Leonard" and Michael.

But there is, as Wordsworth's claim indicates, an important difference: where these other selves are clearly situated at a remove, the "Nutting" poet essentially creates the distance (or difference) to which "Leonard," Lucy's lover, Matthew and Michael are variously removed. In virtual obversion of the poem it most nearly resembles—"Tintern Abbey"—"Nutting" achieves what the remaining poems in *Lyrical Ballads* verge toward in more deliberate, if not always systematic, fashion. "Nutting" manages to "show" the authority that *is* genius, and the authority to which the subsequent poems are, in their various acts of deferment, a prelude.

The emergence of poetic "genius," therefore, makes unnecessary the apparatus where "genius" had been deferred to another figure. And this would presumably account for the retrenchment following *Lyrical Ballads* as well as for the periodic interruption of retrospective allegories like "I travell'd among unknown Men" (1801). Consistent with the other Lucy poems, which may be deemed a postscript to the 1798 *Lyrical Ballads,* this postscript to the Lucy poems underscores the anteriority of the preceding series. Expressing its speaker's resolve to remain in England, "I travell'd among unknown Men," succeeds only in demonstrating the mutability of past affections. In the earlier poems the "men" to whom the poet speaks are, as we observed, literally un-known. Here, in contrast, the men among whom the poet remembers travelling are not

only those along "paths beyond the Sea" (2),[14] but men he once
knew: both the Englishmen to whom he wrote as a man speaking to
men as well as the figure of "England" of whom he was similarly an
extrapolation.[15] Thus, although "England" for whom the speaker
recalls affection is reader and fatherland at once, its influence is
necessarily diminished by association with Lucy. For the figures on
whom Lucy casts her parting gaze— who disappear with her—are
the "men" of whom the poet was previously a part, yet who, in
Lucy's aftermath, are only memorable.

The dissolution of past affinities as evidence of real "genius" is
equally a function of another poem to which Wordsworth returned
at this time, *The Ruined Cottage.* Originally a work whose interest
had been divided between its subject, Margaret, and its speaking
subject, the Poet-narrator, *The Ruined Cottage* had by 1802 become
a poem whose center of interest was the old Pedlar, about whom
Wordsworth now wished to write a separate poem. One consequence of this return, in prompting a return to the autobiographical *Prelude* (begun in 1799), has been often noted. Yet even before
The Prelude and its heroic "Poet," it is important to appreciate the
way the Pedlar is himself a promotion of "greatest genius." With his
unquestionably unique (and ubiquitous) role in the evolution of
Wordsworth's poetry, the Pedlar was an especially fortuitous reminder of the "genius" that Wordsworth had increasingly come to
regard as predestined.

In 1798 the Pedlar (then Armytage) was different from the Poet-
narrator, and was instrumental, as we observed, in uniting the Poet
with his reader. Now, as the sole subject of a poem devoted him, the
Pedlar follows the trajectory of Wordsworth's development in further measuring Wordsworth's movement away from both the past
and a merely common or representative identity. This prefiguration of "genius" is evident in the way the majority of *The Pedlar* was
finally (and self-consciously) revised to represent the Calvinistic
Wanderer of *The Excursion's* first book. More immediately, it is
evident in the way passages from *The Pedlar* shortly find their way
into the "Childhood" books of *The Prelude.* Armytage, the man
formerly opposed to selfhood, is in 1802 a prototype for "the man to
come."

The 1802 lyrics, which for all practical purposes mark the
resumption of Wordsworth's poetic career, are held by their admirers to be something of a "miracle" in light of the poet's numerous distractions at the time of composition. These, as Jared Curtis
details, ranged from Coleridge's personal problems, to the impact

of Wordsworth's own impending marriage, to the prior visit to France (and to Annette Vallon) that engagement required.[16] No one will dispute that there were pressures on the poet at this time. Nevertheless, to call these poems a "miracle" is to overlook the more palpable way in which this miracle was long overdue. This belatedness is no more evident than in "Resolution and Independence," arguably the most characteristic poem of 1802, which was completed only days, in fact, before the transcription in July of the first full version of *The Pedlar*.[17] For in addition to summing up Wordsworth's development to this point, "Resolution and Independence" (initially titled "The Leech-Gatherer") joins the other 1802 lyrics in negotiating passage to the epic or sublime self whose achievement *The Prelude* would then record. In other words, only by reviewing four years, whose developments *The Ruined Cottage* and *The Pedlar* coincidentally chronicle, could Wordsworth fashion a prelude both to *The Prelude* itself and to the equally mystificatory Intimations Ode, which was begun in 1802 and completed in 1804. Indeed, "Resolution and Independence" shows why the structure of differences that I call allegory was no more displaced in 1802 than its appropriation (and the "genius" attendant upon *that* displacement) could have transpired without allegory. Behind the "genius" of which "Resolution and Independence" and the other 1802 poems are evidence lies the "greatest genius," so to speak, of which the poet's is a refiguration.[18]

It is not always customary to think of the 1802 poems either as a unit evincing a self already allegorized, or as a series that makes "genius," for all its momentum, equally retrogressive. Although Curtis, for example, regards the poems as a unit, he also sees a fairly conventional unit: the thirty or so poems Wordsworth composed at this time summon a past in order to make sense of the present and to establish "hope for the future" (*Wordsworth's Experiments* 19). The prevalence of memory, or of personal experience, points to a concern for continuity amid change, making the poems a series of ways to negotiate the passage from the "old man" to the "new" (*Wordsworth's Experiments* 44).

Part of what makes this view so conventional or sentimental is its rearticulation of what happens in more ruthless ways in the poems of 1799–1800, which gradually shift affinity between figures representing the old and new man respectively. Thus, the more remarkable aspect of the 1802 poems is not the even-handedness with which they demonstrate continuity, but the forthrightness with which they make clear the impossibility of being two men at once.

Like the outer world of these poems, which is thoroughly revisioned, the inner world or memory is equally revisioned, limiting access (as in "I travell'd among unknown Men") to any prior orientation. Instead, in confrontational poems such as "Alice Fell," an encountered object simply defers to a perceiver, who (in the absence of an allegorical counterpart) is remembered and remembering subject both. Less about "poverty," as its 1815 subtitle implies, "Alice Fell" is really about perception, and about the *unshared* compassion for the friendless girl that allows the speaker to appear larger than life and allows his subsequent gift of a cloak (actually of money to the innkeeper instructed to buy Alice a cloak), to be a gift of more than physical value:

> "And let it be of duffil grey,
> As warm a cloak as man can sell!"
> Proud Creature was she the next day,
> The little Orphan, Alice Fell! (57–60)

In a recent essay comparing "Alice Fell" to "Gipsies," composed in 1807, David Simpson has argued that the earlier poem is a comparatively radical effort to raise fundamental questions about poverty, specifically the relief available to those for whom there generally was none. In "Gipsies," Simpson maintains, this interrogation is suspended and rendered more ambiguous by situating the gipsies and their plight at a greater, metaphysical distance.[19]

Particularly useful is Simpson's sublimation of Wordsworth's politics, his recognition that political positions in the poetry are (consistent with the question of identity) a matter of displacement. Nevertheless, what Simpson does not emphasize enough (though he has done this subsequently) is the self-consciousness of "Gipsies": how a poem rife with religious typology necessarily exposes the link between a speaker who, as Simpson observes, plays God and the way he represents the plight of the gipsies, which such privilege clearly underwrites.[20] In "Alice Fell," by comparison, what is similarly self-reflexive is, in the way of "Michael" again, unself-conscious. The sudden shift in the poem's final lines from the imperative ("let it be of duffil grey") to the narrative ("Proud was . . . she the next day") is problematic only in that it is offered without a trace of self-irony: it reveals, in its unmistakable echo of *Genesis,* the cloak of authority that the speaker displays more "proud[ly]" than his beneficiary. What the poem demonstrates in a strictly non-satiric manner is that without a benefactor and creator—without a sense of God—there would be no omniscient speaker, no perceiver turned rememberer, to imitate God both as benefactor and observer of his own beneficence. Likewise, the actual effects of the speaker's beneficence, notably the restoration of Alice's pride, are circumscribed by their author and cause, whose "pride" Alice additionally borrows. Unlike "Gipsies," therefore, which is oddly univocal, Wordsworth's efforts in 1802 to advertise a self require the services of an advertiser, whose authority or "genius" fills the gap between the self remembered and the "new man" in whose image the former is recovered.

Other poems in 1802, notably "Beggars" and "The Sailor's Mother," follow "Alice Fell" in focusing on the speaker's perceptual virtues. In "The Sailor's Mother" the speaker goes so far as to imply that what separates the subject from the perceived object (as well as from the audience looking on) are precisely those qualities of mind that divide the enlightened from the unregenerate. All of this, of course, hinges on a suppression of the mother's derangement: the initial description of her as "Majestic" (5) turns out, again, to be the speaker's own gift—even as it is a gift purchased, in differing ways, at both the mother's and reader's expense.

Beyond the alms that the mother actively solicits, there comes a greater gift by way of poetic imagination, by an act of seeing or of "genius" that transforms the female vagrant into something far greater. However, for the reader who has no idea that the mother is mad (and is no more able to forgive her for being otherwise), the poet's representation subverts a readerly way of seeing in deference to a writerly way that is paradoxically non-verbal and non-communicable. When it is finally established that the mother is not "majestic" in the way she has been read, the speaker recalls that even upon observing her in this new light his "pride" did not "abate" (12). The majesty, that is, first perceived (of which the reader is only now disabused) *continues*—albeit as a function of the speaker's own creation. Then, to justify his creation, and the division that now separates him from his once-proud reader, the speaker allows the sailor's mother to recount in her own words the circumstances that compel her to carry a caged bird while begging for charity:

> "The Bird and Cage they both were his,
> " 'Twas my Son's bird;—and neat and trim
> "He kept it—many voyages
> "This singing-bird hath gone with him;
> "And I, God help me! for my little wit,
> "Trail't with me, Sir! he took so much delight in it!"
>
> (31–36)

In tracing the metonymic associations by which the bird is alternately a son to the grieving mother and a mother (retroactively and in fantasy) to the departed son, the sailor's mother is able to acquit herself in grand style. Indeed, her acquittal is enhanced not just by the poetical effects of her grief, but also by her understanding of the pressures which have led to such symbolizing or seemingly irrational flights of imagination. Thus, in the very way that she is vindicated *as a poet,* the sailor's mother is equally instrumental in vindicating her poetic advocate, who initially defends her and finally lets her speak. Although she has the last word here, this prerogative, like Alice's pride, is a bequest which reflects more favorably on the benefactor. To the extent that "The Sailor's Mother" defends the sailor's mother, it is a defense of both poetry and the poet. It is in defense of the primary imagination which initially perceives her as majestic, and of the shaping or secondary imagination which turns the mother's speech into poetic closure.

The emphasis in "The Sailor's Mother," as in "Alice Fell," is on the woman as poetic object to whom the subject alternately lends his pride and genius only to redeem them at a higher rate. Nor are the poet and his objects the only ones affected by this redemption. Also affected is the poem's reader, who demonstrably lacks the capital to give in order to receive. Neither an alms-giver nor one who by the same token warrants alms, the reader, unlike the various women subject to the poet's generosity, has become secondary to that authority —indeed superfluous to it.

Similarly "Beggars," a poem peopled entirely by supplicants, shows the poet's "genius" to be commensurate with his generosity and other attributes, notably self-irony and moral sensitivity. Beginning with a too lofty description of a female beggar (not unlike the majestic image of the sailor's mother), the speaker next recalls his encounter with this "queen" (10), and a subsequent encounter with a "pair of little Boys at play" (21). In the first encounter, he endows the "queen" with a boon for her beauty; in the second, he endows the boys with a mother:

> They spied me all at once—and lo!
> Each ready with a plaintive whine!
> "Not more than half an hour ago
> Your Mother has had alms of mine."
> "That could not be," said one, "my Mother's dead."
> "Nay, but I gave her a pence and she will buy you
>   bread."

"She has been dead, Sir, many a day."
"Sweet Boys, you're telling me a lie;
It was your Mother as I say—"
And in the twinkling of an eye,
"Come, come," said one, and without more ado
Off to some other play they both together flew. (25–36)

There is no evidence that the speaker is correct in his surmise as he (unlike the speaker of "We Are Seven") is aware. He may have made an imaginative mistake, but it is one he turns nevertheless to his advantage. It does not matter surely whether the woman is the boys' mother. In this marginal world of beggars and unfortunates she might as well have been, just as for the boys' part she might as well be dead. It is testament to the speaker's genius that he understands this duality: he enters the world of beggars and enters it as well from a world in which beggars *are beggars*. In demonstrating how his assertions are also an excuse for him to keep his money, or worse, to spend it according to whim, the speaker cavalierly exposes the limitations of privilege (indeed such privilege as both he and the reader enjoy), thereby promoting what he represents in his own right.

That the Wordsworthian speaker shows little understanding of this last turn, that he is taken up less with his good fortune than with demonstrating his unique understanding of class difference, illustrates just how far Wordsworth has progressed in 1802 from "The Brothers" or "Michael" or "The Waterfall and the Eglantine." In these poems degrees of "difference" were established both by the poetical self and by a figure from whom that sympathizing self was himself removed. Now, having removed the self to that state of figuration, having made Michael or "Leonard" or the Waterfall the "I," Wordsworth inadvertently finds himself in the posture of the already excluded reader; he has, like that reader, lost the ability to understand Michael, "Leonard" or the Waterfall. Despite the enormous difference that exists now between the poet and the reader, they are equally products of an allegorical structure. If the reader has been consigned to a secondary or subordinate order, then the poet has been reciprocally removed to a primary role. Thus, for all his genius, the poet no longer has a sense of the hierarchical disposition of the poetical self or of the extent to which genius by its definition is still an allegory. Instead, the lyrics of 1802 promote a self with virtually no awareness that it is already a promotion: that authority in these poems is a mere reflection of that peculiar otherness, the "sense of God," of which "genius" is a reflection in turn.

While the "genius" achieved by the poetics of 1802 differs from the more overtly allegorical poetics displacing Michael (for Michael's state is now the poet's), it recovers—by the poet's removal—the differentiating structure on which the self must continually rely. The apparent union in "Resolution and Independence" of object (the old man) and subject (the man speaking) is not as final or as unequivocal as many readers believe; it is provisional and a prelude to the "independence" to which their sympathy is in fact accessory.[21] More than either Matthew or Michael or the old seaman whom "Leonard" has "now" become, the Leech-gatherer is more an obstacle to the poet than a paradigm: the final barrier, as it were, separating the "man speaking" from the "man to come."[22] Having overcome his representative self in the second series of *Lyrical Ballads*, Wordsworth seeks to overcome the exemplary self's representative, the sympathetic figure, whose exemplariness—beginning with the deceased poet of "A Poet's Epitaph"—has almost always been a function of his age. Thus, by *making* the Old Man an "old man," Wordsworth makes way for a new man whose internalization of allegory constitutes a "resolution" of figures commensurate with his "independence."[23]

Such autonomy on the poet's part will strike many readers as odd because it is generally thought that, without the Leech-gatherer's intervention, the "poet" would not, as he implies, have survived his quandary.[24] Still, in the very way that the "poet" has depended on figures like the Leech-gatherer as a means of "self-defence," that dependence is increasingly a matter of recollection:

> I thought of Chatterton, the marvellous Boy,
> The sleepless Soul who perish'd in his pride;
> Of Him, who walk'd in glory and in joy
> Behind his plough, upon the mountain-side:
> By our own spirits are we deified;
> We Poets in our youth begin in gladness;
> But thereof comes in the end despondency and madness.
>
> (43–49)

By making Chatterton a representative poet, the speaker has created a situation in which the old's man ministry will be directed more toward this "poet," rather than at the speaker, who has already departed the company of those who end in despondency and madness. The question that must be asked of the speaker is not the usual one—does he still have such thoughts?—but whether he ever had these thoughts in the first place?[25] Is there any link between the narcissistic sanctions by which other poets are deified and the spirit by which this one is deified: the "something" that, as the speaker remembers it in the eighth stanza, was "given" him in the form of an old man? Or is it that this something, objectively the Leech-gatherer, ultimately separates the speaker from that anterior deification in highlighting the poet's "own" deification?

My answer may be inferred from the structure of my questions. And it is prompted by the fact that the sections of "Resolution and Independence" devoted to the Leech-gatherer are, no less than the beginning and ending of the poem (or for that matter any of the 1802 lyrics), about the poet's "own spirit." They are about his ability, paradoxically, to suffer with the Leech-gatherer in lieu of being like him (or a son to him). The speaker's deification is a "given" in "Resolution and Independence," commensurate with a trajectory of empathy and autonomy rather than a bond of sympathy. For sympathy (especially in the allegorical configuration) implies an identity or sameness, which is now at odds both with the poetic object and poetic "genius." Just as the poet can only remember having once "thought" himself a poet in the mold of Chatterton, so now, it appears, he no longer practices the self-deification or narcissism which Chatterton and others have failed, in comparison, to sustain:

> But, as it sometimes chanceth, from the might
> Of joy in minds that can no farther go,
> As high as we have mounted in delight
> In our dejection do we sink as low,
> To me that morning did it happen so;
> And fears, and fancies, thick upon me came;
> Dim sadness, and blind thoughts I knew not nor could
>   name. (22–28)

Not even Michael Cooke, who bases the "romantic will" to self control upon such awarenesses, can defend this circumspection; he finds it thoroughly unengaging.[26] No longer despondent, the "poet" can barely convince himself that he ever was so, much less that he owes the recovery from despondency to his interaction with the old man. He may look back perhaps and see in the old man (as he has in Chatterton) an image of his former self, indeed a self whose example he might earlier have emulated. But what the poet can no longer do is defer to the old man as a prototype for the man beholding him. The two are presented in "Resolution and Independence" as a *fait accompli:* a remote speaker, whose despondency is still more remote, and an objectified old man whose suffering the speaker affords as a measure of their mutual remoteness.

It is not the old man's detachment that is at issue; at issue is the speaker's detachment from the old man, whose suffering is again proof of its affordability:

> He told me that he to the Pond had come
> To gather Leeches, being old and poor:
> That 'twas his calling, better far than some,
> Though he had many hardships to endure:
> From Pond to Pond he roam'd, from moor to moor,
> Housing, with God's good help, by choice or chance:
> And in this way he gain'd an honest maintenance.
>
> (106–12)

The old man is ultimately situated somewhere between the poet past, whom Chatterton represents, and the poet present, whom they variously anticipate in their role as representatives. Scarcely denoting a unity with the Leech-gatherer, much less a desire for unity, the Leech-gatherer's "resolution"—and "resolution" (that is, collapsing) of allegorical difference his objectification simultaneously reflects—shows a mutual "independence" and a "genius" finally that need not be figured but is. Where Matthew and Michael were prototypical selves for the poet and thus instrumental to the self-deification to which other poets have apparently fallen prey, the temporal *and* spatial distance separating the speaker from the old man ("I'll think of the Leech-gatherer on the lonely moor" [146]) replaces self-deification (a belated activity) with a deification of the self. Following the separation from Dorothy, and subsequently, from his inferred reader, Wordsworth's separation from the "Old Man" in "Resolution and Independence" marks his separation from the old man *as signifier* as from the other belated man (the "Boy" or "poet" Chatterton) with whom the Leech-gatherer is more immediately aligned.

It is the poem's tone, more than anything else, that belies the connection between the remembering subject and, as it had done with Chatterton, the man "on the lonely moor." Thinking of the Leech-gatherer from the vantage of the present, the speaker cannot resist thinking about him from the vantage of the past:

> While he was talking thus, the lonely place,
> The Old Man's shape, and speech, all troubled me:
> In my mind's eye I seem'd to see him pace
> About the weary moors continually,
> Wandering about alone and silently. (134–38)

It is impossible to tell if this is the way things "seem'd" or the way they appear now, for it is the effect of the poet's independence that it is retroactive: his difference interposes itself—then as now—as a token of his election.[27] Thus, as if to prove his "own" deification, the "poet" dissociates himself in the end from all associations, past and present.

It is with a sense of both futurity and retrospection ("I'll think of the Leech-gatherer"), with a temporality that situates the speaker elsewhere, that "Resolution and Independence" ends. And it ends in this way because of the speaker's ability to catch, confident of his immunity, the language of his former heart. The Leech-gatherer, whose displacement betokens his belatedness, is much less fortunate than the speaker and, like the erstwhile Chatterton, not at all immune to the contagion of desire:

> Once he could meet with [leeches] on every side;
> But fewer they became from day to day,
> And so his means of life before him died away.
>
> (131–33)

These lines, which by 1807 become the only words that the old man is allowed to speak, are in their initial, appropriated form, even more dramatic in implication. Not only do they reveal a speaker sufficiently independent to share the loss of former happiness; they reveal one sufficiently autonomous to imagine present suffering.

For Blake this autonomy was a higher innocence, a triumph of the self over selfhood. For Wordsworth it remained "strength," as he would shortly call it, in what remained behind. The backward movement to Wordsworthian autonomy, its recourse to the very state of desire from which, by definition, it is removed, reminds us that the romantic self—whether in "Resolution and Independence," the "Great Ode" or *The Prelude*—is subject still to a hierarchizing structure of difference. Even though the "man to come" has been "parted as by a gulph / From him who had been" (*Prelude* XI, 59–60), this "parting" or "gulph" has been less the result of the evolution of the poet's soul than of an internalization of "allegorization as such."

NOTES

1. *Personification and the Sublime: Milton to Coleridge* (Cambridge, MA: Harvard University Press, 1985), 106.

2. Knapp treats this problem at length, particularly in "Resolution and Independence," where the "power indicated [in the Leech-gatherer] is not exactly God, or the self, or even the poet's own imagination," but rather "the power itself of poetic representation, conceived by Wordsworth as the repeated dislocation of attention from particular images of the self" (120). While this view approximates my own, I believe that "attention" in Wordsworth proceeds *toward* the self—specifically, the "sublime self"—by means of a deflection that makes "discrepancy," in turn (especially in regard to the Leech-gatherer), a measure of the self's "autonomy."

3. See, again, Fineman ("The Structure of Allegorical Desire"), who argues for the structure, indeed the hierarchizing tendencies of a mode, which only *then* can be regarded as subversive and/or deconstructive.

4. See, again, Bahti ("Wordsworth's Rhetorical Theft"), who emphasizes the "insubstantial state" in which the allegorically constituted self ultimately finds itself.

5. Hartman also includes the "hart's final, gigantic leaps" in the "*preternatural* strength" toward which the poem, in his view, consistently "return[s]" (*Wordsworth's Poetry*, 142). Elsewhere Hartman notes the parallels between the Hunter and Poet, but attributes them to a reflective, contemplative orientation in contrast to the preternatural or supernatural, which is the proper domain of imagination. ("False Themes and Gentle Minds," in *Beyond Formalism*, 292–97).

6. Hartman notes that poems such as "Michael" and "The Brothers" center on sufferers "who cleave to one thing in order to be saved from a still deeper sense of separation" (*Wordsworth's Poetry*, 143). While this would appear to characterize Leonard, his cleaving, particularly to James, ultimately instills "separation," making Leonard in the end a signifier of the very autonomy from which, according to Hartman, he is in flight.

7. This implication is more pronounced in the later version of "The Brothers," where the Priest recalls Leonard's vow to "return, / To live in peace upon his father's land, / And lay his bones among us" (323–25).

8. In an attempt to account for the "moving power" of "Michael," Peter Manning notes the way it reverses the "Matron's Tale" in Book VIII of *The Prelude*, which "depicts the rescue of a son by his father." "The crisis of Michael," Manning observes, "turns on precisely the opposite: the necessity imposed on a son to rescue his father" (" 'Michael,' Luke, and Wordsworth," *Criticism*, 19 [1977]: 202–04). Yet it is precisely this "necessity" that makes Michael—the presumed object of rescue to whom Luke is obligated—as obligated as the father in the "Matron's Tale" and thus more proximate to the authority whose impositions Luke accepts.

9. In an interesting observation that bears directly on the destiny of both "The Brothers" and "Michael," David Simpson counters certain suppositions regarding these poems in noting how the "declines" of the respective families in these poems "are the result of a high degree of self-

determination . . . completely disconnected from any spectre of enclosing landlords or lordly neighbours" (*Wordsworth's Historical Imagination*, 144).

10. John P. Bushnell has written persuasively about the entitlement Michael represents: he is a "perverse hero" who sacrifices Luke as if he *were* God: he sends Luke away "realizing his son will fail." (" 'Where is the Lamb for a Burnt Offering?': Michael's Covenant and Sacrifice," *TWC*, 12 [1981]: 246–52.) Nevertheless, Bushnell views this chiefly as a problem with Michael (and of the agrarian spirit his attachment to nature represents) rather than of the selfhood of which Michael—in the image of God—represents. For a related view, which connects Michael to the patriarchy of Abraham in his mediation between God and son, see Sheldon Halpern, "*Michael:* Wordsworth's Pastoral of Common Man, "*Notre Dame English Journal*, 8 (1972): 22–33. For Halpern, as for Bushnell, Michael fails in his capacity as an authority, but not as an authority that so asserts itself that its behavior might appear perverse.

11. The later version of this speech is more explicit in its reference to "God." But whether this reflects the "religious consolation" that, according to Manning (" 'Michael,' Luke and Wordsworth": 201), "Wordsworth turned to . . . after the failure of nature's support recorded by the poem," is somewhat doubtful. If anything, the conjunction with God—which, not coincidentally, accompanies Michael's more explicit injunction that Luke follow *his* example ("think of me, my Son")—merely exposes the asymmetry by which Luke is instructed to follow authority yet denied a place (with Michael) in the elect, emblematic tradition of "Fathers."

12. Both Manning (" 'Michael,' Luke and Wordsworth": 207–10) and Sydney Lea ("Wordsworth and His 'Michael': The Pastor Passes," *ELH*, 45 [1978]: 55–68) note the doubling of Michael and the speaker and the way "Wordsworth enables it to work on us like the half-submerged intuitions of our own inner lives" (Manning: 208). However, unlike Hartman, neither critic is especially concerned with the fact that "the poet is Michael's true heir" (*Wordsworth's Poetry*, 266). For in this way, the poet, like Michael, has neither need nor want of any heirs that are not also secondary selves.

13. Cited in Moorman, *William Wordsworth: A Biography, The Early Years 1770–1803* (Oxford: Clarendon Press, 1957), 506. Wordsworth's comment was reported by his brother John in a letter to Mary Hutchinson, February 25, 1801.

14. Unless otherwise cited, references to the poems of 1801–02, which subsequently appeared in *Poems, in Two Volumes* (1807), are to the earlier manuscript variants as indicated by Jared Curtis in his edition of *"Poems, in Two Volumes," and Other Poems, 1800–1807 by William Wordsworth* ([*The Cornell Wordsworth*] Ithaca, NY: Cornell University Press, 1983).

15. Frances Ferguson observes quite incisively that the "audience or community of lovers has become England"—though, she adds—"not the England of men, but the England of Nature" ("The Lucy Poems: Wordsworth's Quest for a Poetic Object": 542). I would amend this by suggesting that it is precisely the notion of "community," the "England of men" from whom the man speaking was earlier an extrapolation, that mandates their

displacement (following his extrapolation from the figure of "genius") into "Nature."

16. *Wordsworth's Experiments With Tradition: The Lyric Poems of 1802* (Ithaca, NY: Cornell University Press, 1971), 3–6.

17. For a full biographical account of Wordsworth's progress from the completion of *Lyrical Ballads* to the composition of "Resolution and Independence" in 1802, see Moorman, *William Wordsworth: The Early Years*, 501–48.

18. The idea that 1802 represented a "central turn" in Wordsworth is by no means a new one. Stephen Parrish, for example, notes how in contrast to *Lyrical Ballads* and their "stubbornly experimental style" the poems Wordsworth "wrote in the spring [of 1802] are centered on the poet's own imaginative activity" (*The Art of the "Lyrical Ballads"*, 221).

19. "Criticism, Politics, and Style in Wordsworth's Poetry," *Critical Inquiry*, 11 (1984): 52–81.

20. Simpson's more detailed analysis of "Gipsies" (*Wordsworth's Historical Imagination*, 22–55), and the poem's Miltonic resonances, has subsequently emphasized this very point. But concerned, as he is, with Wordsworth's shifting position in the poem—by which the poet is alternately cast as Messiah, Adam and Satan—and with the social and historical provocations of these transformations, Simpson is reluctant to see the poem as merely ironic, but instead regards it as ambiguous.

21. In a related observation Hartman argues that the encounter with the Leech-gatherer is a "self-confrontation" "unrelieved by myth or allegory or any steadying indulgence" (*Wordsworth's Poetry*, 266–73). It is this lack of relief, then—the way allegory is suspended in deference to the "self" confronting itself—that accounts for the "recalcitrance," as Steven Knapp describes it, whereby the Leech-gatherer is "no more than a cipher for the very medium that makes him seem familiar" (*Personification and the Sublime*, 120). For in a way, the Leech-gatherer embodies (as Knapp suggests) the poetry, indeed the allegory, that precedes him, which precedes the "genius" as well of which the "Old Man" is now a belated precedent.

22. Using a psychoanalytic model, Peter Manning shows how the "reassertion of authority" in "Resolution and Independence" is managed by transforming the Leech-gatherer "into a spectral double" in whom the speaker's " 'untoward thoughts' " are "spli[t] off and embod[ied]." (" 'My former thoughts returned': Wordsworth's *Resolution and Independence*," *TWC*, 9 [1978]: 398–405.)

23. In a more conservative argument, David Eggenschwiller maintains that the acceptance of the Leech-gatherer is a "recognition of [the speaker's] own limits and an acceptance of his humanity," enabling him then to ask "God for help and support" ("Wordsworth's *Discordia Discors*," *SIR*, 8 [1969]: 89). The final appeal to God, as I see it, is more an injunction to God, ordering "Him" in the image of His beholder. This, in turn, considerably neutralizes the "self-mockery," which is more a mockery by "genius" of its former "self."

24. Typical of this view is Albert S. Gérard ("A Leading from Above:

Wordsworth's *Resolution and Independence*," in *English Romantic Poetry*, 118–35), who maintains that "through his ecstatic identification with the Leech-gatherer, Wordsworth raises himself from puzzled recognition to mature acceptance of the positive value of suffering" (132).

25. Anthony E. M. Conran comes very close to asking these same questions by disabusing a tragic view of the speaker's condition in favor a comedic view, whereby the speaker is dissociated from a melancholy attachment to Chatterton and his ilk simply by lingering on the facticity of the old man. ("The Dialectic of Experience: A Study of Wordsworth's *Resolution and Independence*," *PMLA*, 75 [1960]: 66–74.)

26. *The Romantic Will* (New Haven, CT: Yale University Press, 1976), 211.

27. Hartman acutely describes this imaginative phenomenon (in discussing "Resolution and Independence") as an "after-image." "Based on an experience to which the mind has already formally reacted," the "after-image elongates the encounter," placing the mind and its autonomy in the service of very thing (Nature) which it otherwise controls (*Wordsworth's Poetry*, 269–73). One recognizes the dialectic Hartman is exposing; nevertheless, the lack of a temporality, by which the Leech-gatherer comes forward into the present, would appear to privilege his beholder rather than the power of the recollected.

The Great Ode and *The Prelude*: Paradise Regained and Lost

The glance backward to the man on the moor retraces the development of Wordsworthian selfhood from identification to identity. But the consequences of this development, which include contradictions both endemic and inimical to it, are more evident still in the famous complaint with which Wordsworth suspended work on the Intimations Ode at this same time. Having traced his speaker's development from an oceanic state of infancy to a state of individuation, Wordsworth suspended composition of the Ode in the spring of 1802 with two questions: "Whither is fled the visionary gleam? / Where is it gone, the glory and the dream?" (56–57).

It is customary to league these questions (and the two years that intervened before an answer was provided) with a tragic orientation that recognizes the poet's diminished state. Like Freud, whom Wordsworth anticipated in many ways, the speaker argues that in the course of his development he has consigned more and more of what formerly was his ego or conscious self to his unconscious, where it is barely recallable.[1] Further, Wordsworth's speaker laments the "shrunken" nature of this "adult" condition: both that his ego "borrow[s]" its "strength" (in Freud's words) from the very unconscious or "id" it paradoxically "hold[s] in check," and that the adult ego is further subjugated by a division within it that Freud termed the "super-ego."[2] Although properly a part of the mind, the super-ego in Freud's description remains aligned with civilization: with the father specifically in identification with whom the child retains authority in the form of conscience. Observing the diminution that attends upon "birth" and, more memorably, in the transition from "infancy" to childhood, Wordsworth's speaker notes (while essaying an answer to his questions) how "[s]hades of the prison-house begin to close / Upon the growing Boy" (67–68); henceforth the boy resigns more and more of his oceanic self or "Soul" (59) until finally, as a "Man," he "beholds it die away, / And fade into the light of common day" (75–76). Important here is the way "man"-hood is both a chronological progression and a measure of that chronology's internalization. Beyond simply contracting, the infant ego becomes something else or "die[s] away."

By comparing this "becoming" to imprisonment, moreover, the speaker, like Freud, renders a judgment about civilization; for Freud, civilization "obtains mastery over the individua[l]" by "setting up an agency within him to watch over [him], like a garrison in a conquered city."[3] In Wordsworth's version, we see the four-year-old boy (of stanza seven) becoming civilized ("See, at his feet, some little plan or chart" [90]) "[w]ith light upon him from his Father's eyes" (89). This "light upon him" eventually becomes an "agency within him," displacing the still-present mother and the radiance of infancy, both of which fade "into the light of common day."

At this point, the majority of critics are in a quandary with respect to Wordsworth's poem. By effectively endorsing a Freudian or otherwise determined sense of the speaker's development, critics invariably interpret the poem's resolution (and Wordsworth's departure from Freud) as a humanistic counterassertion to apparent loss. This counterassertion may be the speaker's discovery of "new powers" that, as Trilling observes, require a new, more realistic "subject matter" ("The Intimations Ode" 129–59); or it may be the "imaginative power that can bridge [the poet's] separateness and," as Harold Bloom argues, "so intimate an immortality"; or it may be, as Helen Vendler urges, a more modest "acquisition of the power of metaphor," which is the power to transcend "the external world of sense-experience" and the "interior world of [adult] moral consciousness."[4] But in all of these cases the speaker must negotiate a giant leap in which his ego, no longer vulnerable to the ravages of maturation, is empowered to break the bounds of its circumscription.

Nevertheless, a reading of the Intimations Ode, beginning especially with the questions at the close of the fourth stanza, suggests a somewhat different solution and, more importantly, a different problem. In this reading, the Freudian narrative is not the universal paradigm that virtually all readers—regardless of whether they are persuaded by the poem's argument—assume, but a representative condition which the differentiated speaker has evaded. The two questions with which Wordsworth suspended composition in 1802 are more than a complaint against the finitude of "our" existence; they are rhetorical questions by which the speaker claims to have transcended "our" sublunary condition. The problem with the speaker's claim, however, is that in the absence of an allegorical figure with whom to identify, the speaker is both himself and that figure: a "sublime self " who is at once here and "elsewhere" (60) and whose "discrepancy," consequently, is externalized and internalized at the same time.

The speaker's conviction in the existence of the "visionary gleam," his certainty that it "is" at this very moment "fled" in some place or person, must not be taken as his uncertainty about the location of its refuge.[5] This last, again, is a bit of disingenuousness that only the poem renders real and evidence of the "internal difference" (in Emily Dickinson's phrase) which both grounds and mitigates the speaker's notably discrete triumph. Contrary to those readings in which the poet's power and immortality are a "response" to Freud, the speaker of the Ode ultimately resists this very trajectory. In doing so he reveals why Wordsworth was unable to sustain a transcendental posture for much more than the duration of *The Prelude,* which followed the completion of the Ode in 1804. For, as the Ode's 1815 subtitle—"Intimations of Immortality from Recollections of Early Childhood"—would later imply, the speaker is regaining his former strength not through memory and imagination, as he would believe, but through a difference or displacement of which "immortality" is, at best, a reflex. Immortality is intimated because transcendence and power, far from being palpable ends, are a means, a fiction, whose "hierarchies" the speaker has simply internalized.[6]

This distinction holds not a few conflicts, the most important being the "discrepancy" between the man and the myth. Thus, it is not at all surprising that Wordsworth took two years to formulate an answer to his own questions. Now, virtually conceding the fiction of his speaker's exemplariness, Wordsworth subsumes the speaker's subjectivity into an "us" that may or may not include him:

> Our birth is but a sleep and a forgetting:
> The Soul that rises with us, our life's Star,
>   Hath had elsewhere its setting,
>   And cometh from afar:
>   Not in entire forgetfulness,
>   And not in utter nakedness,
> But trailing clouds of glory do we come

From God, who is our home:
Heaven lies about us in our infancy!
Shades of the prison-house begin to close
　　Upon the growing Boy,
But He beholds the light, and whence it flows,
　　He sees it in his joy;
The Youth, who daily farther from the East
　　Must travel, still is Nature's Priest,
　　And by the vision splendid
　　Is on his way attended;
At length the Man beholds it die away,
And fade into the light of common day. (58–76)

Much of this stanza, as we have seen, anticipates Freud's conception of the ego as both separated from the repressed yet restrained by the super-ego. It must be emphasized that the more the Ode coincides with Freud's scheme of development, the less its speaker is directly implicated in that scheme. The further that "we" step westward from childhood, the less the speaker accompanies our procession and the more we are joined by generic figures (the Boy, the Youth, the Man) to whom the speaker refers in the third person. Correspondingly, the "glor[ious]" state to which the speaker is more immediately connected (in consequence of his inability to have forgotten it "entire[ly]") is increasingly indeterminate, and referred to either as "God" or, more vaguely, as "elsewhere."

In stanzas six to eight, the speaker typically is nowhere to be found among the various representative figures he summons to illustrate the systematic contraction of the adult ego. In stanza six, the infant ego that "originally . . . includes everything," most notably Nature, is observed to resemble "that imperial palace whence [it] came" (84). In stanza seven, that state and its maternal/natural mediation are replaced with the boy of four, who by objectifying his mother is observed to have internalized the disposition of his father. The boy's playacting, by which his "whole vocation" is "endless imitation" (106–07), suggests, furthermore, that such internalization constitutes an appropriation *by* "civilization," whose aim will be to make the boy like everyone else.

It devolves to stanza eight to assert what is everywhere apparent in Freud but which, fearful of regression, Freud resisted claiming until *Civilization and Its Discontents:* "our present ego feeling . . . is only a shrunken residue of a much more inclusive—indeed, an all-embracing—feeling which corresponded to a more intimate bond between the ego and the world about it" (15).[7] Or, as Wordsworth puts it in his paean to the little "Child," childhood is not merely a better, more capacious state than adulthood; it represents the best years of our lives. All the same, there is an aspect of sarcasm to this praise—as when the child is referred to as "best Philosopher" (110), "Mighty Prophet" or "Seer blest"(114)—that cannot be overlooked. In addition to reminding us that praise of this sort is not really praise, but rather a dirge over one's own condition, the irony is finally directed at the child himself, "upon" whom "custom [shall soon] lie . . . with a weight, / Heavy as frost, and deep almost as life" (129–31). The speaker's praise, that is, far from measuring his own shrunken-ness, expresses a contempt for the human condition *beginning with childhood,* which in the course of our development appears a high point. Thus, at the very juncture when the speaker most resembles Freud as a tragic thinker, he is—as the real "seer blest"—least like Freud in his unwillingness to accept the dictates of his own wisdom.

This distinction between the speaker and the world, between egos that are increasingly unique and determinate respectively, is dramatically exposed in the ninth stanza, which marks the speaker's return as the "I" last heard in stanza four. Expressing thanks that in "our embers" there is "something that doth live" (132–33), the speaker immediately qualifies his position, and the disposition of his own gratitude: "in me" the "thought of our past years . . . doth breed / Perpetual benedictions" (136–37). What is fugitive for "us" is claimed as perpetual for our representative. Representing us, even as he gives benediction on "our" behalf, the speaker implies (consistent with there being more than one "benediction") a special benediction of his own.

Perpetual rather than mutable, the speaker's blessedness has little to do with the embers of childhood:

> Not for these I raise
> The song of thanks and praise;
> But for those blank misgivings of a Creature
> Moving about in worlds not realiz'd,
> High instincts, before which our mortal Nature
> Did tremble like a guilty Thing surpriz'd.[8]

The difficulty of determining the object of the speaker's "thanks" is partly allayed by recalling the speaker's prior reluctance to praise "the simple creed / Of Childhood" (139– 40). The subject in these lines is a more general one: the adult ego-in-formation or in "disengagement," as Freud described it, "from the general mass of sensations." In childhood such sensations are felt as "misgivings"—erroneously given when, in fact, they are received. In later years, these "obstinate questionings of sense and outward things" (as Wordsworth elaborates them in the 1807 version of the poem) are given back by the contracting ego to the "outside" or "external" world (*Civilization* 14). It is only after the "world" is so "realiz'd," then, that "benediction" is possible; for the speaker's gratitude, no less than the contracted condition for which he is "not" personally thankful, depend equally on the "demarcation" that the developed ego maintains between itself or "I" and what is outside (*Civilization* 13).

There is, of course, a contradiction in this; the speaker's disengagement from "our" disengagement represents a differentiation not unlike our own. Yet as if to elide this contradiction, the speaker moves immediately to distinguish himself further from "our mortal Nature." He expresses thanks not for "the simple creed / Of Childhood" (139–40),

> But for those first affections,
> Those shadowy recollections,
>   Which, be they what they may,
> Are yet the fountain light of all our day,
> Are yet the master light of all our seeing;
>   Uphold us, cherish us, and make
> Our noisy years seem moments in the being
> Of the eternal Silence: truths that wake,
>   To perish never;
> Which neither listlessness, nor mad endeavour,
>   Nor Man nor Boy,
> Nor all that is at enmity with joy,
> Can utterly abolish or destroy! (151–63)

It is easy to see why many readers are confused by this second statement; by reintroducing the "affections" of Childhood, the speaker has essentially erased the parallel construction.[9] Speaking as our representative, the speaker condemns us to the world of stanzas five to eight, where despite growth, contraction, and inevitable despair, we may find recompense in our earliest days: both as our most privileged state ("*the* master light") and, more important, as a foreshadowing of the life to come. The speaker has something different in mind for himself. He would show, in fact, how imagination—his unconscious made conscious—is enabling and ennobling in the here and now. But it is just as characteristic of this stance that its blessedness, like our "immortality," may be only intimated. The only way, in short, that the speaker can identify his "perpetual" blessedness is by *comparing* it to a more determinate condition: one demanding palliatives such as faith or incentives such as guilt to "uphold us" and keep "us" going.

The final two stanzas continue to impose such differences. In the penultimate, the speaker elaborates the deterministic view so as to distinguish his own orientation. This stanza reads, not surprisingly, as if it were the poem's last, and is remarkable in its similarity to the resolution of the crisis described by Freud. Continuing in his role as spokesperson, the speaker observes: "What though it be past the hour / Of splendour in the grass, of glory in the flower; / We will grieve not, rather find / Strength in what remains behind" (172–75 [1802–04]). The "strength" that "remains behind" suggests two things: the unconscious that remains behind, beyond recall, but nevertheless empowers the rest of us; and the ego or "residue" of the present which relies similarly on "borrowed forces" (*The Ego* 15). Then, as if to shore our condition up still further, the speaker continues by observing that we will find strength "[i]n the soothing thoughts that spring / Out of human suffering, / In the faith that looks through death," and last, "[i]n years that bring the philosophic mind" (186–89). Such privileging of the "adult's ego feeling" is absolutely vital to the speaker's purpose, for it privileges the super-ego as well, the civilized faith which employs guilt in order to justify "human suffering" (*Civilization* 13). The "faith that looks through death" is more than religious faith or "monotheism"; it is the "strength" in the "residue" that "remains behind": the guilt that drives us despite our knowledge of mortality on the one hand and our "intimations" of "immortality" on the other.[10]

In the concluding stanza the speaker turns finally to his own state, intimations of which stand entirely in relation to the human condition. Referring to his "heart of hearts" (192) by way of emphasizing this distinction, the speaker argues that despite having "relinquished" (193) the oceanic feeling of childhood (and the need, by implication, to promote it), he has gained recompense in individual perception and in the ability of imagination to transform the world. All of this, however, is little more than protest at this juncture, and worse, protestation dependent on another argument altogether. Observing that "[t]he Clouds that gather round the setting sun / Do take a sober colouring from an eye / That hath kept watch o'er man's mortality" (199–201), the speaker does more than liken his gaze and its transformative power to the sun's; he reveals that this association is underwritten by the object of their "watch," which is of course shrunken man. Were it not for "man's mortality," there would be no basis for comparison and thus no basis for the speaker's immortality.

It devolves to *the poem* to disclose, then, that the speaker's intimations of immortality depend equally on his own shrinking: the ego-feeling or individuation that merely contradicts—so as to render insubstantial—his alleged glory. The final lines, in which the speaker observes that "[t]o me the meanest flower that blows can give / Thoughts that do often lie too deep for tears" (205–06), retain an indeterminacy, both of thoughts and the blessedness they would confirm. And this is probably as it should be. For in accordance with the poetry that has preceded it, the Ode demonstrates how such "thoughts" are inextricably leagued with "our mortal nature"—with "the human *heart* by which *we* live" (203, emphasis added)—that is paradoxically, if unbeknownst to the individuated man speaking, indistinguishable from his own.[11]

* * *

The indeterminacy of immortality in the Intimations Ode owes less to the discrete character of the speaker's grace than to the sublime selfhood which locates the "poet" both here and "elsewhere." Where previously such blessedness was allegorized and sustained by situating the "man speaking" between a "[man] who had been" and one "to come," it is up to the speaker—the man arrived—to demonstrate his portentous difference. But what the Ode ultimately demonstrates is less a separation of "I" and "We" commensurate with the former's blessedness than a discrepancy, or "gulph" within the "I" itself, for which blessedness cannot provide a cover.

That "we" are more determinate in the Ode than the man speaking, that the "human" or Freudian condition remains paramount in the poem over and against the speaker's own, shows, once again, that allegory has been internalized but not suspended. The hierarchical movement by which the self, in acts of identification, has systematically ascended to the rank of "other" may have reached completion. But this does not mean that the self has transcended either figuration or the hierarchy so fostered. Rather, ordination and subordination are sufficiently proximate, both in the Ode and in the poems contemporary with it, to be almost always as proximate in the speaker himself. Thus, in one way or another, Wordsworth's claim to power—in the Ode, in "Resolution and Independence," and in the contemporaneous lyrics—reflects a difference within "the poet" by which power and "immortality" are more often imitated.

It devolves, then, to a supervention of allegory—brought on the instability of this internalization—to uncover the hierarchy of which the poet is both signifier and signified. The hierarchy which privileges the poet of the Ode remains, as his internal difference shows, a structure on which he is still reliant. In becoming that self whose distinguishing feature is (as Hartman rightly notes) its autonomy, the poet must still defer to something—what in 1805 he describes as "[t]he sense of God, or whatsoe'er is dim / Or vast in its own being" (*Prelude* XIII, 72–73)—of which he is only provisionally the referent. Thus, it is up to allegory of a more displaced sort, to an allegory *beside* its internalization, to turn the poet's figuration to more constructive (and more deconstructive) ends. This is certainly the case with *The Excursion* (whose "Poet" resigns his identity to various other figures and to God whom they variously promote), and it is the case too with *The Prelude*, which oscillates, as we shall see, between promoting the character of the "Poet" and promoting the poet, or man writing, as a demystification of the former.

It is also the case with the epigraph added to the Intimations Ode in 1815, which in typically allegorical fashion returns the speaker to the "God" who is his "home." The epigraph, taken from the conclusion of the 1802 lyric "My heart leaps up," is significant in that it eliminates the sighting of a rainbow, which provided intimations of immortality, and begins with the statement "The Child is Father of the Man" as the paradigm for the wish, "And I could wish my days to be / Bound each to each by natural piety." To remove the beginning of "My heart leaps up" is to alter the basis of its subsequent intimations, making them contingent upon the inverted parentage whose trajectory the speaker will oppose. Moreover, to emphasize this reversal, Wordsworth allows the "and" of "And I could wish" the force of disjunction. As it introduces the sublime "I," it simultaneously inaugurates a movement away from the preceding maxim, effectively orphaning the speaker from his childhood and transforming his "wish" (whose fulfillment had earlier been so certain) into something ever more conditional. Unlike the initial epigraph from Virgil ("Paulo majora canamus"—"let's sing a nobler song"), the revised epigraph to the newly retitled "Ode" neither introduces the poem nor, as Peter Manning argues, evades "the conflicts actcd out by the Ode." Consistent with its allegorical function, the epigraph is a representation *of* representation, whose "epigrammatic density" uncovers the differentiation within the speaker by exposing the subsumption of allegory by (and into) the "sublime self."[12]

With the resumption of *The Prelude* in 1804, allegory gradually assumes a supervening function, whose purpose now is to expose allegory's function of identifying the poetical self with God. Like the Ode, where such identity in the end requires the services of the epigraphic ironist, *The Prelude* makes a similar requirement by blithely exposing the conflicts inherent in its overarching scheme. And, as in the Ode, where this exposure takes the form of a series of questions, the originating questions of *The Prelude* engage a rhetoric turned similarly against itself. I refer specifically to the questions beginning "Was it for this" which open the poem of 1799 (the then "two-part" *Prelude*), but which by 1804–05, in the context of a thirteen-book personal epic, register a somewhat different meaning:

> Was it for this
> That one, the fairest of all rivers, loved
> To blend his murmurs with my nurse's song,
> And from his alder shades and rocky falls,
> And from his fords and shallows, sent a voice
> That flowed along my dreams? For this didst thou,
> O Derwent, travelling over the green plains
> Near my 'sweet birthplace', didst thou, beauteous
>   stream,
> Make ceaseless music through the night and day,
> Which with its steady cadence tempering
> Our human waywardness, composed my thoughts
> To more than infant softness, giving me
> Among the fretful dwellings of mankind,
> A knowledge, a dim earnest, of the calm
> Which Nature breathes among the hills and groves?
>
> (271–85)

If there is an echo of "Tintern Abbey" in these lines it is because they are from a stage in the poet's development in which he found himself poised between the relatively tragic (if representative) identity of "Tintern Abbey" and the "genius" prophesied in "Nutting."

In the questions above "this" signifies the pinnacle that the 1805 speaker has by his own claim achieved, but in 1799 the word is initially less definite. Both "Preludes," to be sure, are informed by an intentional or narrative structure that means to connect the glory of the past with the glory of the present. In the 1805 poem, Wordsworth the "Poet" underwrites this structure with over two hundred lines of unqualified confidence, beginning with the invocation of the "correspondent breeze."[13] In the 1799 poem, however, the narrative is immediately written over by an interrogative mode.[14]

Nor is the referent of "this" the only point of difference between the two "Preludes." Where the 1805 version makes copious use of the initial poem in conjunction with a still larger design, the 1799 version is necessarily unclear as to how to proceed. The individuation, for example, which in "Tintern Abbey" had opposed the integration of the past, is both retroactive and cautionary. Disposed to represent his past in the image of his present solitude and in anticipation of his election, the speaker of 1799 is similarly obliged to warn against that state—and the autonomy it portends—and to invoke a more powerful, more sublime providence. This obligation is clearly at work in the way key recollections are narrated and evaluated. The narrative that accords progress to the present simultaneously withholds judgment in 1799 in deference to an authority represented as more advanced and more impressive than the speaker himself.[15]

This duality is repeated in even bolder relief in the overall trajectory of the 1799 *Prelude*, whose second and concluding part actually shows the "Poet" moderated by virtues of community and Nature.[16] Such moderation, as we saw in Chapter III, had in the months preceding enabled the speaker to become a self in the image of his reader. Thus, unlike the Ode, where "We" and "I" are at once strange yet familiar bedfellows, the sudden shift in Part II from the singular "I" to the plural "We" essentially gives credit where credit is due. The movement from exemplary to representative man in 1799, no less than the gender shift between the patriarchal authority of Part I and the maternal/natural mediation of Part II, remain an etiology of self capable of crediting both the community (from whom the man speaking is an extrapolation) and the broader, cultural agenda that (unbeknownst at this stage) makes the individuated speaker a representation of God, the father. Removed in the first part from both community and Nature, the speaker in the second is associated with these as a measure of his dependency: both as a counterpoise dissociated from them *and* as a kindred spirit

inclined consequently to mystify the "self-sufficing power of solitude" (Part II, 77):

> An auxiliar light
> Came from my mind, which on the setting sun
> Bestowed new splendour; the melodious birds,
> The gentle breezes, fountains that ran on
> Murmuring so sweetly in themselves, obeyed
> A like dominion, and the midnight storm
> Grew darker in the presence of my eye.
> Hence my obeisance, my devotion hence,
> And *hence* my transport. (Part II, 417–25)

The sequence of dependencies, transforming the speaker's reverence of the other into a species of self-worship in which he becomes,
by turns, the thing reverenced ("my devotion hence, / And *hence* my
transport"), brilliantly formulates the complex etiology that made
the first *Prelude* a more accurate account of the "growth of a Poet's
mind" than the epical version of 1805.

Furthermore, this sequence shows why subsequent poems became more allegorical, more inclined to negotiate passage *to* self-
enclosure, than the autobiography that immediately deconstructed
the very self it promoted.[17] The incorporation of the two-part *Prelude* into the first two books of the 1805 epic did more than give
Wordsworth a running start; it also put a pressure on his poem
similar to that placed on the Intimations Ode.[18] And like the Ode,
which persists despite all manner of pressure, the initial books
of *The Prelude* have a similar effect of upholding their speaker's
grace—the paradise or "immortality" he has claimed to have regained—while invariably sliding from it. These sections, which an-
nounce the superimposition of biblical mythos on the represented
Poet's history, necessarily promote this "representation" as somehow distinct from the writing poet's "will," or as accessory to the
business at hand. This is clear, for example, in the questions
imported from 1799, where "this," no longer shifting between the
antipodes of alienation and immortality, hovers over the "gulph" between signifier and signified: asking, in effect, whether the speaker's present grace is merely art or, as the questioning amid telling
suggests, a version of life imitating art?

Nor is *The Prelude* at all wrong to register this uncertainty. What
the initial books disclose, as they narrate their speaker's triumph, is
an internalized allegory: the speaker claims as his own those virtues

previously assigned to a sublime presence, while still presenting them as a model to which he must conform. The loud wind, for instance, which in 1799 was a power admonishing the Poet-to-be from without, is demonstrably less powerful in 1805— thanks largely to the "mild creative breeze," whose arrival "within" (I, 42–43) is prefigured by the more violent wind. So, too, the stolen boat episode, where an "act of stealth / And troubled pleasure" (I, 388–89) receives admonishment by the "huge cliff" (406), retains less of its former fear and, moderated by the surrounding text of Book I, is more generally self-enclosed. Initially a submission to authority, the episode in 1805 follows the Intimations Ode in also departing from Freud by allowing paternal authority to be internalized still further in what Michael Cooke has called the "romantic will." The rising eminence, as Cooke shows, is dependent on the boy's actions, making its "contrar[iness]," in this instance, corollary to an opposing self.[19]

In becoming, as it were, the authority earlier privileged, the Poet no longer requires an authority to prevent his becoming. Both the Drowned Man episode and the spots of time, whose task had been to mystify a force greater than the Poet, are no longer part of the initial book, having been reassigned to Books V and XI respectively, where they perform a decidedly different function.[20] Prevalent in the meantime are less significant "memories" (the word or variant of which appears no fewer than five times in the hundred lines concluding Book I). Yet even their recovery of the past is gradually exacerbated by another function, which is the reconstruction of the past. As a result, one must separate the tension where memory simply contradicts itself in *The Prelude*, from the tension alleged in memory's "other" function of forgetting for art's sake.[21] In expressing hope, that is, that "[i]nvigorating thoughts from former years, / Might fix the wavering balance of my mind" (I, 649–50), such "wavering" is subsumed already by the "balance," or fulfillment of hope, that rewrites former years.

A more proper index of memory's subversive function, of contradictions as opposed to "contrarieties" (X, 899), involves those situations where, as in the Intimations Ode, tension is for the Poet nonexistent. This is the case, for example, in the well-known paean to the "infant Babe" in Book II (237–80), which appeared initially in the 1799 poem. A celebration of the affections of childhood reminiscent of the Ode, the description of "the babe / Nursed in his mother's arms" (239–40) clearly resists the irony into which the Ode descends. Yet it does so prelusive to a still greater irony on whose brink it is at present poised. That the description is unself-conscious is necessarily the point. For the ironization to which the passage is eventually subject is dictated by the way it is both an anatomy of the Poet's selfhood, consistent with the representational scheme, while still an anatomy of self, sufficient to reverse that process.

The crux of this exchange remains the displaced father in whose admiring gaze the "blessed . . . babe" is beheld, yet whose displacement concurrently revises the identity to which the child aspires. In the most basic sense, of course, Wordsworth means to argue that the "self" into whom the child has grown was initially ministered to by maternal forces with whom "he" (both child and Poet) was intimately connected. Yet in negotiating the child's movement from integration to individuation—to the identity putatively fostered by the "filial bond" (263)— Wordsworth not only interrupts the movement by making *himself* the father of the child (as opposed to making "the child . . . father of the Man"); he defers negotiation in the very act of projecting it: so that "poetic" identity remains a prolepsis now to which the child is heir in lieu of not being "outcast . . . bewildered and depressed" (261). Where in the first case the child remains an antetype for the man watching him, anticipating the man to come; he is reduced, in the second, to imitating a future, relatively shrunken self, whose prototypical status is registered in the way the beholder, distinctly individuated from the present scene, remains the only example or "earthly soul" (242) now present. The narrative that valorizes the past so that the affections of childhood are "verily . . . the first / Poetic spirit of our human life" (275–76) is undone by a selfhood that demands severance from the past and from maternal/natural connection in "manifest kin[ship]" (242) with the man watching.[22] This accounts for the simultaneity of father and son—wherein the presence of the former makes it literally impossible for the babe to become him—as well as for the speaker's absence *as father,* or for his reluctance in the passage to claim paternity. So long as the speaker is father of the child—the poetical self waiting to be reborn—the child cannot also be father of the man, or that figure whose grace the Poet claims to have inherited.

Like the Intimations Ode, where contradictions are both proven and resolved in intimations of immortality, *The Prelude* initially presents a self whose instability, or in this case absence, is continually checked by the very narrative whose arbitrariness it would expose. As *The Prelude* continues, however, away from the earlier sections that had been adapted for present purposes, the tension of memories—sublated thus far as one function of memory—issues in an ever greater tension between the writing Wordsworth and the written, figurative Wordsworth: both as speaker and as the character of the Poet. An important dimension of this latter tension is the supervention of allegory, which follows in accordance with the internalization of the allegorical structure. A concomitant aspect—and no less important in that it explains the existence of *The Prelude* as a personal epic—is an ever-increasing association of the poem's primary narrative with a reader, nominally Coleridge, to whom intentionality is often given in the form of readerly expectation.

This association, to be sure, reenacts a much earlier one in which obligations to a reader were fundamentally obligations to self. The difference now is that by serving society in such a way that "my song" (I, 56), as Wordsworth initially calls it, may become "[o]ur song" (XI, 8), the self correspondingly served—that imperial self the "babe" is destined to become—is continually identified as the product of idealization.

That *The Prelude* is at one level the result of obligation, of expectations whose fulfillment is also tantamount to the poem's intentional structure, helps explain why the poem persists despite Wordsworth's growing disaffection with it. And it would explain, too, the disaffection of Matthew Arnold, who made a point of excluding Wordsworth's "poems of greatest bulk," both "the *Excursion* and *The Prelude*," from his "best work" ("Wordsworth" 42). As Arnold (I believe) correctly intuited, the humanistic or otherwise liberal "application" promoting both the Poet and the power of his imagination (which Arnold elsewhere lauds) is resisted in *The Prelude* by an increasingly separate referentiality, from whose vantage the poem's obligation to self is shown to be a fairly conventional (dare one say "Hebraic"?) obligation to culture. Further, in keeping this referentiality and the allegories by which it is exposed separate or indirect (or even by eliding it as happens with "Vaudracour and Julia" in Book IX), Wordsworth simultaneously shows how the hierarchical structure is sufficiently internalized at this stage to make its exposure *as hierarchy* adversarial rather than primary. Barely secondary, therefore, to the impulse to complete *The Prelude*, to make it a "history" of the poet's triumph by imagination, is the counter-impulse (in addition to such counter-testimony as the letter to Beaumont and the suppression of the work from publication) by which completion of the poem is increasingly a matter of bringing *The Prelude* "[t]o its appointed close" (XIII, 270).

NOTES

1. For additional discussion of the Ode along these lines, see Lionel Trilling, "The Immortality Ode," in *The Liberal Imagination* (New York: Scribners, 1976), 144–45. I use the formulation from *Civilization and Its Discontents* because it is ultimately implied throughout Freud, especially when Freud allows (following Ferenczi and his appropriation of Platonic myth) that infantile sensations—though ungoverned by the ego—constitute a kind of consciousness. Nevertheless my use of Freud differs from Trilling's use of him in that it is comparative not normative.

2. *The Ego and the Id,* trans. Joan Rivière, ed. James Strachey (New York: W. W. Norton, 1962), 15, 18–29.

3. *Civilization and Its Discontents,* trans. and ed. James Strachey (New York: W. W. Norton, 1962), 70–71.

4. I quote, in order, Bloom, *The Visionary Company,* 170–77; Vendler, "Lionel Trilling and the *Immortality Ode,*" *Salmagundi,* 41 (1978): 66–86. For a parallel view, see also Hartman, *Wordsworth's Poetry,* 273–77 and Ferry, *The Limits of Mortality,* 44–50. Although Ferry is generally skeptical about the vagueness of Wordsworth's counterassertion, he nevertheless evaluates the poem in light of "its failure really to convince us that the childhood vision of things *is* the 'fountain-light of all our day,' the 'master light of all our seeing' " (49).

5. Susan Wolfson similarly notes that the questions which "forc[e] a two-year break in composition at the end of Stanza 4" are voiced by a "representative, rather than empirical, 'I' " (*The Questioning Presence,* 170), the latter of whom provides a a relatively confident answer (172–73). In this context, it is interesting, too, that by the publication of the poem in 1807 Wordsworth had revised the question, replacing "gone" with "now," emphasizing even more the coexistence of what, for the representative man, is necessarily and otherwise "fled."

6. Frances Ferguson also notes the "title's reticence about its own hierarchies": "it alternately appears as a profession of belief, and as uncertainty which chooses not to advertise itself " (*Wordsworth: Language as Counter-Spirit,* 100).

7. Trilling also cites this passage in his analysis, yet committed, as he is, to a view of the poem's tragic sense, he elides the ultimate subject of Freud's study, which is guilt and its effects.

8. The line numbers in the 1802–04 version of the poem are, because of the (as yet) unadded material regarding "obstinate questionings / Of sense and outward things," 140–45; otherwise the line references, the arrangement of the lines, and the spelling here derive from the version of the Ode first published in 1807, which is also the "reading text" in Curtis, ed., *Poems, in Two Volumes," and Other Poems, 1800–1807.* In all substantive matters, the text of the Ode that I discuss represents the earliest full version of the poem as documented in Curtis's edition.

9. A notable exception is Cleanth Brooks who attributes the problem to "Wordsworth's paradoxes," the "method" of which shows the blindness of

childhood to be the possession simultaneously of "rare sight," establishing a "relation" between "analytic reason" and the "synthesizing imagination" ("Wordsworth and the Paradox of Imagination," in *Wordsworth: A Collection of Critical Essays*, ed. M. H. Abrams, 175–76).

10. For the relationship between institutionalized orthodoxy and Freud's psychoanalytic theory, see Freud, *Moses and Monotheism*, trans. Katherine Jones (New York: Vintage, 1955). See also Jerome Christensen, " 'Thoughts That Do Often Lie Too Deep For Tears': Toward a Romantic Concept of Lyrical Drama," *TWC*, 12 (1981): 52–64, which explores the "guilty" dynamic whereby the poet is at once "the father's child as he is the child's father" (57).

11. In a somewhat related argument, Ferguson observes how the "continuities and connections" of the Ode's final stanzas are affirmed "in a rhetoric which suspends itself over a gap in demonstrable truths" (*Wordsworth: Language as Counter-Spirit*, 125). The problem, as I see it, has perhaps less to do with the poet's rhetoric *per se* than with the "[dis]continuities and connections" in which that rhetoric is grounded.

12. "Wordsworth's Intimations Ode and Its Epigraphs," *JEGP*, 82 (1983): 539–40. I am grateful to Manning for detailing the differences between the two epigraphs, although I am less convinced than he of the evasive quality of the latter. Manning, too, notes the shift from "I" to "We" in the poem as a way of allowing the narrator to "declare his fidelity to the vision [of loss] while remaining removed from its demands" (531)— however, as I see it, this removal remains, along with the narrator's fidelity to the vision, simultaneously greater *and* smaller than in Manning's conception.

13. Following Abrams' notion of the "correspondent breeze," Harold Bloom speaks for most readers of the poem in noting that from the very beginning "*The Prelude* is a song of triumph rather than a song of experience" (*The Visionary Company*, 143).

14. For a similar view, see Wolfson (*The Questioning Presence*, 156–57), who notes that "self-reproach" inherent in the "interrogative syntax" of the "earlier manuscript" is subsequently "divert[ed] into self-affirmation."

15. My conception of the 1799 *Prelude* differs clearly, then, from that of Jonathan Wordsworth ("The Two-Part *Prelude* of 1799," in *The Prelude 1799, 1805, 1850*, 567–85), who regards the two parts as "a single unit," which compared to the 1805 version is "more tightly constructed" and of a "single theme"—"the birth and growth of imagination" and/or the "primacy" of the individual mind.

16. In noting the relationship between the 1799 *Prelude* and the various components of *The Recluse* (of which the first *Prelude* was manifestly a part), Kenneth Johnston similarly stresses the poem's "movement . . . from Wordsworth's solitary, free-spirited relation to nature in the First Part to the socially determined relations suggested in the Second." (*Wordsworth and "The Recluse"*, 66).

17. This view contrasts with Kenneth Johnston's; in the determination

to see the 1805 *Prelude* as part of *The Recluse,* Johnston notes how this *Prelude* exposes the "underlying structural principles" of the 1799 version (*Wordsworth and "The Recluse"*, 104–06). I would argue that it is the reverse that takes place: the 1799 version exposes the structural principles of the epic version.

18. For the chronology of *The Prelude* in its various stages of composition, see Reed, *Wordsworth: The Chronology of the Middle Years*, 1–15, 628–55. See also Jonathan Wordsworth, "The Five-Part *Prelude* of Early Spring 1804," *JEGP,* 71 (1977): 1–25. Following both Reed and Jonathan Wordsworth, I regard 1804 as the year that *The Prelude* was composed—certainly in the form that Karl Kroeber has called a "personal epic" (*Romantic Narrative Art*, 78–103).

19. *The Romantic Will*, 89. Although the "will," in Cooke's formulation, essentially opposes the romantic autonomy celebrated by critics such as Hartman and Bloom, this opposition is based essentially on affinity with authority rather than a difference.

20. For analysis of the various revisions of the Drowned Man episode and the different challenges the episode poses to the poet's authority, see Wolfson, "The Illusion of Mastery: Wordsworth's Revisions of 'The Drowned Man of Esthwaite,' 1799, 1805, 1850," *PMLA*, 99 (1984): 917–35.

21. Paul Jay has also noted the forgetting or pervasive "absence" that necessarily accompanies "the double activity of both remembering and imagining [the] past" in *The Prelude* (*Being in the Text: Self-Representation from Wordsworth to Roland Barthes* [Ithaca, NY: Cornell University Press, 1984], 78–82). Nevertheless, by attributing these "confusions" and the poem's "unwieldy size" to the fact that "writing *The Prelude*" was "an act of becoming" for Wordsworth, Jay allows neither the poem nor the poet a life of their own.

22. Here, while recapitulating Freud, Wordsworth also anticipates other psychoanalytic theorists, including Nancy Chodorow (*The Reproduction of Mothering: Psychoanalysis and the Sociology of Gender* [Berkeley: University of California Press, 1978]), in positing an object-relational approach to selfhood or difference, which (regardless of gender) requires a severance from the mother in imitation of the self/father. More important, perhaps, is the anticipation of Julia Kristeva's promotion of mother-child interaction (or the "semiotic") as a subversion of the hierarchic structures of meaning (or the "symbolic" as Lacan initially calls it) impressed by agency of patriarchal authority. (*Revolution in Poetic Language*, trans. Margaret Waller [New York: Columbia University Press, 1984].) Thus, the "meaning" of this passage is simultaneously undone by an assault on its meaning, foreshadowing its subsequent ironization.

SEVEN

"The man to come parted . . . from him who had been": *The Prelude* (Dis)continued

The discord—by which *The Prelude* remains willed in being obligatory and "willed" in necessarily resisting its obligations—is more apparent in the books following the 1799 sections. Beginning with Book III, Wordsworth's "public voice" continually oscillates between the private and dramatic by way of becoming, in Herbert Lindenberger's description, the voice of "the poet addressing [his] audience" (*On Wordsworth's "Prelude"* 5). Whether it is the "loneliness" (III, 379) at Cambridge, different in its dependencies from the "enfranchise[ment]" (I, 9) it prefigures, or the regression homeward in Book IV that reverses the Poet's alleged progress, there is insistently something private in *The Prelude* in continual conflict with what is public, reconstructed and readerly in orientation.[1]

This "private," then, is not simply a function of the way memory often stands in opposition to the poem's reconstruction of events. The Discharged Soldier episode at the close of Book IV, for example, in some ways is less a memory than an allegory that contests the public voice of the man speaking and the idealized Poet of whom he speaks. In the episode, which was composed originally in 1798, Wordsworth projects himself, his represented self, in the image of the soldier, whose reflexivity is implied both in the "unseen" (405) vantage from which the man is first observed and, more explicitly, in the "self-blame" that the speaker confesses feeling as he "prolonged [his] watch" (433–34).[2] Thus, although a memory like those preceding it, the encounter with this "double" differs from these recollections in being a text adapted for present purposes.

Two things are important with respect to this adaptation: the perceived "stature" (405) of the soldier who, like the character beholding him, is felt to be larger than life, and the soldier's actual *lack* of stature, which the Poet's perceptions, no less than his perceptions of himself as character, initially conceal. The "enfranchise[ment]," already characteristic of the Poet's condition, is revised in the example of the soldier to a state of discharge or "dismiss[al]" (448), thereby wresting freedom from the very character who at the outset (and in the memory immediately preceding the encounter) appears free and "alone" (415). Likewise, the soldier's subsequent claim that he is "travelling to his native home" (449)—in paralleling the "journey home" that is *The Prelude* itself—becomes a journey whose necessary futility casts the Poet's journey into dubious relief. When, following their encounter, the Poet remembers having "sought with quiet heart my distant home" (504), his separation from his goal (indeed, his revision of the soldier's "native" to "distant") is prompted by a backward look to the very "hero," whose typicality finds a further register in his absence.

The allegorical function of the Discharged Soldier episode—its effect in paralleling the memory of the Soldier to the larger work of which that memory is also a part—is immediately confirmed in Book V, the book on "Books." Continuing to avert to certain "accidents" as a way of distancing himself from the poem, Wordsworth begins Book V in the first person only to digress suddenly to a dream about an Arab experienced by a "friend" (49). Because the recital of this dream was apparently provoked by a vision of the speaker's own in which books (the "consecrated works of bard and sage" [41]) are destroyed, critics have often questioned Wordsworth's motive in assigning the dream to a friend, especially as the Poet so obviously shares the Arab's fear of apocalypse. Yet it is precisely the identity of Poet and Arab—exposing the idealization to which the former has been subjected—that makes the friend's mediation necessary.

Apocalyptic vision, the Arab dream reminds us, is a function of memory, hence a repetition of the past (the Flood) at variance with the progressive sense of history on which the Poet's "sovereign[ty]" and conditions of heroism in *The Prelude* both depend. Like the Poet, the Arab fears imminent destruction, and fears for the fate of books which he hopes to preserve by burying them—in this case, a shell signifying poetry and a stone representing Euclid's *Elements*. Yet, unlike the Poet, the Arab is manifestly a failed hero or "semi-Quixote" (142), whose blindness to the futility of his enterprise preconditions his heroic stance to life. Most immediately, the Arab

ignores the fact that the world's "drowning" (136), as he has prophesied, will negate his effort to preserve monuments of intellect
from destruction: books themselves will not vanish— their transformation into stones and shells ensures otherwise. But human culture,
which arbitrarily "consecrate[s]" books or, more pointedly, stones
and shells, will.[3]

From another point of view, however, both the Arab's "backwar[d
look]" (128) and the fact that the flood he fears actually "chace[s]
. . . him" (137) suggest that he is tilting at windmills of his own
device—that is, at memory. "Quixote"-hood, in other words, is less a
function of human inadequacy than of the heroism at which "Quixote" fails: Quixotehood attests to the failure of "Sovereign Intellect" (14) and the failure of that myth to accommodate the escha-
tological predisposition to looking backwards. What fails in the
dream is not man but man *as figure*, not memory or personality, but
the mythologized intellect vulnerable to memory. The myth and the
progressive conception of history with which it is aligned make one
vulnerable to becoming a Quixote, and to a heroism doomed to
failure.

Similar to the Discharged Soldier episode, the Arab dream depicts a crazed, deluded wanderer, who resembles the "written" Poet
this time in the way he is implicated in a predestined or intentional,
yet uncompletable, structure. In the Poet's case, the past or private—what is observed in "looking backward"—gives the lie to a
more public, represented past which is a future as well: an idealized
"home" to which (as Abrams describes it) the Poet will "journey."[4]
Far from assisting this "journey," memory is more like the flood
chasing the Arab. It will likely provoke movement, but "looking
backward" necessarily renders the idealized conflation of selfhood
and sovereignty—and the conflation simultaneously of past, present and future—a negation.

The meaning of this episode or its "drift," as even the speaker
concedes, is "scarcely . . . obvious" (290–91). But it remains, however cryptic, the "drift" of Book V and, in the allegorical configuration of this book, of the poem as a whole. This drift is equally
apparent in the subsequent examples of the "infant prodigy" (290–
349), the "Winander boy" (389–449), and the drowned "man"
(450–81). These three figures are, of course, variously implicated in
the "obvious" drift of "Books," specifically its attack on modern
education. Nevertheless, they also resemble the Arab in the way
they allegorize as examples—the prodigy's growth is stunted, the
Winander boy dies prematurely, and the man, a school teacher,

drowns unexpectedly— the *arrested development* by which the Poet otherwise progresses in his poem from infant to boy to man.[5]

In the books that follow "Books," Wordsworth gradually discloses— while bringing *The Prelude* to "its appointed close"—that the real problem before him has less to do with the transcendental myth and its claim to enfranchisement than with those obligations consistent with the need to bring the personal epic to its proper end. The authority appropriated for the character of the Poet, no matter how radical or agnostic that appropriation, corresponds by rights to a conventionally hierarchical or (as we initially see with Matthew) patriarchal orientation. This disclosure, I believe, underlies the Poet's "grie[f]" (453) in experiencing the long-anticipated sight of Mount Blanc in Book VI and is further indicated in the Blind Beggar (VII, 611–23), whose autobiographical "pro[p]" and paternal visage provoke a similar "admonish[ment]" (623).[6]

In the latter incident, remembering and reconstructing, the mutual supports of autobiographical representation (pinned to the beggar's chest is "the story" of his life), are covered by a pervasive blindness and, in the speaker's case, by an additional confusion of figures:

> My mind did at this spectacle *turn round*
> As with *the might of waters*, and it seemed
> To me that in this *label* was a *type*
> Or *emblem* of the utmost that we know
> Both of ourselves and of the universe.
>
> (616–20, emphasis added)

If the man's blindness is an "emblem," a "type" or "label" of what "we know," it is because his writing, the "written paper [upon his chest]" (613–14), exposes the gap between the self and its representation. Through the veil of memory, the blind man becomes, as it were, the speaker reading, making the mutable object ("spectacle . . . label . . . type . . . emblem"), and additional referent of "we," the Poet—turned poet—remembering. This explains furthermore why the admonishment recalled upon looking into the man's "sightless eyes" comes "*[a]s if* . . . from another world" (623, emphasis added). With the proximity suddenly of the more immediate object to the remembered one, and the emergence simultaneously of a new subject (in whose self-reflexive gaze "sightless[ness]" is a property of objects past and present), the admonishment is no longer part of the remembered past. It belongs properly to the remembered present or "world" of the poem, to the moment when in recollection of the blind, paternal, supplicatory author, Wordsworth at last sees and is corrected by himself.[7]

Finally, in Book VIII, this awareness burgeons in the "unforgettable" image of paternal solicitude (842–59), which reinscribes and ironizes the "blessed . . . babe" of Book II. Entrapped in what is paradoxically an "open square" (845), a man—an "artificer" (854) as the Poet remembers him—is observed ministering to "a sickly babe . . . whom he had thither brought / For sunshine" (849–51). Taking "no note" of "those who passed" (including the Poet, "who looked at him" [852–53]), the man "bend[s] over" the child as if to protect it from the salutary elements ("the sun / And . . . the air which he had come to seek") and "eye[s] it with unutterable love" (856–59).

The significance of this scene is registered in several ways: in the various images of enclosure (the "square," the "fenc[e]," the "iron paling," the "wall" [845–48]); in the isolation of the perceiving Poet, emphasizing his correspondence to the perceived artificer; and last, despite claims to its "tenderness" and "delight" (841–43), in the activity itself. Here, the man tends to the child as much out of love as out of self-love, or in virtual defiance of the futility of his enterprise. This is underscored by the child's sickness and more crucially in the man's impulse to shield it in sickness from the salutary elements. Equally significant is the character of these elements. They are aspects of nature circumscribed—and, insofar as Nature is earlier tantamount to "mother," marginalized—by civilized, idealized constraints: both the narcissistic completeness of father and son and a geography that extends metonymically to the encircling arms of the "artificer . . . to the elbow bare" (854). "Unutterable love" becomes, in the self-reflexive gaze of Wordsworth writing as he remembers, the equivalent of utterance—the utterable love of self-representation—itself.

To say, then, that *The Prelude* has gone from an essentially mystified view of mother and son in Book II to a demystified view in Book VIII is not to dismiss the intervention of an authoritarian structure nor to deny the progress of the Poet's soul. As the retroactive ironization of Book II reminds us, allegory of this sort is beside progress rather than progressive—a rhetoric of perpetuity that is always there and always "scarcely . . . obvious."[8] David Simpson is quite blunt about this aspect of the poem. *The Prelude*'s "rhetoric of affirmation," he submits, is "completely . . . coloured by the language of retraction" (*Wordsworth's Historical Imagination* 120). Consistent with this configuration, therefore, with the "drift" that contests the drift or meaning of *The Prelude,* is the "tragic tale" of "Vaudracour and Julia" in Book IX ("Residence in France") in which the most conventional of forms—the love story—rewrites the "story of the man" (VII, 615) speaking.

Regarded for many years as a clumsy appendage to *The Prelude* whose excision in 1832 was entirely warranted, "Vaudracour and Julia" has recently come to fashion as a crucial moment in the poem. Following the general belief that the story is a substitution for Wordsworth's relationship with Annette Vallon, both Gayatri Spivak and Mary Jacobus have identified the story as an exemplary instance of the distortions and mystifications (especially involving gender) endemic to the poem as a whole.[9] And yet, without debating the merits of "Vaudracour and Julia," either as an artifact in its own right or as an episode that fortuitously tries the formal virtues of the larger poem, the story can be shown to wage a feminist argument remarkably consonant with those waged against it. What the story performs in its supervening function is an assault on authority by communication of what Julia Kristeva, in her particular modification of irony, has termed "she-truth": a truth that "never presents itself as such" (which is of course the feminist supposition about "Vaudracour and Julia"), "but rather captures, points, withdraws, hides itself in its veils."[10] While the love story is, as Spivak and Jacobus maintain, indivisible from *The Prelude* as a whole, its indivisibility is in the fact that as a tale of the Revolution, "Vaudracour and Julia" contests the patriarchal underpinnings of *The Prelude*'s humanistic, revolutionary narrative. Thus, this story of the Revolution is simultaneously a "revolution in poetic language," allowing "mimesis," as Kristeva observes, to "go through its truth (signification, denotation) to tell the 'truth' about it."[11]

The story of the two lovers follows upon a series of recollections noteworthy in the way they circumvent Wordsworth's ability to have assimilated the "language" (37) of France. Recalling his conversations with Michel Beaupuy, the "patriot" whom he befriends, the Poet is careful not to distinguish Beaupuy's voice from his own voice in the discourse they share:

> We took, and let this freely be confessed,
> In painting to ourselves the miseries
> Of royal courts. . . .
> > We added dearest themes,
> Man and his noble nature. . . .
> We summoned up honorable deeds . . .

Of truth preserved and error passed away,
Of single sprits that catch the flame from heaven.
(351–76)

These lines imply not only that the Poet spoke the French language, but that he had assimilated the various idealizations—the hope of a renovated society and the sanctity of the individual—to which the "language" had been put.

However despite their commonality of discourse, the speaker seeks to differentiate himself from its common subject: from the "patriot" (that he says he had become [124]) and, more dramatically, from the "we" of Wordsworth-Beaupuy. Sitting amid the ruins of the Bastille, the speaker remembers "pocket[ing]" a "relick in the guise / Of an enthusiast," and adds that "in honest truth" he was "[a]ffecting more emotion than [he] felt" (66–71). Later, having recounted his interaction with Beaupuy and the circumstances of Beaupuy's death in battle, the speaker recalls how "often," amid their "dialogues," he "slipped in thought,"

And let remembrance steal to other times
When hermits, from their sheds and caves forth
     strayed,
Walked by themselves, so met in shades like
     these. . . .

Or "saw methought a pair of knights"

Joust underneath the trees . . .
                              . . . anon the din
Of boisterous merriment . . .
                      . . . burst from haunt
Of satyrs in some viewless glade, with dance
Rejoicing o'er a female in the midst,
A mortal beauty, their unhappy thrall. (445–64)

With these allusions to solitude and desire, and their extensions in autonomy and requital respectively, it is perhaps no surprise that "the force" which, as the speaker observes, "did often mitigate the force / Of civic prejudice, the bigotry / So call it, of a youthful patriot's mind" was "Imagination" (497–501).

A faculty that *The Prelude* must, in one sense, continually privilege, "Imagination" is similarly "the force" that recognizes and "might[ily]" opposes the very itinerary in whose service it remains pressed. Wordsworth distinguishes the quality of what he imagines from the ideals that drive Beaupuy. Although "Imagination" is something Beaupuy possesses, both in his revolutionary hope and delectation in the misery of the ruling class, it is also a power he lacks. This difference enables Wordsworth to behold Beaupuy "in perfect faith," as one who wanders "through the events / Of that great change . . . [a]s through a *book,* an old *romance,* or *tale* / Of Fairy, or some dream of actions wrought / Behind the summer clouds" (305–09, emphasis added). There is a relationship between the speaker's ability with *another* language in Book IX, his "half-learned speech" (195), and this ability to identify Beaupuy's fidelity to "romance"—since with this identification, the speaker is able suddenly to stand outside the "great change" in the certitude that he was then a "stranger" (194). The language that the speaker partially masters (or refuses to have mastered in retrospect) becomes an index now of his ability to have recognized and also to have resisted the narrative that language had earlier constituted. As it was then (as now it seems), the Revolution in France comes to signify "romance" or representation, allowing Wordsworth to contest *his* representation even while as representer (the poet writing of himself as Poet) he must, like Beaupuy, bring *The Prelude* to its prescribed end.

The equation of Revolution with narrative, and its contestation on these grounds, occurs in "Vaudracour and Julia"—a story, it is important to note, that was told first by Beaupuy, but which in *The Prelude* is recounted by the speaker. This metonymic swing makes the relationship between the represented, Beaupuy the hero, and the representer, Beaupuy the teller, also a relationship between Beaupuy and the main character of *The Prelude.* This equation, in fact, is the basis for their separation—and for the separation (by extension) of the man writing from the one written of.[12] The Revolution turns out to be two things, then: a political or historical reality in Beaupuy/Wordsworth's story as well as a "romance," whose antagonist and host remains (in this "revolution in poetic language") the authoritarian father.[13] The phrase "his father's house" appears no fewer than six times in the story, and this is no accident. Without the authoritarian father, who prohibits Vaudracour from marrying beneath his station, and who enforces the prerogatives of rank and class over those of the pursuit of happiness, there would be no story and no cause for revolt. Correspondingly, when this nostalgia for the father subsides, when Vaudracour refuses upon his son's birth to imitate his father's example, Vaudracour's insurrection concludes with the cessation of all action—or what can be represented.[14]

Somewhat like *Romeo and Juliet,* its obvious (and admitted) analogue, "Vaudracour and Julia" involves two lovers who, although friends from childhood, are prohibited from marrying for reasons of class difference. They are prevented, literally and figuratively, by the patriarchy that grounds the reigning social structure. Thus, the tale's further complication—the illicit love affair that follows in reaction to these paternal "bars" (598) and the pregnancy that finally results—proves as much an expression of the will to happiness, a revolutionary impulse, as it remains a will to power. Patriarchy, with no small irony, begets patriarchs in "Vaudracour and Julia." Apprised of his impending fatherhood, Vaudracour redoubles his efforts to persuade his father to consent to the union and bless its issue. Each effort involves a "return" to "his father's house" (764) during which Vaudracour is invariably spurred to reaction and revolt. In one, he is imprisoned and nearly killed by "three armed men" (677) one of whom he slays in self-defense. In another, he returns to Julia only to flee again to avoid pursuit by the authorities. In a third, he returns willingly as an alternative to imprisonment but soon finds himself imploring his father's consent to his marriage.

Vaudracour's returns point as much to the pervasiveness of patriarchy as a social phenomenon as to its persistence in matters of aesthetics. Action and heroism, in that they are provoked by these encounters, depend on the father for their existence, making representation a filial piety of sorts.[15] Without the father, either Vaudracour's father or Vaudracour himself, there would be neither an authority nor "his" narrative to tell. Furthermore, from the moment Vaudracour vows not to follow his father's example until the end of the tale when, following Julia's retreat to a convent, he assumes the offices of mother, there is a noticeable "slack[ening]" (855) in both revolution and representation. His actions no longer bear retelling and his stance toward his father is far less severe—though, again, to little effect. Finally, with the death of his son, Vaudracour stops speaking altogether, retreating to a world whose veritable "abjection" (to use Kristeva's term) casts the world of the tale (and the symbolic order to which it refers) into dubious relief.

Vaudracour's reduction to a state of "imbecili[ty]" (935) is often taken as evidence of the overkill that warranted the story's excision. Yet the non-verbal imbecility to which Vaudracour is reduced, indeed reduced upon reenacting the mother-child interaction, must be weighed not only against the idealized backdrop of the Revolution but, following Kristeva's notion of abjection, "as a kind of oblivion that is constantly remembered" and, as such, proves a challenge to the more transcendent, authoritative selfhood dictated by the law of the father (*Powers* 8). Vaudracour's reduction to a pre-linguistic or "maternal" state, in the aftermath of his maternal offices, effectively charts his departure from the paternal order he had previously inhabited. So long as revolution *is* repetition, a "return" effectively to one's father, the only alternative to revolution is a return, by turns, to one's mother. In terms of poetic representation, such withdrawal means silence.

The correspondence in the tale between Vaudracour and Wordsworth, between one "patriot" and another patriot destined likewise to become a "stranger," reflects equally on the relationship between Wordsworth and Beaupuy: each man—to the extent he is hopeful of a renovated world in time—is a hero of "romance." But ultimately the movement from hero to hermit in the tale, from Vaudracour the father to Vaudracour the silent "mother," parallels the movement in this same book from "we" to "I," from Wordsworth the "patriot" to Wordsworth the "stranger." When at the end of the story Vaudracour so removes himself from "all intelligence with man" that neither "the voice of freedom" ("which through France / Soon afterwards resounded"), nor "public hope," nor "personal memory" can "[r]ouze him," (929–34), it is these *and their alignment*—the way gender and hope, public and private, language and liberty are variously conflated—that are reciprocally "[c]ut off" (929). An "intelligence with" Vaudracour, the displacement of these various elements represents a movement "with" him from the poem. The end of "Vaudracour and Julia," it cannot be emphasized enough, is also the end of Book IX. In a silence finally coincident with Vaudracour's, Wordsworth's "intelligence with" *The Prelude* gives way in Book IX to an intelligence *of The Prelude* which, like the order from which Vaudracour is simultaneously estranged, appears more and more to be another "man"'s song.

Proceeding less by authority of the writing poet and more by authority of the Poet writing, *The Prelude* progresses finally by authority of "we"—the Poet and his expectant audience—over the protests of a "stranger" grown suspicious of utterance. Many critics, myself included, have noted Wordsworth's capitulation in *The Prelude* to an ideal image of himself.[16] But far more noteworthy is Wordsworth's resistance to that capitulation. Beginning indeed with Book V and continuing in Book VI ("Cambridge and the

Alps") something nearly akin to identity consists with something other than itinerary—and, in contrast to the goal of narrative (which in Book VI is notably a *"soulless* image" [454]), with the "hope that can never die" (VI, 541) or be fulfilled. Wordsworth thus dissociates the "soulless" character of the Poet from the man writing. Identity and "Imagination" (VI, 525) come to oppose their mystifications in the poem's humanistic narrative by opposing the structuring of individual experience into forms such as the poem, where "first . . . and last" (VI, 572) are disingenuously one "and" the same.[17] In their place, with assists from memory and imagination, is an "unfathered" (VI, 527), more feminized consciousness whose story is "end[less]" (VI, 572), and in which there is no distinction, nor need of link, between a remembered past and a writing present. A faculty whose time and place are both there and now, "Imagination" in *The Prelude* (in accordance with the supervention of allegory) belongs equally to "another world"—is part of a movable present—of the very writer who, as he remarks in Book VI, was "[f]our years and thirty . . . this very week" (61).[18]

In conjunction with this writerly defection, Wordsworth, as I have suggested, foists responsibility for *The Prelude* on the reader Coleridge. Although accessory to the poem initially and to the Poet's "confidence in things to come" (I, 67), Coleridge becomes, in *The Prelude*'s second half, the Poet's better half: a figure, like Beaupuy, with whom the Poet is aligned, yet from whom—on the basis of their alignment—the writing poet is dissociated. "Not with these (i. e., "unhappiness . . . guilt . . . [a]nd lastly, utter *loss of hope itself*") began / *Our* song," Book XI begins, and "[n]ot with these *our song must end*" (1–8, emphasis added). And it is clear, both in the restoration of the narrative framework and in the deliberate accession to "hope," that *The Prelude*—which later culminates in the image of Wordsworth and Coleridge as "[u]nited helpers" (XIII, 438)—has become a "joint labou[r]" (XIII, 439). No longer "my song," the poem is emphatically "our song," usurping by form and function "another" song which, with ever fewer exceptions, has become a song of silence.

Nevertheless, the scarcity of these exceptions, especially as the poem wends its way to triumph, has the effect of dismantling the silence by identifying its purport. All of which makes silence, in the image of Vaudracour's "intelligence," a revolution in poetic language that the audibility of the thirty-four-year-old writer will additionally confirm. This dynamic is most evident in the "spots of time," whose "effective meaning" opposes the poem's more obvious drift. Enlisted to help close the narrative, which chronicles the achievement of the grace already claimed Book I, the spots (as their name implies) resist this reclamation by stopping or breaking the circular progress.

Not surprisingly, Wordsworth makes a distinction regarding the "spots of time" in Books XI and XII that is almost always overlooked: these incidents are so designated in order to separate them from the climactic ascent of Snowdon, the memory that begins Book XIII. Taken customarily to be a spot of time, the Snowdon ascent is more a spot *in* time insofar as it defends both the poem's narrative structure and the hierarchies that ground it.[19] Thus, a proper assessment of the "spots of time," while recognizing the "renovating virtue[s]" (XI, 259) asserted on their behalf, must measure them as much against these public assertions as against the ascent of Snowdon without which *The Prelude* could not have been brought to its "appointed close." The distance separating the Snowdon scene from the incidents that precede it, particularly the Sarum incident in Book XII, attests silently to the spots' audible if otherworldly testimony: their reminder that individual authority is another form (indeed a representation) of a still earlier tyranny.

"[T]aking their date / From our first childhood" (XI, 274– 75) rather than from adulthood (as in the Snowdon scene), the "spots of time" protest the growth, the ascension to authority, that the representational scheme demands. While these incidents, we are told, show an independence from sensory constraints—from perceptions associated either with Nature or, as in the "blessed . . . babe" of Book II, with the mother herself, this must not be confused with a larger, ostensibly freer assumption of male authority. The "mind," to be sure, remains by association with the spots "lord and master." However this same mind is also observed to exert a feminine "will" over the "outward sense," deemed the "obedient servant of her [the mind's] will" (270–72). Amid the typology of enfranchisement Wordsworth is able to dissociate his terms from their origins and, as he could not in 1799, to deconstruct them. Using patriarchy (i.e., lord and master) to underscore *his* emancipation at this juncture, he allows that this autonomy—the inarticulate freedom to be inferred from the "spots"—differs in this same regard from the represented, idealized freedoms of individual enfranchisement and revolution. These last are, in the absence of a feminized "will," utterly paternalistic.[20]

Such autonomy clearly differs, then, from what Geoffrey Hartman ascribes to "Imagination" in *The Prelude*, where the fear of autonomy (he famously shows) is registered in the continued conflict between the primacy of Nature and that of the individual mind. As most readers are aware, Hartman sees the reverence for the natively human in *The Prelude* as different from, and even subversive of, other orthodoxies in the poem, notably the reverence for Nature. Thus, for the very reason that humanism is not an orthodoxy in Hartman's conception, the failure of *The Prelude* to promote the individual "Imagination" by adopting a less conciliatory stance to Nature is, in his view, primarily a failure of will not of representation. Hartman, of course, presupposes that Nature is aligned entirely with the deity in *The Prelude*. He does not consider at all the ways Nature is virtually synonymous with the unrepresentable: with the silent, "unfathered" orientation that as early as Book II contrasts with the individuated authority of the father and self. Thus, while he is perfectly right in observing how *The Prelude* fails to uphold the myth of enfranchisement, Hartman cannot allow how it is the myth itself that fails to uphold the poem, indeed to make it the very poem he would prefer it was.[21] Hartman's ultimate disaffection with *The Prelude* and concomitant affection for "Imagination," both in Book VI and in the "spots of time," are curiously a measure of Wordsworth's own disaffection—of a conviction, amid detachment, that the poem may succeed, but only on its own terms.

Given this "autonomy," not only of the man writing but also of the poem itself, the "spots of time" can do no more than protest the progress of *The Prelude* to its appointed closure. Alleged to be salutary in their effects, these incidents are cryptic at best: how can a "reverie" of a "waste" animated by bloodlust, human sacrifice and primitive druidic rites have at "its *base* / That whence our dignity originates" (XII, 373–74, emphasis added)? How can the guilty memories of a father's death bring sustenance for a "later time" (XI, 385)? Plainly, they cannot—and do not—yet the point is not that *The Prelude* turns on itself in this very literal way; it is that the poem achieves closure in veritable ignorance of its own content or in defiance of the gap between argument and evidence.[22] Included less finally to bring the poem to an unexpected halt, the "spots of time" serve to lament the capitulations that prevent *The Prelude* from stopping, in silence, before the end—before the "man to come" *becomes* the man he was destined to be.

The incident at Penrith beacon—and first of the "spots"—illustrates this point. Conflating two separate incidents—the sighting of the inscription beside the gibbet mast and the sight of the woman "vexed . . . [b]y the strong wind" (XI, 314– 15) beneath "the melancholy beacon" (321)—Wordsworth negotiates a complicated dissent in which dissent itself becomes (as in "Vaudracour and Julia") a matter of consenting to authority. "Disjoined" (285) from a parent figure in the incident, the speaker discovers himself unremoved from paternity and unable, by virtue of this disjunction, to rebel. To rebel is simply to be coopted by a narrative which registers nostalgia (in Derrida's axiom) for a now absent father. Thus, the young boy's removal from his "guide"—or suppression of that presence conveyed in the image of the *nonexistent* man in chains—is inevitably undone by the "monumental writing [carved]" by "[s]ome unknown "hand" (XI, 294–95), which arrests the young boy in his "[f]altering . . . ignoran[ce]" (299).[23]

A similar interchange is evident in the sight of the "girl" that immediately follows. Conspicuous in its recourse to a maternal or feminine authority, the experience similarly charts the futility of this counterturn. The experience, whose "dreariness" appropriately defies representation ("I should need / Colours and words that are unknown to man / To paint the visionary dreariness. . . . " [308–10]), manages in any case to represent both the subjugation of the "mother" by Nature (dramatizing the contradiction of feminine authority) and, more important, a subjugation by the "beacon on the lonely eminence," which presides over "her" vexation in virtual response to the boy's renewed search for his "lost guide" (311). Denial of paternity in these two movements is both futile yet necessary, or necessary first *and then* futile. It is not resistance or revolution, but always (already) a capitulation whereby a "guide" is "lost" so that guidance may be found.[24]

The two other "spots of time"—Waiting for the Horses and the reverie on Sarum—are inured, if similarly unresigned, to the narrative, or "written"-ness, of Penrith beacon. The ascent to the "eminence" (XI, 350) by which the Poet hopes to gain "sight" of the "two horses" that will "bear [him] home" for Christmas (347–48) becomes in the aftermath of his vacation, and after his father's death during that vacation, an *assent* to the eminence. The trip "[u]p to the highest summit" (355) is at first functional, aligned solely with the young Poet's anticipation of freedom from boarding school. Yet by sad coincidence it remains linked to freedom from the sponsor of that anticipated freedom, the father: the same horses anticipated here (though this knowledge is elided) are presumably those used to convey the "body to the grave" (367). In this way, the initial ascent becomes, by agency of guilt, an insurgence for which the boy at once seeks and achieves expiation:

> . . . and when I called to mind
> That day so lately past, when from the crag

> I looked in such anxiety of hope,
> With trite reflections of morality,
> Yet in deepest passion, I bowed low
> To God who thus corrected my desires. (369–74)

Although seemingly administered by God the father, the correction of desire, as the categorical and causal "thus" suggest together, is enacted by the Poet himself, whose initiatives include the corrective as well as the trespass. It is the initial journey, circumscribed by the patriarchal scheme, that is the key one. Not only does the enfranchising ascent lead inevitably to a second, inhibiting assent. The latter becomes, in due course, an ironic echo of the former.

We see, then, how self-reflexive, how much like "Vaudracour and Julia," Waiting for the Horses remains. By merely allowing the narrative to work its course, Wordsworth is able to acknowledge the authority, God the father, in imitation of whom the ascending or remembered Poet becomes his own adversary. A similar pattern will reoccur atop Mount Snowdon; but there the movement from ascent to assent is unself-conscious, caught up entirely in the narrative scheme. Here, in contrast, Wordsworth exposes the irrevocable drift of the Prelusive scheme and, at the same time, its irrevocability: there are no means left to write against *The Prelude* without writing it all the same.

The reverie of Sarum makes evident both the autonomy of *The Prelude* and the detachment of the writing (as opposed to written) Wordsworth. Based on an experience of 1793, by which time Wordsworth had parted from Annette Vallon (and from the evidence and intelligence, not coincidentally, of his paternity), the incident in Book XII confirms all that he has relinquished, in literature as in life. As such, the episode stands in distinct contrast to the poem that surrounds it: both the utterly prosaic book for which it provides an uncharacteristic close, and finally, the Snowdon incident and conclusion proper in Book XIII. Moreover, unlike the two other "spots," the Sarum incident stands in contrast to the Poet himself, who is less a participant in the incident than a witness both to his and the poem's contestation.[25]

The account begins characteristically with an image of the solitary Poet "disjoined," as in other incidents, from a predestined or anticipated itinerary:

> There on the pastoral downs without a track
> To guide me, or along the bare white roads
> Lengthening in solitude their dreary line,

While through those vestiges of ancient times
I ranged, and by the solitude o'ercome
I had a reverie and saw the past. (XII, 315–20)

Yet recalling this much, the speaker declines participation in the "past," bowing instead to the "single Briton[s]" (322) who, comprising "multitudes" (321), are exemplary still in their "barbaric majesty" and "strength" (325–26). The result of an overarching system or scheme, what appears unusual, singular and heroic about these men is in the present vantage participated in by all, obeyed by all. Accordingly, the "sacrificial fire," which suddenly illumines the night, is "fed," as the speaker conceives it, "[w]ith living men" (331–32)—men, that is, who, like the living man himself, are subsumed by a larger order whose "imitative forms" include this druidic "pomp" as well as the "[l]ines, circles" and other mysterious "shapes / Such as in many quarters yet survive" (340–41).

Nor is it a coincidence that the image that concludes this "antiquarian's dream" (348) effectively admonishes *The Prelude* as perhaps the most extant and mystified of these "imitative forms":

[I] saw the bearded teachers, with white wands
Uplifted, pointing to the starry sky,
Alternately, and the plain below, while breath
Of music seemed to guide them, and the waste
Was cheared with stillness and a pleasant sound.
(XII, 349–53)

In this image of patriarchal mediation, of teachers situated between heaven and earth, we are shown for perhaps the first time the truly seductive character of an otherwise arbitrary, culturally "engraven" (XI, 294) scheme. "Uplift[ing]" what is "below" (or, as the speaker earlier remarks, in "rais[ing]" one "above all" [313–14]), the narrative of *The Prelude* is self-congratulatory because it is "guide[d]" by music that, while "seem[ingly]" distant or "unknown" (XI, 293), is nevertheless proximate to its own. By internalizing allegory in the manner we have previously observed, the Poet, like the elevated teachers, becomes equivalent to the authority he merely signifies. Both the Poet's passivity and the pervasive "stillness," which the remote music interrupts, hint at this equivalence. However they depend as intimations on the Snowdon incident that immediately follows. For it is in the Snowdon scene that the character of Wordsworth—the written Wordsworth—conclusively silences the silent, writing Wordsworth by annexing with "Coleridge" (XIII, 247) the roles of "teach[er]" (XIII, 445) and of prophet "blessed" (XIII, 437).

To ascribe so different an authority to the Snowdon incident, especially in its proximity to the "spots of time," requires less justification than might seem necessary. Indeed, this requirement may be answered simply by reiterating that this proximity, punctuated by the stillness of Book XII and by the silence between the books, is the issue. Unlike the other three incidents, the Snowdon incident is neither cryptic nor at odds with the poem, save in its inability to restore at last the wholly "enfranchised" Poet with whom, and in whose voice, *The Prelude* began. This inconsistency derives partly from the actual circumstances of the Snowdon experience, the walking tour of 1791; for Wordsworth, then twenty-one, neither needed nor sought to reject a fellow-traveller or guide—in this case Robert Jones. Yet for this reason too, the recourse to the plural "we" in place of the singular, exemplary "I" seems equally odd, particularly on the heels of the Sarum incident. It is as if the companion in the Snowdon scene were crucial precisely in that he is not, that the memory of him gave the Poet cause to adopt what at one level is simply a more natural form of self-reference. And this is so because, unlike the Sarum incident, there *is* a guide here, and more proper referent of "we," than Robert Jones.

This guide, again, is the reader Coleridge, whose "expectations" are, as Wordsworth imagines them, identical to *The Prelude*'s. Indeed, like Beaupuy's expectations or young Vaudracour's expectations, Coleridge's are guided by a structure that makes "we" a spontaneous acknowledgment of the indebtedness by which the poem's autonomy is purchased with its main character's.[26] Moreover, like the "Intimations Ode," where similar acknowledgments are equally spontaneous, the cost at this stage appears slight, making "we" a sign of how the mythology has taken over, rather than a conscious register of that initial allegory (or structure of identity) on which a Poet's house and now his "ante-chapel" are built. The extent to which Wordsworth's "we" replaces "I" cannot be underestimated any more than it can be ascribed simply to historical fact. Without this plural, after all, or in absence of the prefiguration "we" credits, the success of *The Prelude* as a personal epic (even in conjunction with the collective disposition of the Poet's person) would be irremediably diminished.

Beginning with a deliberate account of the physical ascent of Mount Snowdon, Wordsworth's speaker gradually becomes a single self whose remembered sensations render him a second self or imitation of God. Intimations of this rendering are already apparent in the geography of the experience where the Poet finds himself, like the teachers on Sarum, between heaven and earth. But it devolves to the experience itself and the subsequent "meditation" to authenticate matters by establishing a link between creation and Creation: between a privileged perception and the fiction which mystifies and legitimizes the former:

A meditation rose in me that night
Upon the lonely mountain when the scene
Had passed away, and it appeared to me
The perfect image of a mighty mind,
Of one that feeds upon infinity,
That is exalted by an under-presence,
The sense of God, or whatsoe'er is dim
Or vast in its own being—above all,
One function of such mind had Nature there
Exhibited by putting forth, and that
With circumstance most awful and sublime:
That domination which she oftentimes
Exerts upon the outward face of things,
So moulds them, and endues, abstracts, combines,
Or by abrupt and unhabitual influence
Doth make one object so impress itself
Upon all others, and pervades them so,
That even the grossest minds must see and hear,
And cannot chuse but feel. (XIII, 66–84)

As the seemingly needless condescension to "grossest minds" indicates, the assignment of a will to Nature signifies a hierarchy in which Nature, like these other minds, is ultimately subordinate. It is often argued that Nature's actions confirm the "wedding" of mind and matter constitutive of Wordsworthian grace.[27] It is equally clear, however, that Nature's will is no longer the subversive, feminized will of the "spots of time," but an adjunct—subordinate *by being feminine*—to the paternal or "fathered" will of which the marriage of mind and Nature is a similar, yet smaller, synthesis.

If in Book XI the "will" (pace Schopenhauer) opposes "representation," then in Book XIII it coincides both with representation and with the hierarchy that grounds the "revolutionary" ideal of individual enfranchisement. When the Poet observes that Nature had "above all . . . one function of such mind . . . there / Exhibited," the words "above all" are as much an introduction or bridge to Nature as a confirmation of the "sense of God" inherent in the incident as in the larger poem.[28] In the first books of *The Prelude,* the vaguely incestuous "correspondence" of Poet and Nature portended their resistance to an oppressive, authoritarian presence. Now, at the poem's appointed close, Wordsworth shows how much his "mind" has grown: as an exemplary, more than representative, man he has overcome Nature by becoming his own father. His revolution, accordingly, is more a counter-revolution and merely a re-presentation.[29]

NOTES

1. I wish to distinguish this countermovement in the poem from what Paul Sheats perspicaciously terms the "retrogrades" in *The Prelude* ("Wordsworth's 'Retrogrades' and the Shaping of *The Prelude,*" *JEGP*, 71 [1972]: 473–90): those movements both temporal and formal in which the poem's progress, or the assumption that the Poet has progressed successfully to the present, is opposed. By allowing these movements to be "retrogrades," Sheats allows also for their cooptation by the Prelusive scheme. By contrast, the counter-movements with which I am concerned maintain a less congenial, less dialectical, relationship to *The Prelude* in the same way that "loss" or "debasement" are no longer, as Sheats maintains, a precondition for gain. Rather, in instances such as the Arab dream, "retrogrades" of the kind of which Sheats speaks are identified as foils to progress and thus necessary to the humanistic, if merely idealized, movement they provisionally oppose.

2. Although Onorato (*The Character of the Poet: Wordsworth in "The Prelude"*, 245–53), does not identify the soldier as a surrogate for the Poet, he nevertheless stresses the importance of the former's "solitude" which mirrors, as it disrupts, the Poet's "pleasurable quality of self-possession" (251).

3. In "Spirit and Geometric Form: The Stone and the Shell in Wordsworth's Arab Dream" (*SEL*, 22 [1982]: 563–82), Theresa M. Kelley argues that the stone and the shell, rather than signifying an opposition of science and poetry, are "emblems for the past and future products of the intellect" (579).

4. *Natural Supernaturalism*, 278–92. For a particularly succinct refutation of Abrams based on *The Prelude*'s failure to correspond to a smooth pattern, indeed on the contradiction inherent in its "correlative fascination with origins," see Jonathan Arac, "Bounding Lines: *The Prelude* and Critical Revision," *Boundary 2*, 7 (1979): 31–48.

5. This point is made even more boldly by Paul de Man ("Autobiography as De-facement": 919–30), who, in emphasizing the indeterminate character of autobiographical representation, urges that the "figures of

deprivation [throughout *The Prelude*]"—"maimed men, drowned corpses, blind beggars, children about to die"—"are figures of Wordsworth's own poetic self " (924). Still, as is the case with our respective views of allegory, de Man is concerned with the poem's flight from referentiality rather than with the alternative or resistant meaning to which, in my view, many of these figures refer. For a fuller treatment of Book V along these lines see my essay, "Authority and Deconstruction in Book V of *The Prelude*," *SEL*, 26 (1986): 613–31.

6. Although it is not uncommon to assume that the beggar is an older man—Onorato, for example, likens him to the Leech-gatherer in "Resolution and Independence" and the Old Soldier in Book IV, whom he calls "figures of the world" (*The Character of the Poet*, 235–60)—there is no mention, in fact, of the beggar's age. This would be in keeping, then, with the beggar's function as a projection of the Poet who, though young, is necessarily part of a patriarchal or hierarchizing scheme.

7. In a similar observation in conjunction with a larger argument about the sublime, Neil Hertz observes that the "difference between what Wordsworth can see [in the Beggar's blank face] and what he can read . . . is . . . almost no difference at all" inasmuch as "the encounter with the Beggar triangulates the poet's self in relation to his double, who is represented, for a moment, as an emblem of minimal difference fixed in relation to itself." ("The Notion of Blockage in the Literature of the Sublime," in *Psychoanalysis and the Question of the Text*, ed. Geoffrey H. Hartman [Baltimore: The Johns Hopkins University Press, 1978], 83–84.)

8. Allegory for de Man—what he, again, calls the "rhetoric of temporality"—is a counter-rhetoric in the romantic period, subverting through figural displacement the symbolic or "intentional" structures that presume a stable or otherwise "organic coherence" ("The Rhetoric of Temporality," 173–209). For Theresa M. Kelley, on the other hand ("Proteus and Romantic Allegory," *ELH*, 49 [1982]: 623–52), symbol and allegory are in romantic writing "competing yet cooperative modes." My position, then, is in-between these insofar as allegory, as *The Prelude* shows, is *meant* to compete with the symbolic by more nearly approximating what de Man, to distinguish it from allegory, calls "irony." As I conceive it, allegory opposes the representational structure of a still greater *and symbolic* rhetoric of temporality—*The Prelude*—making the poem the register now of a consciousness that is also skeptical of self-representation.

9. In "Sex and History in *The Prelude* [1805]: Books Nine to Thirteen" (*TSLL*, 23 [1981]: 324–60), Spivak argues that the suppression of the relationship with Annette Vallon, specifically Wordsworth's paternity, issues in a series of rhetorical sublimations—notably "Vaudracour and Julia" and the account of the French Revolution in Books IX and X—in which fatherhood and sonship are "sublated" in deference to a more convenient myth of androgyny; in turn, this allows poetry to be privileged over Revolution. For Jacobus, by contrast, the episode redeems "sexual love as romance . . . and rededicates it to revolution" by "putting a woman's face on the Revolution." However, in the same way that the story's excision neverthe-

less leaves us with a poem—indeed a genre—in its image, so it is the effect of this feminization, Jacobus argues, to render the woman redundant in contrast to both Vaudracour and the narrator Wordsworth. ("The Law of/and Gender: Genre Theory and *The Prelude*," *Diacritics*, 14 [Winter 1984]: 47–57.)

10. Alice Jardine, "Gynesis," *Diacritics*, 12 (Summer 1982): 61. This follows obviously from Kristeva's distinction between the symbolic and the semiotic, where the feminized consciousness provides an alternative language (in Wordsworth's case, irony) in contrast to the symbolic language whose meaning is dictated by structures of authority.

11. *Revolution in Poetic Language*, 60. Kristeva, of course, is concerned chiefly with a pre-symbolic, maternal language which originates in the semiotic chora of the mother's body and is recovered oftentimes in literary texts. Nevertheless, Kristeva's insistence on the decidedly "feminine" aspect of this revolution both in *Revolution in Poetic Language* and *The Powers of Horror: An Essay on Abjection* (trans. Leon S. Roudiez [New York: Columbia Univ. Press, 1982]), is equally evident in her recuperation of meaning— what she terms the "effective meaning" of a text (*The Powers of Horror*, 202)—by which literature is wrested from the stranglehold of authorial intent, on the one hand, and from the indeterminacy, on the other, that renders all authority a mystification.

12. Jacobus is surely right to call Beaupuy "the real hero of the tale." Yet if he is, as she suggests, an "idealized revolutionary self" ("The Law of/and Gender": 53), it is because Wordsworth, following Vaudracour, is increasingly willing to resign that function.

13. In his illuminating discussion of *The Prelude*'s attempt to discover a genre adequate to the poet's experience in France, Alan Liu notes Wordsworth's disaffection with "romance" as being "the very emblem of the *ancien regime* that necessitated revolution in the first place" (" 'Shapeless Eagerness': The Genre of Revolution in Books IX and X of *The Prelude*," *MLQ*, 43 (1982): 16–18). I agree with Liu on the point of the poet's disaffection, as on his larger point of the representational or generic disposition (however skewed) of the Revolution in the poem generally. But I am less convinced, as I believe Wordsworth was, that there is a "genre" adequate to the "Revolution" that is not romance and therefore not complicit with the larger patriarchal structure that the "genre" of *The Prelude* recapitulates.

14. In observing the dialectic of self and society in *The Prelude* (as part of *The Recluse*), Johnston notes the "symbolic conflict" between Vaudracour and Beaupuy as representatives respectively of tradition and revolutionary promise (*Wordsworth and "The Recluse"*, 177–88). Within the larger context of Wordsworth's development (before and after *The Prelude*), however, the conflict between Vaudracour and Beaupuy renders them (in my view) versions of each other.

15. Here Wordsworth anticipates Derrida's argument in "Plato's Pharmacy" (*Dissemination*, trans. Barbara Johnson [Chicago: University of Chicago Press, 1981], 63–172) that representation is at base a nostalgia for an "absent father" or presence.

16. See, for example, my essay, " 'Turns and Counter-Turns': The Crisis of Sincerity in the Final Books of *The Prelude*," *MLQ*, 40 (1979): 256–74. See also Simpson, *Wordsworth's Historical Imagination*, 113–39. Simpson observes how certain "moments of enlightenment" in *The Prelude*—predicated on a "social dimension" that, as he conceives it, challenges Wordsworth's "epic of self"—"ente[r] the narrative as a positive redirection" only to be "negatively contextualized" (115).

17. Wordswort's allusion to the "one mind"—"first, and last, and midst, and without end"—whose "workings" the Poet remembers witnessing while crossing the Simplon Pass (VI, 568–72), is an allusion, most notably, to the description of God in Book V of *Paradise Lost:* "Him first, him last, him midst, and without end" (165). Thus, the elimination of the pronoun "him" not only undermines the authority to which all things previously defer; it defers this now undermined authority to the perceiving Poet, whose humanistic representation of "God," so to speak, is of a God at once imitated and thereby subverted.

18. In acknowledging his birthday, Wordsworth is, however consciously, also acknowledging his paternity. Yet just as the "unfathered" imagination "lift[s] . . . itself / Before the eye and *progress* of [the Poet's] song" (VI, 525–26, my emphasis), so this shift suddenly to the writing present, in simultaneous acknowledgement the speaker's *maternity*, can be said to halt the progress of a song which also celebrates the "fathered" or, in this case, "unfathered" imagination whose vessel, as Hartman shows (*Wordsworth's Poetry*, 31–69), is consequently both origin and father.

19. Typical of those who regard the Snowdon scene as a "spot of time" is Jonathan Bishop ("Wordsworth and the 'Spots of Time,' " *ELH*, 26 [1959]: 45–65). Unlike the initial two spots, however, which were composed in 1799 and subsequently removed from Book I to Book XI, where they perform a different function, the Snowdon incident belongs to the representational present of *The Prelude* and was actually composed in 1804–05.

20. Tilottama Rajan has written how the "will," as conceived by Schopenhauer and Nietzsche, accurately describes an impulse prevalent in English romantic poetry (though not in Wordsworth's) to expose a gap between the represented or idealized and the real (*Dark Interpreter: The Discourse of Romanticism*, 35–57). It is noteworthy, then, that the introduction of the spots, identifying them with such a "will," was revised to incorporate the will in 1804.

21. *Wordsworth's Poetry*, 208–59. Where Hartman persuasively reads the Snowdon scene as an instance of failed apocalypse, as a reassertion of "akedah" or binding of imagination to "this world," I attribute this failure to the failure of apocalypse *as a myth*, which presumes autonomy where there, in fact, is none. Similarly, Book VI— which Hartman sees as a representation of apocalypse—is simultaneously an imaginative attack, in my view, on the narrative that privileges "Imagination."

22. I have argued elsewhere that this discontinuity points to an unresolved conflict in *The Prelude* between public and private (" 'Turns and Counter-turns': The Crisis of Sincerity in the Final Books of *The Prelude*").

For a particularly compelling view of the inscrutable nature of the spots of time, see Thomas Weiskel, *The Romantic Sublime* (Baltimore: The Johns Hopkins University Press, 1976), 167–204. Concerned, as he is, with the "liminal" aspects of these moments, Weiskel is even less willing than I to assign them a specific function. But this reluctance, it turns out, is in keeping with *The Prelude*'s idealization of self, since it ultimately privileges a highly discrete, personalized sublime. Thus, the "writing" that arrests the young boy at Penrith Beacon is of significance to Weiskel not because it is writing, but because it is writing that resists reference. Similarly, the dynamic of guilt and authority in Waiting for the Horses is eschewed by Weiskel in deference to "the liminal place" where, as he asserts, the speaker's spirit works.

23. Although composed, again, in 1799, the relevance of the the first two spots remains their preoccupation, now as then, with paternal constraints. In the first incident this preoccupation is enhanced by what de Selincourt (*The Prelude*, 614) and, more recently, Theresa M. Kelley ("The Economics of the Heart: Wordsworth's Sublime and Beautiful," *RPP*, 5 [1981]: 22) perceive as a confusion with respect to memory, geography or both. As these scholars observe, the gibbet marker below Penrith Beacon in Cowdrake Quarry memorializes no crime whereas the gibbet at Hawkshead, from which no beacon is visible, does. Furthermore, the crime is a crime of patriarchy—the murder of one's wife—and becomes, in light of the poet's confusion, identified with an orientation for which the writing Wordsworth also holds himself culpable. Indeed, the "crime" is even reenacted as Wordsworth replaces his "lost guide" with the beacon, which usurps and overcomes the woman with the pitcher. Finally, the power that the monumental writing exerts over the young boy anticipates Derrida's deconstruction of the Platonic distinction between speech and writing (*Dissemination*, 63–171) in the way the "other" of this writing (at present absent) virtually imitates the presence which the boy alternately yearns for and resists.

24. Both Onorato (*The Character of the Poet*, 205–19) and, more recently, David Ellis (*Wordsworth, Freud and the Spots of Time: Interpretation in "The Prelude"* [Cambridge: Cambridge University Press, 1985], 17–34) have, with various degrees of specificity, underscored the relationship of "fathers and sons" in this and in other spots of time. While my argument certainly parallels theirs—particularly Onorato's—in associating these incidents with "family romance" (as Freud would later conceive it), I see the function of the spots as *exposing* the "narrative" of which both Freud's "romance" and *The Prelude*'s revolutionary romance are further manifestations.

25. Johnston similarly notes the difference between the "spots of time" (which he also distinguishes from the Snowdon vision) and the "contexts" in which they are placed. Yet, for Johnston, "[the spots] gain persuasiveness" by their placement and "tend," consequently, "to silence objections rather than answer them." In short, these "visionary episode[s] of conclusive power" serve to "overrid[e] obscurities in [Wordsworth's] argument" for his restoration (*Wordsworth and "The Recluse"*, 194–95).

26. Frances Ferguson has argued that the "account of the growth of the

poet's mind yields a poet and autobiographer who . . . is nothing more or less than a web of perceptions derived from the sum of his loves (and their loves)": in short, "that no self can be created as an isolated entity" (*Wordsworth: Language as Counter-Spirit,* 152–53). While this observation is particularly apt with respect to the origins of selfhood in the poetry prior to 1799, the turn to community at *The Prelude*'s close is as much a recourse to the self's dependencies as it represents a resignation of selfhood in recognition of its origins.

27. See, for example, Jonathan Wordsworth, "The Climbing of Snowdon" (*Bicentenary Wordsworth Studies,* ed. Jonathan Wordsworth [Ithaca, NY: Cornell University Press, 1970], 449– 74) in which the Snowdon scene effects "a complete reconciliation" of "straightforward perception on the one hand, and the Creative Imagination on the other" (465).

28. Weiskel, too, is uncomfortable with the "archaic voice of Godhead" here, yet as it remains, in his view, a typology somehow adequate to the romantic sublime, the "Snowdon vision," he asserts, "does not cancel the opposite motion of the spots of time" (*The Romantic Sublime,* 194–95).

29. The remainder of Book XIII is even more dramatically opposed to (and by) the spots of time. Seemingly reconciled to the Prelusive scheme, the Poet becomes, for example, the omniscient authority in whose gaze we observe "the lamb / And the lamb's mother, and their tender ways" (XIII, 154–55). This apparent recourse, then, to the "blessed . . . babe" of Book II, is perfectly in keeping with *The Prelude*'s close, since it also cancels the ironization to which the babe and mother are subsequently subject. A Prophet now, whose authority is descendent from God, the Poet's paternalistic stance remains the only stance by which *The Prelude* can (and does) come full circle.

EIGHT

Ironizing Authority

The lyrics clustered around *The Prelude,* which attest in often bewildered fashion to the mind's cooptative powers, have been justly celebrated (and anthologized) as "major" works by a major poet. Yet many of these poems show a disquietude with the poet's "majority" that distinguishes them from works committed (in one way or another) to an allegorical function. We have already seen how the Intimations Ode, a poem sometimes regarded as a *Prelude* in miniature, attests to the instability of identity, revealing that the "sublime self" is no more, or less, than a figure for the self. In the Ode this disclosure is a virtual function of the figurative apparatus by which "immortality" is gradually intimated in the poetry preceding it. In contrast, such contemporaneous works as "Composed Upon Westminster Bridge, Sept. 3, 1802," "The Solitary Reaper" (1805) and "I wandered lonely as a Cloud" (1804) appear more detached from this apparatus and more knowing in their subversions.

This is especially evident in "The Solitary Reaper" which, as Hartman has shown, remains one of the more compelling demonstrations of Wordsworth's humanistic imagination (*Wordsworth's Poetry* 3–18). Here, in his recollection of a highland girl "[singing] in the field," the speaker is consumed less by the memory of his encounter than by the memory of other memories that had suffused the experience, compelling him to ventriloquize through the girl:

> Whate'er the theme, the Maiden sang
> As if her song could have no ending;
> I saw her singing at her work,
> And o'er the sickle bending;—
> I listen'd till I had my fill:
> And, as I mounted up the hill,
> The music in my heart I bore,
> Long after it was heard no more. (25–32)[1]

And yet, while the world beheld in "The Solitary Reaper" is clearly consumed by the speaker's self-consciousness, it is the beholder, rather than highland girl over whom he writes, who is more properly in this sway. The desperate plea for an auditor who might provide a more accurate perspective on things—"Will no one tell me what she sings?" (17)—is not only testimony to the authority and power of which separation, as Hartman shows, remains a fearful consequence; it is testimony as well to the narrowness of the speaker's perspective which, with the introduction of another perspective, is thereby judged. This latter vantage, where "authority" is both "questioned" and "demystified," or in which a "metacommentary," as David Simpson terms it, rises against more direct commentary in the poem, may be distinguished from the allegorical countermovements previously noted in *The Prelude*. For it is *reading* in this instance that is a subversive or "deconstructive" activity, all of which makes writing (in a not so obvious sense) a pretext for being read and for being distanced from oneself (*Irony and Authority* 21–55).

Such complementarity of writing and reading must be distinguished from the rapport of 1798, where the reader was a prototype for poetic authority. Where in "Simon Lee" "irony" measures "superiority," intimating a consciousness or identity to which (in imitation of the reader) the "poet" simultaneously lays claim, irony in 1805 is opposed to superiority. What may be testimony in "The Solitary Reaper" to the power of imagination is evidence also of a contraction of which the speaker is both author and subject. While he remains, as Wallace Stevens might describe him, the single artificer of the world he sings, the speaker of "The Solitary Reaper" is also maker of a world that, when read, has shrunk to the parameters of a rather finite mind.[2]

In a similar way, the worlds beheld by the speaker in both "Westminster Bridge" and "I wandered lonely as a Cloud" manage, in the "double structure" of their irony, to demonstrate authority and, in that way, to contest it.[3] In the "Westminster Bridge" sonnet, this contestational dynamic is similarly suggested by a passerby, or figure for the reader, who bears the imprecation of being too "dull" to appreciate "[a] sight so touching in it's [*sic*] majesty" (2–3). Nevertheless, at the poem's close, when the speaker admits to having colored London according to his inner disposition ("Ne'er saw I, never felt, a calm so deep!"[11]), his ensuing apostrophe ("Dear God! the very houses seem asleep"[13]) uncovers the "majesty" which, as the passerby may have already surmised, has been appropriated in a too-human capacity.[4]

In "I wandered lonely as a Cloud," by contrast, the irony or metacommentary is virtually tantamount to the commentary about the daffodils, making the speaker at once a passerby and the subject he represents. Unlike the above two poems, whose internalizations attest to the primacy of imagination, the internalization of reading in "I wandered lonely" makes epiphany—the imposition of imagination—something less than majestic. Beginning with the refiguration of the speaker as a lonely cloud and culminating in the image of ten thousand daffodils "dancing" gleefully (6–8), poetic imagination is forever on the cusp of fancy, setting the "beautiful" en route from the sublime to the ridiculous. Consequently, the speculation afterwards on "what wealth the shew to me had brought" (12) implies (along with the interrogative) somewhat dubious compensation: a "bliss" or privilege where intimations of distinction are a cover under which there is mostly "solitude":

For oft when on my couch I lie
In vacant or in pensive mood,
They flash upon that inward eye
Which is the bliss of solitude,
And then my heart with pleasure fills,
And dances with the Daffodils. (13–18)

The image of the poet in isolate recumbency, animated by memories whose blessing is already in dispute, is certainly a far cry from the triumphant image of him atop Mount Snowdon. And yet, it is a measure of how far Wordsworth has come from (and in) *The Prelude* that he can submit to this subordination without a protest. To be sure, such willing suspension of belief in oneself is not altogether submissive. As Wordsworth shows later in *The Excursion,* this renunciation amounts still to an oppositional stance that has too much in common with the authority it would oppose. Nevertheless, it is vital to an understanding of the development of Wordsworth's poetry, both in *The Prelude* and after, to recognize the way irony and its attendant metacommentary remain, after Wordsworth's "ambiguous allegorizations," more constructively pitched toward a renunciation of individual authority.[5]

Wordsworthian irony, therefore, differs from the increasingly deconstructive posture of Wordsworthian allegory in that it is not specifically aligned with the hierarchizing tendencies that gradually make the self—certainly, the sublime self—its own worst enemy. This is an important point. Although usually seen as a device through which a writer confers authority on the reader in order to retain authority as an author—a means whereby he or she invites the reader to "join the wise and the just in looking down on repudiated worlds"[6]—irony comes to have a different application in Wordsworth. In the development of Wordsworth's poetry irony becomes a way to relinquish authority so as to initiate a revolution *in* poetic language. This is to not suggest, of course, that irony is necessarily removed from all will or authorial intention. It is to argue simply that this will, in ever-increasing measure, is a will to powerlessness, issuing in a more renunciatory, more democratized poetics.

Of interest in this respect is Tilottama Rajan's argument that such "displace[ment]" of "responsibility for producing meaning from the text to the consciousness of reader and author" is evident in both biblical hermeneutics and romantic poetry: together, Rajan submits, these discourses "initiated an awareness" in the eighteenth and nineteenth centuries of the "[problematical] relationship between signifier and signified" ("Supplement" 587). While romantic texts, as deconstructionists remind us, remain vulnerable to the dynamics of signification, the Romantics, according to Rajan, understood the problem well enough to have used it in a recuperation of meaning. Romantic writing, she maintains, invites "a hermeneutics of reversal in which the positive essence of the work must be grasped across the barrier of the text's negativity, and in which the reading process does not simply complement and complete the creative process but compensates for the deconstructive momentum of the latter" ("Supplement" 583).

It is tempting to view the development of irony in Wordsworth as a similar compensation. But there is a crucial difference. Where the function of reading, in Rajan's scheme, is to "supplement" and complete the text (thereby compensating for "the disestablishment of authoritative meaning" implicit in the linguistic system ["Supplement" 578]), irony in Wordsworth is really compensation against authority and pitched toward the deauthorization of meaning. Wordsworth in this way actually allows for meaning—what Kristeva calls an "effective meaning" (*Powers* 202)—provided that such meaning is also at cross-purposes with meaning. For it is in being *read* that Wordsworth's texts are marshaled against poetic consciousness. Schlegelian or so-called "romantic irony" differs equally from Wordsworth's irony by virtue of being formative in function: as Anne Mellor writes, the romantic ironist "consciously deconstructs his mystifications of the self and the world. . . . in the expectation that such deconstruction is a way of keeping in contact with a greater creative power" (*English Romantic Irony* 5). Wordsworth's irony is, in contrast, unromantic and pitched increasingly to the loss of power.

The irony that comes to characterize the later Wordsworth is itself subject to change. Beginning as a protest against the authority of which the poet is possessed, irony eventually modulates to a less reflexive, more meditated retrospection. Removed, by turns, from the authority it initially opposes, irony becomes a method by which authority is displaced and made examinable. Not only does Wordsworth eventually renounce his role as *The Excursion*'s spokesman; he reassigns "his" authority in such fashion as to erase the distinction (*given* their opposition) between the Solitary and the more conventional versions of authority embodied in the Wanderer and the Pastor. This is the true irony of *The Excursion*: there is no difference, no real grounds for opposition, in what purports in form and function to be a "spiritual debate." The irony is that all of *The Excursion*'s participants, with the occasional exception of the reticent narrator, are on the same side of the argument.

Nevertheless, there is in the very nature of this retrospection enough of an opposition between subject and object, between the poet present and the various versions of the poet past, to allow deauthorization its own authority. And, indeed, both *The Excursion* and the poems contemporary with it generally manage to do two things: to recollect authority as testimony to its displacement, and to reenact it as a measure of its retrievability. The version of "I wandered lonely" published 1815, for example, includes several added lines which emphasize the arbitrariness as well as the sublimity of the speaker's experience. Such double emphasis similarly characterizes the ram scene at *The Excursion*'s close. We have already observed the way this seemingly passive recollection interrupts and contests the Wanderer's particularly assertive discourse. But this is only one of its functions. As Stephen Spector observes, the scene pretty clearly "serve[s] as a proof of both the Wanderer's godliness and the truth of his principles" (100). The point, then, is not that Wordsworth's overall sympathy with the Wanderer ultimately subsumes any and all opposition to him. Rather, the poem's point is altogether more subtle: the Poet, in opposing the Wanderer's oppositional position, theoretically and necessarily represents it.

Such opposition to opposition (however futile) is also a factor in "Laodamia," in the two poems "To Lycoris," and in the *River Duddon* sonnets, all of which follow *The Excursion* in marking passage from a fairly aggressive, humanistic orientation to a more conventional, seemingly Christian form of resignation. The irony and, to some extent, the liability of these poems is not just that they reveal the affinity between the "new" and the "old," whose roles are typically reversed; it is also in the *"vertige"* (to use de Man's description of irony ["Rhetoric of Temporality" 198]) by which they keep the passageway open, allowing the present to be linked with, and alternately mystified by dissociation from, an equally authoritarian past.

It becomes necessary, therefore, to recover irony from the contradictions to which it is prone. This is the achievement of those poems which, for all practical purposes, mark the conclusion of Wordsworth's career. Here, in both the sonnets later appended to the *Ecclesiastical Sketches* and the rather notorious *Sonnets Upon the Punishment of Death*, Wordsworth abandons the retrospective posture for the sake of what appears to be something infinitely worse. What is almost never appreciated, however, is the way this "something worse" —Wordsworth's ultraconservatism—follows from the preceding phase in moving to eliminate the *vertige* previously endemic to the ironic posture. What the late poetry says in appallingly obvious fashion is not what the late poetry means or represents. On the contrary, Wordsworth's speaker in this final phase is more properly a "straight man" whose utter assumption of authority, whose blind belief in the utter rectitude of his position, are sufficiently foregrounded to relieve the poet and his poetry of the need to comment on them.

The various stages of irony, leading to this unmaking of "Wordsworth's anti-climax," are nicely represented in the three poems about visiting the Yarrow. Composed in 1803–04, the first of the poems, "Yarrow Unvisited," resembles other lyrics of this period such as "The Solitary Reaper" in its unease over the primacy of the poetic imagination. Beginning in the middle of a dialogue during which the speaker has apparently convinced his auditor not to visit the Yarrow, the poem is sufficiently one-sided to make the speaker, not the auditor, the figure more in need of persuasion. The uncertainty at this juncture involves the speaker's assumption that Yarrow "unseen" is better than the river itself—that the river recreated in its absence will make for a better memory (with better results) than any memory of Yarrow seen:

"If Care with freezing years should come,
"And wandering seem but folly,
"Should we be loth to stir from home,

"And yet be melancholy;
"Should life be dull, and spirits low,
" 'Twill soothe us in our sorrow
"That earth has something yet to show,
"The bonny Holms of Yarrow!" (57–64)

Ronald Schleifer has observed that the final line of "Yarrow Unvisited," taken (as he notes) from a Scots ballad "Leader Haughs,"
makes the world unseen a "song" as well as a repetition *in* song of
what already is a "re-vision."[7]

But there is more to this configuration than simple repetition or
the humanization of nature that, according to Schleifer, is necessarily celebrated in such a gesture. For accompanying the quotation,
which is a reassertion of human authority, is *another* vision or "song"
that opposes the self in the very act of asserting it. This, of course, is
the vision of old age, conceived apparently as a way to justify the
speaker's imaginings, but which indicates all the more that "earth"
indeed "has something yet to show." That the speaker willingly
consigns his future to a melancholy prospect points to more, in
other words, than his determination to have his way. It is testimony
to the self-enclosure, and ultimately to the melancholy, by which the
exercise of will prohibits him from actually submitting to more
worldly delights. It is in this prohibition that the borrowing from
"Leader Haughs" becomes crucial. For the Yarrow so authori-
tatively envisioned remains, like the highland girl in "The Solitary
Reaper" or Westminster Bridge or the daffodils, a *fiction*, making
the river no different in the end—quite literally no different—from
the "bonny Holms of Yarrow," whose inauthenticity is thereby admitted.

In "Yarrow Visited" (1814), by contrast, "sadness" is no longer
simply a projection or the consequence of imagination, but, in
keeping with the poems at this juncture, a result of setting the poet's
past and present in juxtaposition. The "sadness" (8) that the speaker
experiences upon actually seeing Yarrow for the first time is less an
index of the river's meagerness (as might be expected) than of the
very opposite—of the visible plentitude that has managed to do the
speaker's work for him:

—a silvery current flows
With uncontrolled meanderings;
Nor have these eyes by greener hills
Been soothed, in all my wanderings.

And, through her depths, Saint Mary's Lake
Is visibly delighted;
For not a feature of those hills
Is in the mirror slighted. (9–16)

Where in "Yarrow Unvisited" Saint Mary's Lake was a conceit, a
mirror on which a swan was directed to "[f]loat double, Swan and
Shadow" (44), here it is a more passive register that the poet manages actually to imitate. The mimetic precedent in this poem is no
longer a revision of the lake by imagination (i.e., "Leader Haughs").
It is the lake itself which, unlike imagination, merely mirrors the
environment.

Still, for all his success in imitating the lake, the speaker cannot
resist the impulse to re-vision the world in more idealized fashion.
Turning (as in the previous poem) to a Scottish ballad, *The Dowie
Dens of Yarrow*, whose central character is metamorphosed into a
flower, the speaker allows a narrative structure to be imposed suddenly on the world viewed. This time the imposition is short-lived as
the speaker concedes that Yarrow *seen* "[d]ost rival in the light of
day / [Imagination's] delicate creation" (43–44). But what is clearly
not short-lived is the *memory* of the speaker's authority, persistent
even in spite of its rebuffs. In resisting, for example, a subsequent
impulse to mythologize the present in conjunction with "Newark's
Towers" ("[r]enowned in Border story" [55–56]), the speaker is
moved, in regarding a cottage, to speculate on the stages of life:

Fair scenes for childhood's opening bloom,
For sportive youth to stray in;
For manhood to enjoy his strength;
And age to wear away in!
Yon cottage seems a bower of bliss,
A covert for protection
Of tender thoughts, that nestle there—
The brood of chaste affection. (57–64)

It may be objected that the surmise about the cottage is as much an
appropriation of the real as are the balladic narrative or the narrative of history inspired by the castle's ruin. Yet the speaker's appropriation, I would argue, is a belated counterthrust to the loss of
authority admitted in his survey of mutability.

Nor is the speaker unaware of this double-movement, or of the
authority for that matter additionally echoed in his recourse to

paternalistic language. Turning once again to the river, he allows
having "see[n the river] . . . not by sight alone," but as having "won"
it by agency of "fancy" (73–75). The conception of winning by fancy
is something of a paradox for Wordsworth, for it is "imagination"
(already broached) with which the speaker is generally accustomed
to winning. Resisting the speaker in his various appropriations, the
ministry of fancy is more properly a way of assigning victory elsewhere:

> The vapours linger round the Heights,
> They melt, and soon must vanish;
> One hour is theirs, nor more is mine—
> Sad thought, which I would banish,
> But that I know, where'er I go,
> Thy genuine image, Yarrow!
> Will dwell with me—to heighten joy,
> And cheer my mind in sorrow. (81–88)

The genuineness of Yarrow's image, somewhat compromised by its
recollection in tranquillity, is made authentic by the poet's sorrow.
For this is what lets him admit to having lost or relinquished what he
was vain enough to have thought he had controlled. This admission
is implied by his recourse to visible particularity, as well as by his
reluctance to turn the visible scene into a pathetic fallacy. If it is the
case that the "vapours" have an hour to live, then it is a coincidence
that the poet's time is similarly limited. Underlying the poet's sadness is no longer the "thought" of mutability *per se;* it is the recognition that Yarrow obeys an authority all its own that cannot be
"banished" any more than the river itself can be appropriated.
Thus, although the final lines of "Yarrow Visited" assert that the
memories of Yarrow are sufficient to sustain the speaker amid
despair, they ultimately contradict this assertion (and the human
authority that informs it): the consoling agent is not Yarrow *unvisited* and consequently imagined, but the river's "genuine image,"
whose "cheer" is inextricably "sorrow."

　　The sadness characteristic of Wordsworth in 1814, at which point
he had reluctantly resigned faith in imagination, is less apparent in
the poetry a decade later—though not necessarily because Wordsworth had gained faith in something better. Rather, as we see in
"Yarrow Revisited" (1831), the systematic resignation of authority
ultimately enabled Wordsworth to set all authority, including the
authority of resignation, in greater perspective. Beginning with its

form, which jibes uncomfortably with the speaker's gravity, Wordsworth's paean to Sir Walter Scott (whom he did not especially admire) transforms very quickly into a critique of human greatness. Recalling the day he had spent with Scott on the banks of the Yarrow, the poet cannot resist linking Scott with an earlier and, in retrospect, identical version of himself:

> For busy thoughts the Stream flowed on
>   In foamy agitation;
> And slept in many a crystal pool
>   For quiet contemplation:
> No public and no private care
>   The freeborn mind enthralling,
> We made a day of happy hours,
>   Our happy days recalling. (17–24)

If Wordsworth finds himself disposed to unite with Scott, as "we" implies, then this is because Scott remains, in aftermath, a figure for days bygone—a man whose "freeborn mind" remembers the enfranchisement characteristic of individual authority.

No sooner is the union established, however, than it is disrupted by the actuality of Yarrow, which helps separate the poet from the "character of the Poet" embodied in Scott:

> And if, as Yarrow, through the woods
>   And down the meadow ranging,
> Did meet us with unaltered face,
>   Though we were changed and changing;
> If, *then*, some natural shadows spread
>   Our inward prospect over,
> The soul's deep valley was not slow
>   Its brightness to recover. (33–40)

The shift to a singular subject for the "soul's" recovery allows the speaker to distinguish himself from a self suddenly disposed to brood on its mortality. It is not that Yarrow is unchanged. It is that the river is unchanged so long as it wears the "face" of the *human* subject, whose "immortality" it better intimates. As in "Yarrow Visited," the "shadows" or sadnesses "revisited" in this poem derive from the failure to forget (or, in suddenly "recalling" it, to relinquish) the myth of enfranchisement. While there is clearly a difference between the projection of immortality in the river and the projection of authority in Scott, it is because Scott, as a displacement of the freeborn mind (or the vessel now to whom human authority is resigned), is also a means by which the speaker's "freedom" is resigned and his "brightness" restored.

And yet, the vision of Scott in "divine employment" (42), like the vision of Yarrow as immortal, forces the speaker to imagine Scott as necessarily vulnerable to his alleged immortality. Indeed, as he reflects on Scott's convalescence in Italy, the speaker cannot refrain from hoping that "classic Fancy, linking / With native Fancy her fresh aid, / Preserve thy heart from sinking!" (54–56). The notion of "fancy . . . with . . . fancy" as a stay against despair is a most peculiar wish at this point, since it is a wish that actively militates against fulfillment. Not only is the unlikeliness of fancy's success already intimated by using it in place of imagination; it is intimated as well in the way such sinking, as we have seen, is a virtual condition of allowing one's "native" perception to be subsumed by a "classic" or intentional structure. In the very way that the vision of Yarrow in "Yarrow Unvisited" is subverted by making it equivalent in the end to the "bonny holms of Yarrow," so the piling here of fancy on top of fancy seems a virtual prescription for the slackening it would reverse.

Unlike Wordsworth himself, whose earlier self-enclosure led increasingly to such slackening, Wordsworth's poem makes Scott apparently immune to the very ravages that the speaker consequently projects onto him. And this immunity, not surprisingly, owes to a certain obtuseness:

> For Thou, upon a hundred streams,
>   By tales of love and sorrow,
> Of faithful love, undaunted truth,
>   Hast shed the power of Yarrow;
> And streams unknown, hills yet unseen,
>   Wherever they invite Thee,
> At parent Nature's grateful call,
>   With gladness must requite Thee. (65–72)

Here, in possibly the most ironic stanza in the poem, the image of Scott as nature poet is allowed to founder on that very contradiction. To be a poet of nature is not to defer to Nature nor to celebrate her; it is rather to "shed" nature's power in favor of one's own. The idea of having made "a hundred streams" conform to a narrative structure is more than heroic to the point of ridicule; it is a prelude to the far subtler image of "parent Nature" which replaces mother Nature: the world, at whose urging Scott *proceeds,* is essentially a reflection of the traveller himself. Nor is this narcissistic self-enclosure—the image of the world wearing a poet's "face"—the only circularity in these lines. The assumption that streams as yet unvisited "must" satisfy their visitor places Scott within a narrative at once arbitrary and predetermined. Moreover, it suggests by counterexample that only by being "unknown," "unseen," or otherwise subordinate to human authority may nature function in this manner.

Such regency is no longer characteristic of the man speaking who, having made Scott into his former self, proceeds in equally ironic fashion to confront poetic authority in all of its privilege. Recalling his earlier encounter with the Yarrow where, as we have noted, he remained "[u]nwilling to surrender / Dreams treasured up from early days" (78–79), the speaker continues by protesting the tendency to write over the world according to the "voice . . . within us":

> And what, for this frail world, were all
>   That mortals do or suffer,
> Did no responsive harp, no pen,
>   Memorial tribute offer?
> Yea, what were mighty Nature's self?
>   Her features, could they win us,
> Unhelped by the poetic voice;
>   That hourly speaks within us? (81–88)

Although these questions are plainly rhetorical, they elicit two very different answers. At the level of commentary, whereby Scott, the representative poet, remains the object of praise, the answer is tantamount to a defense of imagination in its ability to humanize and enhance the outside world. Yet because humanization necessarily renders nature a "mighty self" or reflection of the beholding subject, the second, more ironic answer returns to the uncertainty already indicated in the interrogative mode. Here, the answer is more than just nature or nature uninformed by an authority apart from itself; it is "Life as she is—our changeful Life" (95), whose resistance to "Romance" (89) allows for a world where there is neither sublimity nor, as a counterweight to humanism, the "suffering" and mutability that are equally idealizations.

In the concluding stanza Wordsworth returns to Yarrow itself, whose personification, unlike the idealizations to which the river was previously subject, reveals a capriciousness that is also a rebuff. Reflected now, through the veil of "memory's . . . moonshine," is the merely foolish disposition of the beholder:

> Flow on for ever, Yarrow Stream!
>   Fulfil thy pensive duty,
> Well pleased that future Bards should chant
>   For simple hearts thy beauty;
> To dream-light dear while yet unseen,
>   Dear to the common sunshine,
> And dearer still, as now I feel,
>   To memory's shadowy moonshine! (105–12)

In assuming the role of straight man, to whose besotted directives the river performs, Wordsworth completes the trajectory of opposition to poetic authority begun in 1804. Nevertheless, it took many years for Wordsworth to resign such authority to the status of textuality—allowing himself to be read by someone other than himself—and for irony to be the sole basis for meaning. Before that point Wordsworth's resistance to the totalizing tendencies of art is most evident in his recourse to sequences or groups of poems. In these, as we shall see, comprehensiveness is mitigated by individual components, and these parts, in turn, are sublated within the larger, now fragmentary, whole.

Representative of the way these later groupings actually resist a unitary purpose is the reorganization in 1815 of the poetry thus far under headings beginning with "Poems Referring to the Period of Childhood" and culminating with "Poems of Old Age" and "Poems of Death." As James A. W. Heffernan observes, this monumental project begs comparison with the 1814 observation (in the Preface to *The Excursion*) that the poems exclusive of *The Recluse* could "be likened to the little cells, oratories, and sepulchral recesses, ordinarily included in [a gothic church]."[8] Yet such "monumentalization" is also fraught by complications: both by the mutability to which the autobiographical arrangement is plainly subject, and by the way the architectonics of the 1815 arrangement are as fragmentary as the edifice of 1814.

The "church" to which Wordsworth was referring in the Preface to *The Excursion*—whose "ante-chapel" remained *The Prelude* and whose "body," the projected *Recluse*—would never be completed. With this in mind, Heffernan regards the edition of 1815 as a kind

of "self-monumentalization" to redeem the failure to monumental-
ize oneself in more constructive fashion. But what of the larger
monument of which the "canonized" self (whether in *The Prelude* or
in the now autobiographical structure of the 1815 volume) was an
extrapolation? Is this not already a ruin—a *gothic church*—and thus
a fragment from which only other fragments can issue? What I am
suggesting, in other words, is that far from "unconsciously report-
ing the death of [Wordsworth's] own shaping powers" ("Mutilated
Autobiography" 110), the consignment of the self to the status of
ruin, replete with its confinement to a rhetoric of temporality
(youth, old age, death and so on), belongs to a *conscious* effort to
return power—such shaping authority embodied in the gothic or
sublime self—to a totality or to a textuality of which the self itself is
no longer an extrapolation. The self, as Wordsworth now conceives
it, is only part of something much larger, which poetry may likely
adumbrate but can never, given its fragmentary nature, wholly
comprehend.

This strategy is powerfully reinforced by the metaphor of the
gothic church, which proves both a concession and resistance to
fashion. While many gothic churches had been restored in the
eighteenth century, it was fashionable and certainly nostalgic by
century's end to associate the gothic with ruination. The nostalgia,
of course, was for a departed (and thus recoverable) wholeness of
which the fragment, as Thomas McFarland has detailed, represented a synecdoche.[9] What is distinctive about Wordsworth's
church, however, is its fragmentariness *before* the fact. This last is
suggested as much in its merely hypothetical ruination as in the fact
that it is a gothic *church* (not a cathedral) and of a style— specifically
the "Late Gothic"—that implicitly resists the "total" or "synthetic"
vision of its predecessor.[10] Beyond the shambles of his totalizing
vision, Wordsworth's "gothic" projects an art whose comprehension
of the world is conditional upon a willingness to defer wholeness.

This aversion to totality is widespread and is apparent in Wordsworth's secondary writings as well. In the "Essay, Supplementary to
the Preface" included in the 1815 collection, Wordsworth not only
goes so far as to admit the supplementability and thus the incom-
pleteness of his previous defenses—both the Prefaces *and* the
poems that had already supplemented one another; he makes this
deficiency a condition of art's totalizing agenda. His rather bombastic claim for the similarities of "poetry and religion" suggests—in
the way poetry now supplements religion—a deficiency in any poetry that would necessarily follow religion's example. Similarly, the

definition of "originality" as the ability to create the taste by which one's work is to be enjoyed bridles against the various instances of taste which, as Wordsworth details, were affected by forces *other* than originality. Along with the overall arrangement of the 1815 volume, then, or the metaphor of the gothic church, the supplementary essay characteristically subverts a more bombastic, more monumental sense of the artist's function in the very guise of promoting it (*Prose Works,* III 62–84).

All the same, as the preoccupation with the gothic simultaneously suggests, Wordsworth's resignations of authority are almost always accompanied by the memory of its assertion. In the two "Lycoris" odes composed in 1817 Wordsworth clearly vacillates between an acceptance of the world (and of the mutability to which he is consigned as a human) and a humanistic resistance, or contempt for "life," that renders mutability a tragic destiny.[11] In the initial "Ode to Lycoris, May, 1817," the speaker recalls how "[i]n youth" (19) the change of seasons was less a threat than grist for an imagination accustomed to transfigure Autumn in "a feeding gaze" (34). However, having witnessed the disappointment to which such regency is heir, the speaker proposes a new "*art*"

> To which our souls must bend;
> A skill—to balance and supply;
> And, ere the flowing fount be dry,
> As soon it must, a sense to sip,
> Or drink, with no fastidious lip. (39–44)

The image here of "drinking in" the world clearly contrasts to the earlier image of engorgement where the world had to "bend" to the will of the subject. Needed now is both an art that bends to the world and an artist whose supplies to "life" supplement the world and its offerings.

Nevertheless the very notion of "art" or supplementation, no matter how deferential, carries intimations of authority. Hence, in welcoming Spring, as the "new" artist is directed to do, there is "recall[ed]," unexpectedly, "the Deity / Of youth into the breast" (47–48). Earlier, at a more expansive juncture in Wordsworth's career, the deity of youth remained a foreshadowing of the sublime self to which the mature poet would eventually be privy. However in the aftermath of this immortality, the "deity" recovered through the artist's function marks something of a retrenchment that the speaker seems unable to reverse. Turning to the "Spring" before him, he cannot refrain from situating it in a narrative structure, whose consumption of the world is reflected in the way Spring is virtually inseparable from the particular malaise of its beholder:

> While blossoms and the budding spray
> Inspire us in our own decay;
> Still, as we nearer draw to life's dark goal,
> Be hopeful Spring the favourite of the Soul! (51–54)

The deference to Spring—in contrast to the youthful deference to Autumn—is no different in its subsumption of the actual from the earlier "feeding." All that has changed is the "gazer" who, as he grows old, finds Spring a more companionable object. Following the affinity for Autumn underwritten by his eternal Spring, the eternal Winter to which the speaker is subsequently heir makes it impossible still for him to respond to the *world*. The "Guest" (45)—Spring—is no sooner "welcomed" than consumed by the speaker's hospitality.

The futility of the "art" recommended in the first "Ode to Lycoris" was arguably responsible for the decision some months later to compose a second poem "To The Same." Beginning this time with a more vigorous complaint against the ascendancy of the individual "dwarfing the world below" (6), the speaker's gaze is again directed outward to the very world that "the *heart*" (12) is quite inclined to leave behind:

> The umbrageous woods are left—how far beneath!
> But lo! where darkness seems to guard the mouth
> Of yon wild cave, whose jagged brows are fringed
> With flaccid threads of ivy, in the still
> And sultry air, depending motionless.
> Yet the cool space within, and not uncheered
> (As whoso enters shall ere long perceive)—
> By steady influx of the timid day
> Mingling with night. . . . (19–27)

That nature literally wears a human face in this description does more than emphasize the idealization to which nature is apparently subject; it points to an entrapment to which the speaker is similarly subject.

Once in the cave, the speaker is sufficiently consumed by imagination to recognize an alternative. Turning to his auditor, with whom he has brooded (if only speculatively) upon various creations of "fancy," he observes how "shutting up thyself within thyself" she will perhaps

> sink into a mood
> Of gentler thought, protracted till thine eye
> Be calm as water when the winds are gone,
> And no one can tell whither. (41–45)

The auditor's self-enclosure, recapitulating the more dramatic image of the speaker within a head of his own imagining, is abruptly checked by the image of her eye. In contrast to *her* self-enclosure, this image yields an altogether different reflection of her beholder. Gazing passively upon the passive image of the eye "calm as water," the speaker is, in the *example* of his friend, suddenly capable of relinquishing control or, as his extended simile suggests, of resigning the ambition to know. As a result, "were power granted to replace [such happy hours]" as he and his friend had earlier "known" (46–47), the speaker "should . . . be [loth] to use it" (50). For the "power" the speaker hesitates to assume may be recovered simply by remembering it. It is the "passing" of memory, then, the memory of having had power, that the second ode to "Lycoris" celebrates, since only with the relinquishment of this memory "[a]re the *domains* of tender memory [sweet]" (50–51, emphasis added).

A similar pattern can be seen in "Laodamia" (1814), where poetic authority remains equivalent to religious, specifically Evangelical, authority—providing a crucial backdrop for the major sequences that follow: both the *River Duddon Sonnets* (most of which were composed between 1819 and 1820) and, more importantly, the *Ecclesiastical Sketches* published in 1822. Although drawing from a number of classical sources including Book VI of the *Aeneid,* Wordsworth gives a contemporary twist to the parable involving Laodamia's demands for the restoration of her slain husband and the reincarnation of him that follows. The most obvious instance of this contemporaneity is Laodamia herself, whose entreaties to the gods are really imperatives, and so evidence of an authority of which she evidently feels possessed:

> 'With sacrifice before the rising morn
> Vows have I made by fruitless hope inspired;
> And from the infernal Gods, 'mid shades forlorn
> Of night, my slaughtered Lord have I required;

Celestial pity I again implore;—
Restore him to my sight—great Jove, restore!' (1–6)

An equally important index of the parable's relevance for Wordsworth is the fact that Laodamia's demands are "answered" in such a
way as to make the "consummation" (26) of mind and nature a
figure of wish fulfillment. Indeed, the Protesilaus who returns is not
the husband, but a "spectre" sent "in reward of [Laodamia's] fidelity" (40). The question thus is: to whom has Laodamia been faithful?
Her fidelity, like Margaret's in *The Excursion,* appears more to herself and to her desires rather than to the gods who are apparently
willing to defer to her.

By way of emphasizing that Laodamia's power is a mystification,
that it remains of little moment in a world she does not control,
Wordsworth gives Protesilaus a similarly reflexive function. Having
revealed that his death in Troy was also a self-fulfilling prophecy—
he had merely obeyed what he had "wished for" by listening to the
"oracle" (121–22)—Protesilaus proceeds to instruct Laodamia in
the proper conduct of life:

'Learn, by a mortal yearning, to ascend—
Seeking a higher object. Love was given,
Encouraged, sanctioned, chiefly for that end;
For this the passion to excess was driven—
That self might be annulled: her bondage prove
The fetters of a dream, opposed to love. (145–50)

Although it is undoubtedly tempting to use Protesilaus as a mouth-
piece for Wordsworth, he exposes more immediately the necessary
relationship between the humanistic authority embodied in his wife
and a sententious, Evangelical authority, which attempts similarly
(and with equal success) to have its way. Laodamia's sudden death,
which may be interpreted as annihilation of "self" commensurate
with Protesilaus' injunction, merely recapitulates Laodamia's previous failure—which is now Protesilaus' failure—to transform the
world. Hence, the apathy with which the gods are subsequently
charged in allowing this cycle of disappointment to play itself out is
not apathy any more than their passivity will have proven Laodamia's authority. No longer signifying fate or some overarching
providence, the pagan apparatus of "Laodamia" recovers a world
whose very recalcitrance should be sufficient to discourage woman's
(and man's) attempts to see themselves reflected.[12]

NOTES

1. References to this and to all subsequently discussed poems that first appeared in 1807 are to the "reading texts" in Curtis, ed., *"Poems, in Two Volumes," and Other Poems, 1800–1807*. Citations to poems after these, unless otherwise noted, are to the texts in *The Poetical Works of William Wordsworth*, ed. Ernest de Selincourt, 2d. ed. rev. Helen Darbishire (Oxford: Clarendon Press, 1952–59), 5 vols.

2. For a related view of "The Solitary Reaper," which makes the continued "integrity" of the "object" a necessary precondition for the observer's awareness "of what is most personal about himself," see Frederick Garber, *Wordsworth and The Poetry of Encounter* (Urbana: University of Illinois Press, 1971), 3–27.

3. In referring to the "double structure" of irony in Wordsworth, I am making use of de Man's distinction between irony and allegory in "The Rhetoric of Temporality." According to de Man, irony differs from allegory in its impulse toward a more stable differentiation: an "activity of consciousness"—or "a relationship, within consciousness, between two selves," which is "not an intersubjective relationship." Irony is a means, then, by which the "subject comes to know itself by an increasing differentiation from what it is not" (195).

4. My sense of the poem's "doubleness" differs somewhat from that noted by J. Hillis Miller in *The Linguistic Moment: From Wordsworth to Stevens* (Princeton, NJ: Princeton University Press, 1985), 68–76, where the various negatives, as Miller observes, reflect the poem's "oscillation between consciousness and nature, life and death, presence and absence, motion and stillness" (74). While the world, in Miller's view, effectively resists the imposition of the speaker, this resistance, as I see it, is initiated by the poet against the impositions of the "I."

5. I have, in speaking of poems contemporary with *The Prelude*, not mentioned either "Ode to Duty" or "Elegiac Stanzas," which are customarily viewed as harbingers of the poet's more orthodox posture. In both of these poems, Wordsworth's orthodoxy is not only purposefully vague, but is also juxtaposed with an antecedent posture, thereby borrowing from the very thing it would supersede. It is the speaker, for example, who summons Duty—not Duty who summons the speaker. Likewise, the blindness, or innocence from which the speaker allegedly awakes in "Elegiac Stanzas" is "deplored" with a conviction clearly equal to that of the "dream" it has dispelled. The sobriety we normally assign to these works ignores an ironic posture that deconstructs the "conversion" each allegedly portends.

6. Wayne C. Booth, *A Rhetoric of Irony* (Chicago: University of Chicago Press, 1974), 42–43.

7. "Wordsworth's Yarrow and the Poetics of Repetition," *MLQ*, 38 (1977): 353–55.

8. "Mutilated Autobiography: Wordsworth's *Poems* of 1815," *TWC*, 10 (1979): 107–112.

9. *Romanticism and the Forms of Ruin: Wordsworth, Coleridge and Modalities of Fragmentation* (Princeton, NJ: Princeton University Press, 1981).

10. In *Gothic Architecture and Scholasticism* (Cleveland, OH: Meridian, 1957), Erwin Panofsky argues that the High Gothic cathedral may be likened to the contemporaneous High Scholastic *Summa* in representing a "totality" and in "tend[ing] to approximate, by synthesis as well as elimination, one perfect final solution." By contrast the Late Gothic—whose edifices were mostly "parish churches"—undermines this "principle of *manifestatio*": "Its barnlike shell encloses an often wildly and always apparently boundless interior and thus creates a space determinate and impenetrable from without but indeterminate and penetrable from within" (43–44).

11. For an especially relevant discussion of the two "Lycoris" poems and "Laodamia," see Stelzig, "Mutability, Ageing, and Permanence in Wordsworth's Later Poetry." According to Stelzig, however, the consignment of authority to the world, or to such inexorable processes as "mutability," in the later poetry is not a contestation or refiguration of Wordsworth's more subjective orientation, but rather a reversion to a "tradition," which privileges the "permanence of process." Thus, one whole gives way in the later Wordsworth to a more traditional sense of wholeness.

12. It is interesting to note that in 1820 Wordsworth changed the ending of "Laodamia," making the poem less sympathetic to the heroine. Although Mary Moorman attributes this to Wordsworth's "fidelity to Virgil, not vindictiveness to Laodamia" (*William Wordsworth: The Later Years,* 274–75), it is clear that the years 1815–17 were also something of turning point for Wordsworth, after which he was better able to manage and to move away from his "humanistic" legacy.

Unmaking Wordsworth's
Anti-Climax

.

As the examples of the previous chapter indicate, there are numerous instances that, in and of themselves, illustrate Wordsworth's growing opposition to individual authority. However, it is in the *groups* of poems, particularly the sonnets, that the authority customarily associated with romanticism—notably its mythopoeic tendency—is most clearly contested. Of these groups, the *River Duddon Sonnets* and the *Ecclesiastical Sketches* (later, the *Ecclesiastical Sonnets*) are undoubtedly the most crucial and, along with the notorious *Sonnets Upon the Punishment of Death,* can be counted as the most sustained efforts of the poet's later period.

These projects, which direct attention *from* themselves and from the committed vision of their author, are well served by the sonnet form. For more than the recourse to either rhyme or conventional meter, the sonnet, particularly in sequence, marks a repudiation of the "greater romantic lyric" and the "personal epic," both of which are assertions of personality.[1] What is more, the sonnet upholds tradition both as a counterpoise to individual talent and in order to expose their not-so-strange relationship.[2] In the absence, that is, of individual talent, of any real difficulty or "art," the sonnet characteristic of the later Wordsworth fails additionally to uphold tradition in refusing to re-vision the world. Not only do the *River Duddon* sonnets refer to something other than William Wordsworth (in comparison to either *The Prelude* or *The Excursion*); the referent or represented itself poses a challenge to its recoverability. The dominant figurative mode in these poems is not metaphor—often regarded as a trope of power or authority—but simile, which more than metaphor uncovers the gap between poetic authority and what it strives generally to dominate. What is most mimetic about these poems turns out to be the impossibility of representation, just as their remarkable determinacy—their continued deference to a world apart—is achieved through a renunciation, whereby poetry and poetic language are brought to crisis as a condition of their recovery.

Thus, both the *River Duddon* and, by turns, the *Ecclesiastical* sonnets are notable in their preoccupation with visible particularity, with the "matter-of-factness" or external reality that, as the Yarrow poems have already shown, increasingly contests the drive of imagination to overcome the world. In the notes dictated to Isabella Fenwick in 1843, Wordsworth, as Thomas McFarland observes, "again and again stresses the factuality of incidents that underlie his poems, often with a curious sense of revealing something that makes the poem more important."[3] To McFarland, this "something" involves a paradox central to Wordsworth's greatness, whereby the urge to fantasy "was held in a fructifying tension" with "a drive to realism" that was also a resistance to "imagination" ("Creative Fantasy" 5). Yet it is clear too that for McFarland this resistance is fairly minimal in Wordsworth; it merely allows, as Coleridge wrote, "the charm of novelty" to be given "to things of every day" and cultivates "a feeling analogous to the supernatural" (*Biographia*, II 7).

The cultivation of such "feeling" may well characterize the poems for which Coleridge and McFarland have particular admiration. But the Fenwick Notes are another matter, and the issue of their resistance to imagination is very real. By insisting, as they do, on the factual basis for poems such as "Resolution and Independence" and "Nutting"—instances both of what the poet earlier termed "genius"—the Fenwick Notes seek to deflect attention from these poems' most important feature: namely, their perceiving subjects. It is equally crucial, then, that these deflections are by and large failures—that the Notes' resistance to the poems never quite subsumes the poems' "genius." For it is the function of the Fenwick Notes, as it is the function of the later poetry, to write over so as to displace the poet's earlier achievement.

The *River Duddon Sonnets*, Wordsworth's first sustained compositions in the aftermath of *The Excursion* and its reception, are very clearly a reaction to the poetry that had preceded them. As is well known, *The Excursion* did not fare well among Wordsworth's contemporaries, the majority of whom found the work tedious. This, coupled with the virtual lack of interest in his collected poems of 1815, posed an interesting dilemma. However searing, public opinion had echoed the very skepticism toward authority that both *The*

Excursion and the fragmentary nature of the collected works had in various ways espoused. Wordsworth's reaction to his reception, by all accounts, was one of despair and bitterness.[4] Yet whether Wordsworth was reacting to a perceived lack of respect, or to an awareness that his two "monuments," however contestational, were *as monuments* contradictory and unquestionably a problem, is perhaps best explained by his decisions henceforth. The most remarkable of these was his decision to abandon *The Recluse;* despite the entreaties of Dorothy and Mary he never really resumed it. A more immediate decision yielded the *River Duddon Sonnets* which, following the reception of *The Excursion* and *Poems by William Wordsworth,* may be taken both as a resumption and as a clarification of the project that these, in their own way, had already initiated.[5]

Beginning, indeed, with the opening dedication to the poet's brother, "The Rev. Dr. Wordsworth," the ostensible (and conventional) contest of town and country, of civilization and the renovating virtues of the rural world of Duddon, quickly modulates to a more ironic conflict. Here, the idealizing tendencies of art (chiefly its subsumption of the actual) are continually chastened by a world that expressly assaults "tradition." In the dedicatory poem, both Christmas and, more startlingly, the infant Christ are no sooner broached than described in natural, *factual* terms—already anticipating the way the Duddon and its surrounding landscape resist humanization, specifically the narrative structures underlying art's appropriative bent.

In Sonnet I, mythologies old and new—both the "Latian shades" (1) of the ancients and the sublime "Alpine torrents thundering" (7) of the moderns—are eschewed in deference to the visible particularity of the present. From this latter vantage the history of representation becomes a "needless sleep" in which men have simply "toil[ed] . . . from dream to dream" (12).

Yet what does it mean to wake from the history of art into the "morning light" (I, 10) of the present? Is the poet able suddenly to produce "verse" (I, 13) whose sole "intent" will be to "[m]ake to the eyes of men [the river's] features known" (III, 2–4)? Or is this impossible in light of the difficulty the poet admits at the beginning of Sonnet III: "How shall I paint thee?" The answer to these questions is fairly complicated: only by exposing the sonnets' failure to accomplish their announced aim—which is to represent the Duddon with a clarity unknown to art—can the poet at least dream of a world cognizant that he is only dreaming it. "Such intent" as he "give[s] way" to (III, 2), he realizes, is not one to which nature need accede. Thus, the employment of the phrase "Child of the clouds" to refer to the river in Sonnet II (1), moves in two directions simultaneously: toward a literal description of the river's origins and to a highly figurative reconstitution of the actual that the originating river, in turn, renders artificial.

In this way, Wordsworth has moved beyond *The Excursion* (and those aspects of *The Excursion* that perplexed many of his contemporaries) in finding a partial alternative to his oppositional, authoritative stance. Imbedded in the opposition now—in the resistance, specifically, to art's idealizing tendencies—is a resistance to opposition per se. This does not mean that Wordsworth fails also to convey his point about the self-congratulatory disposition of poetry. It is that the opposition he wages in the Duddon poems derives its sanction from the "unrepresentable," from the river and world that Wordsworth can only adumbrate—and not, as customarily believed, from the nature Wordsworth succeeds in representing. It is not the speaker, who casts the river in mimetic relief as he would hope; it is the river, instead, whose otherness continually highlights that "intent," again, to which both the speaker and the representable world must variously "give way."[6]

For the most part the "intent" that Wordsworth at once represents and opposes takes the form of civilization or "tradition," beginning indeed with the actual traces that man and his culture have impressed upon the environment—and including just about anything whose "purpose" would by definition "rival" (IV, 12) or resist the actual. This last may even include such natural phenomena as the "mountain" in Sonnet IV, whose significance is culturally inscribed. Noting initially how comparing the river to a "cradled Nursling," a "loosely-scattered chain," and a "glittering snake," remains "to the gazer's eye untrue" (1–6), Wordsworth is still disposed to prefer this river, whose visibility contains the *potential* for truth, to the adjacent mountain. The mountain, which is personified (and appropriately invisible), has been coopted by an order whose "achievement" (14) it can only symbolize.

The subsumption of the actual as a condition of art is the subject as well of Sonnet VII. Here, in a critique of the sonnet tradition, the various metamorphoses to which the "love-sick Stripling" would be subject—whether it be the flower "[o]n Laura's breast" or "her [caged] bird" into whom "he would" also "pass" (1–5)—are "choice[s]" that for the speaker are "too daring" (10). The daring is not only in the captivity for which the stripling perilously yearns. It is in the poet's "choice" to have invested the stripling with that very volition. The imposition of will in a series of pathetic fallacies involves, by curious reversal, the imposition of "tradition" in the form of volition, making the poet and the stripling versions of one another.

The perils that "tradition" poses are further warned against in the two sonnets (IX and X) on "the stepping-stones" where, as the utilitarian function of these rocks portends, appropriation and control are the principal "subject." In the first, "The Stepping-Stones," the actuality of the river coursing swiftly through the stones "[w]ithout restraint" makes their "studied symmetry" (6–8) no different from the thoughts on "[d]eclining Manhood" (12) that the scene finally evokes. In both instances, the observed or seen remains peripheral to the visible yet an imposition nonetheless. The second sonnet, entitled "The Same Subject," is more pointed. Ostensibly delighting in the actions of a young "Pair" as they negotiate the stones, Wordsworth records a continuous cycle of utilization, beginning with the couple themselves and continuing in the use to which the male puts the female:

> Blushing she eyes the dizzy flood askance;
> To stop ashamed—too timid to advance;
> She ventures once again—another pause!
> His outstretched hand He tauntingly withdraws—
> She sues for help with piteous utterance!
> Chidden she chides again; the thrilling touch
> Both feel, when he renews the wished-for aid. (4–10)

This economy of appropriation and submission—neither the man nor the woman will be excited unless they are dominant and submissive respectively—dramatically reenacts the problem of art in general which must abuse in order to represent. The difference is that where the "unrepresentable" or the actual will expose the arbitrariness (and the limitations) of the artist's authority, the woman, in consort with her partner here, wages no similar act of resistance.

If anything, the compliance she displays remains one in which her partner colludes, since his domination of her remains a "victory" in the end over man and woman "both" (12–14). The "betrayal" that, as the speaker warns, will affect "both" parties "[s]hould [their fluttering hearts] beat too strongly" (11–12) is irrelevant at this stage. As the final lines make clear, they are already betrayed by a pervasive *structure* of domination:

> The frolic Loves, who, from yon high rock, see
> The struggle, clap their wings for victory! (13–14)

Whether Wordsworth here alludes to cherubim, or to birds neatly rendered into expressive subjects, is less important than the fact that the "victory" they applaud is quite literally a victory of *something* over both man and woman. And since the speaker's vantage is similarly from "on high," he is able with this one gesture both to judge the structure that informs the man's stance to the world and to judge his own viewpoint as similarly structured. As surely as the winged creatures applaud the victory of man over woman, their approbation marks another victory to which they, like the "He" whose victory they applaud, are equally subject. The world of man, as the poem's title ("The Same Subject") indicates, may be nothing more than the same subject or subjugation over and over again: a *mise en abyme* in which the narrative of human authority is virtually inescapable.

Where just about all of the River Duddon sonnets deal with this "same subject" in one way or another, certain sonnets, including "American Tradition" (XVI), are particularly indicative of the irony pervading the sequence as a whole. Certainly, the very notion of an "American Tradition" would have struck some of Wordsworth's audience as an oxymoron, implicitly admitting the superiority of the old world to the new. But with an irony typically militating against such a posture—deconstructing the artist's position from "[o]n high"—Wordsworth proceeds to show that America is just as traditional, just as apt to write over the actual, as is England. If Europeans are inclined to patronize the Indian as uncivilized, so the Indian similarly pities "the White Man's ignorance" (5), particularly his unfamiliarity with those narratives that for the Indian both explain and domesticate certain natural phenomena. Beginning with the presumption that the American Indian somehow lacks a "tradition," Wordsworth moves immediately to show how the American way is equivalent to his own "tradition": both in its self-congratulatory disposition and, more importantly perhaps, in its refusal to grant what is visibly *"[t]here"* (4) an autonomy apart from the authority of man.

The unrepresentable world, forever opposing the impulse to represent it, remains a world toward which the River Duddon poems usually do no more than gesture. To do more, after all, would mandate the appropriation of what, thanks to the arbitrariness of the traditional stance to the world, is continually *"there,"* visible and free. And yet, such gesturing as the sonnets manage would be impossible (and unnecessary) were there nothing here for the world to contest: nothing, that is, of which the speaker is not in some way culpable. So it is frequently the case in these poems that the speaker receives the stigmata of "tradition" in order to relieve it. His imperative at the beginning of Sonnet XVII—"A Dark plume fetch me from yon blasted yew, / Perched on whose top the Danish Raven croaks" (1–2)—initiates a "return" (as the title indicates) to "[d]eparted ages": specifically, the Romans who had earlier "fetch[ed]" the bird by making it a symbol, "the imperial Bird of Rome" (3–4).

Yet here the similarity ends. The Romans, for their part, are unaware that they constitute tradition, that their dominion, as it were, reflects their domination in turn. The speaker is less naive, though no more capable of possessing the world according to his design. While his remembrance of things past separates the things of the past that need be imagined (the Romans) from those aspects of the past that are forever present and necessarily unimaginable (the fragmented sound of the raven echoing among "the rocks" [5–6]), he also demonstrates, in actually recurring to "departed ages," that the past *not* present is present too. The Romans are clearly obliged, as the speaker remembers them, to bend their "knee to Jove and Mars" (11). Yet having thus recalled them, the speaker is similarly subjugated to a narrative which, having displaced the unimaginable, prohibits contact with what is past *and* present—namely, contact with the "Earth" (14).

The tendency for tradition to repeat itself with a regularity that makes the "earth" equally adamant in its resistance to tradition is a recurrent pattern from which there really can be no escape. Escape would entail either being sufficiently like the Romans not to know the earth, or being sufficiently removed from tradition to have forgotten the Romans altogether. At once a nightmare from which the speaker would awake, and a nightmare to which, having woken, he is simultaneously consigned, "tradition" remains, for present purposes, both the speaker's and its own worst enemy. It is significant, therefore, that in the very sonnet entitled "Tradition" (XXII), the narrative of the "Love-Lorn Maid," who gazing into a pool "saw that Rose" she "longed to ravish" (1–8), does more than disclose the vanity and self-absorption that preconditions the maid's appropriative tendencies. It creates a dichotomy between subject and object sufficient to grant the rose a respite from "tradition." That the rose is quite literally "[u]ntouched" by poem's end, that it is absent from the mimetic plane in which it is initially seen, is absolutely crucial to the poem's function. For as the flower's absence shows, Wordsworth has used representation to get beyond art to the unrepresentable. How well he can succeed in this, of course, is another matter. Like the maid, in fact, who remains subject to "hapless doom" (14), the poet, in failing to represent the world, is fated to represent representation. Indeed, his failure to represent—the poem's achievement—ironically repeats the maid's failure to gain her goal.

A similar paradox exists with respect to religion which, like the poet's own art, is at once traditional and a means to get beyond tradition. The "Sacred Religion" ostensibly lauded in the opening lines of "Seathwaite Chapel" (XVIII) is not a specific religion—in this case, Anglicanism—but a human legacy: the "[d]read arbitress" forever "[ordaining n]ew rites . . . when the old are wrecked" (1–3). The speaker seems hopeful of an alternative—a mechanism for religion "to purge the vapoury atmosphere / That seeks to stifle it" (8–9). Yet the mechanism he proposes—"A Pastor such as Chaucer's verse portrays; / Such as the heaven-taught skill of Herbert drew; / And tender Goldsmith crowned with deathless praise!" (12–14)—does little more than reenact the "ordination" earlier criticized, allowing "religion" the responsibility of healing itself.[7]

In response to toiling thus "from dream to dream," Wordsworth offers another option more in keeping with the contingent, paratactic reality to which religion and art are mutually opposed. Returning once more to a church, "The Kirk of Ulpha" (XXXI), the speaker distinguishes finally between a wish fulfilling narrative, by which the church is as "welcome [to the pilgrim's eye] as a star" (1–2), and an anti-narrative which proceeds *from* the churchyard outward, away from tradition, toward the world that is noticeably "there": "to the summits hoar / Of distant moon-lit mountains" and the "unseen River's gentle roar" (12–14).

In privileging the "unseen" over what was earlier sighted by the pilgrim, Wordsworth does not diminish the power of the sight in deference, say, to the "power of sound." He simply reiterates, as he has throughout the *River Duddon Sonnets,* that mere visibility is not always sufficient to rescue the world from what, in the example of the pilgrim, is clearly an intentional structure or "choice." It is often the case, in fact, that what is "seen" in the sonnets is no sooner sighted than "unseen" or transformed by agency of thought. Thus, if we frequently find Wordsworth promoting sensory perception in the sonnets, it is chiefly to warn against the mythologizing or symbolizing tendencies by which sight and sound are, as the sonnets themselves show, continually written over.

The final poem of the sequence ("After-Thought"), appropriately following "The Kirk of Ulpha," reiterates this claim: the sonnets' function has not been to eschew thinking, but to get beyond it. Only "after" thought, by gazing "backward" over "what was, and is, and will abide" (XXXIV, 3–4), does the "Eternity" (XXXIII, 14) that resists history—the past that is visibly the present—oppose the eternity that is history: those "dreams" past, passing, and to come, that idealize and reformulate what is simply "there."

* * *

It might seem foolhardy to argue that the *Ecclesiastical Sonnets*, composed shortly after the *River Duddon Sonnets* between December of 1820 and March the following year, are as antagonistic toward tradition, specifically cultural tradition, as the preceding group of poems. In systematically tracing the history of the English Church from the Romans to the present day, the sonnets (or "sketches" as the initial one hundred and two were called) clearly celebrate Anglicanism as an ideal form of Christianity. Yet even so, these poems do not promote Christian doctrine. Instead, they trace an evolution and a disposition that, correctly or not, Wordsworth thought endemic to English character.

This disposition is toward renunciation and the ameliorative stance it takes. Proceeding from the example of Christ, Wordsworth equates the "Christian" and the selfless so as to distinguish them from the authoritarian—in this case, Rome— which not even the conflation of Rome and Christianity will alter. It is the English, indeed, and no other Europeans who, as the history of their church attests, most faithfully reenact Christ's example.

From the early example of Alban, who "for his friend . . . died" (I, vi, 11 ["Persecution"]), the initial sonnets trace the origin of English Christianity in a way that continually distinguishes "conquest" as an end, or an act of submission, from the action which privileges the conqueror. This does not mean of course that all of the English and all of the Romans are conquered and conquerors respectively. Pope Gregory, for example, is commemorated for having submitted to "commanding sympathies" (I, xiii, 11 ["Casual Incitement"]) and the English Dunstan is berated for his selfish "ambition" (I, xxviii ["Influence Abused"]). In the main, however, Wordsworth means to promote and to represent a gradualism (or an ameliorative stance) characteristic of Christianity in England:

one that actively mitigates the more impulsive, authoritarian tendency to enlist Christ in the service of non-Christian ends. Anxious, therefore, to remember such figures as the "war-worn Chieftain," who forsook war in favor of penitence (I, xxi ["Seclusion"]), and the "pious Alfred," who gave rather than received (I, xxvi), Wordsworth is just as eager to deplore both Papal abuses (I, xxxvii) and, in the conclusion of Part I, the Church authority that found its most dramatic expression in the Crusades (xxxiv).

If it is the position here that the *Ecclesiastical Sonnets* are a timely utterance—consumed, like the *River Duddon Sonnets,* with the poet's own humanistic legacy—then this is assuredly not the way that they (or the Duddon poems for that matter) are customarily read. Edith Batho and, more recently, Peter Manning, have argued that Wordsworth's Anglicanism not only contests his revolutionary phase, but also that Anglicanism is sufficiently native to the poet's upbringing, and of a piece with him, to require a reassessment of Wordsworth's achievement. According to Manning, the poet's "revolutionary ardors," however appealing, are in many ways "an aberration" from Wordsworth's fidelity to the English Church and "from a pattern of family service to the Lowthers"—a fidelity that renders the *Sonnets* and, in Manning's example, the poem on St. Bees, representative of an aspect of Wordsworth that criticism has been unwilling to confront.[8]

One welcomes Manning's point about the humanist or "revolutionary" bias in the reception of Wordsworth in our century. Yet for Manning Wordsworth's resistance to such valuation does not diminish criticism so much as it diminishes Wordsworth. And this, it seems to me, raises an issue of genuine concern with respect to Wordsworth studies and current criticism generally. As most critics are by now aware, it has become common, and undoubtedly useful, to reassess those values by which canonical judgments have been made. Yet for all their circumspection, such reassessments are sometimes fraught with blindnesses of their own. This is particularly evident in the so-called "new historicism" with which Manning is in this case aligned, and which apparently has little quarrel with the general consensus regarding Wordsworth's later conservatism. This unwillingness to challenge the consensus, specifically the notion of the poet's anti-climax, is to my mind highly problematic. For by accepting (and even extending) the conventional wisdom on the late Wordsworth, critics such as Manning and Jerome McGann do not simply join forces with those commentators (including deconstructionists) who are otherwise objects of disagreement. They refuse, more crucially, to follow their own precedent in granting the late Wordsworth an ironic dimension and thus a partnership in the challenge to posterity.[9]

If Wordsworth's earlier poetry can be deemed a poetry of elision, one that, as Manning, McGann, Levinson and Simpson have variously argued, suppresses or studiously avoids a referentiality conspicuous by its very absence,[10] then the same may be said of Wordsworth's later poetry and politics. Behind the poet's "service to Lowthers," for example, particularly his campaign in 1818 against Henry Brougham ("the most prominent Demagogue in the Kingdom" [Moorman, *The Later Years* 344]), was not merely the "tradition" to which Wordsworth was always committed; it was the specter of his own, individual authority, which had already shown both the strength and flimsiness of that tradition's hold. This specter, initially recognized in "character of the Poet," and subsequently in both the Wanderer and the Solitary, later found additional representation in the Whiggism about which Wordsworth was similarly antipathetic and in the figure of Napoleon with whom the Whigs had carried on an unfortunate liaison.[11]

Wordsworth's "relationship" with Napoleon had been long-standing, beginning indeed with the oddly sympathetic sonnet "1801" ("I Grieved for Buonaparté") composed in 1802 when, as we have noted, Wordsworth was increasingly convinced of his identity as an autonomous subject. In time this sympathy dissipated, but it did not dissipate independently of the dissolution of other sympathies. Before Wordsworth came to revile Napoleon, or came oppose to Brougham in support of the landed interests, or before he came to write *The Excursion* and the *Ecclesiastical Sonnets*, the poet had come to oppose *himself*, particularly the enfranchised figure of whom *The Prelude* was to have been a celebration. To argue, then, that Wordsworth's conservatism simply reestablished loyalties from which his earlier humanism was a clear departure is not only to posit a "revolutionary" agenda where none, in retrospect, may have existed; it refuses, more modestly, to see (as the Victorians saw) a consistency or corrigibility to Wordsworth's poetry that only canonical practice seems to want to overlook.

Nor do I mean, in speaking of this "consistency," to argue the structuralist position that there was effectively no difference between the authoritarian nature of Wordsworth's later poetry and the bourgeois humanism that led earlier to the authoritarian self. I mean to argue something very different: the consistency of which Wordsworth can be accused was a consistency he was unquestionably the first to recognize and, in the very way he was disposed to write it, to write against it. "Wordsworth's relations with the 'great'," writes David Simpson, "were always complicated" (*Wordsworth's Historical Imagination* 73). And it is in light of these perenially complicated relations that Wordsworth's orthodoxy must be viewed. Far from being an apostasy, therefore, or worse, a development that merely uncovers the apostasy that was revolution, Wordsworth's "anti-climax" *continues* the quarrel with authority that, to be effective, had to be communicated indirectly now—or without specific authorization.

We have seen how Wordsworth's recourse to the sonnet, which visibly exposes the limits of traditional representation, receives its sanction in the tendency of these poems to gesture toward the unrepresentable. This is equally characteristic of his defense of the English Church which, in the absence of doctrine, merely foregrounds the poet's own renunciation—his deference to a world apart—rather than the authority of the institution to whom he is ostensibly subject. And then, of course, there is the example of "Napoleon," who reinforces this stance in the way that he, like the Wanderer or the Solitary before him, is a figure for the poet himself. While the Wanderer and the Solitary repeat one another simply by repeating the "Poet," Napoleon, by reenacting the revolution that is representation, by exposing the authoritarianism inherent in the millenarian narrative, remains the very figure against whom Wordsworth writes in poetry and in public life.[12]

This does not mean that Wordsworth's texts are always equal or even faithful to their referent. The assumption that England is ultimately less authoritarian than Continental Europe on the evidence of its Church flies directly in the face of the very palpable way Protestantism led quite directly to the kind of selfhood exemplified by Napoleon. Similarly, Wordsworth's aversion to change and insurrection, reflected in his defense of landed interests and his horror at workers' uprisings, is too much like the authoritarianism to which his earlier "revolution" was akin. However, on balance, there is enough that is independent or sufficiently irregular about the later Wordsworth—be it his continued opposition to Evangelicism or his wary association with the Oxford movement —to recover the irony that makes his "career," like his poetry, subject to interpretation.[13] If it can be said of the *Ecclesiastical Sonnets* that they do not often provoke interpretation, then this consensus about their meaning has perhaps less to do with the poems themselves than with a blindness both to their irony and to the basis for that irony that has robbed these works of their justification as poems.

In conjunction with the recurrent theme of renunciation, there are two other aspects to the *Sonnets* that deserve comment. One is the anti-narrative or paratactic nature of the arrangement, in which individual moments comprise a whole that is ultimately less than, or can be said (paradoxically) to bear a synecdochical relationship to, its component parts. The other is the tendency of these parts to embrace a factuality that, like the episodic nature of the poems themselves, actively militates against any larger mythopoeic function. The gradualism, in other words, that Wordsworth privileges over more willful efforts to alter the disposition of things actually finds a correlative in the collected "sketches," which inscribe in large the very constancy endemic to each station.

Moreover, these facts of "life" as Wordsworth glimpses them are, in the first two parts particularly, "facts" of history as well, further deflecting attention outward, away from any bias or intentionality. Nor is "factuality" the sole method of deflection. In reconstructing the development of the English Church, Wordsworth consistently relied on more than one source: Bede, Eusebius, Stillingfleet and Sharon Turner for the early period; Fuller, Daniel, Stowe, Drayton and Foxe for the Middle Ages through the reign of Elizabeth; and Walton, Heylin and Milton for the seventeenth century (Moorman, *The Later Years* 392–93). Such manifold reliance is perfectly in keeping with Wordsworth's project. Wordsworth's "history" is simultaneously a theory of both history and art that explicitly warns against the idealizing tendencies characteristic of any single point of view. In addition, then, to the acts of deference that signal a renunciation of authority, there is a deference here to authorities whose remarkable diffuseness effectively places the represented (i.e., England) beyond the reach of representation.[14]

The parahistory that Wordsworth practices in the *Ecclesiastical Sonnets* achieves it is fullest articulation in the third section. Here, the "present," like the River Duddon before it, becomes an objective correlative for the past—relegating history to the realm of the ideal. Recapitulating the past so as to annihilate the myth of progress, the *Sonnets'* present is quite visibly a counterpoise to the millenarian narrative that either subordinates the present to some future ideal or, as we saw earlier in *The Prelude,* makes the "present" the future suddenly arrived. In opposition to revolution and to the progressive history with which it is always leagued, the "present," these poems show, is a past that has always been.

Wordsworth reaffirms this theme at the very beginning of Part III in the seemingly uncharacteristic poem "I saw the figure of a lovely Maid." Recalling the beloved figure "[s]eated alone beneath a

darksome tree" (2), Wordsworth juxtaposes the memory of her—
the "bright corporeal presence—form and face" (9)—to its eventual
"dissolution" (14) as a memory. In contrast to a poem such as "I
wandered lonely as a Cloud," where the daffodils are dissolved in
order to be recreated, the actuality of the maid in the past ensures
her "presence" in a way that her recreator, to whom she was once
visible, cannot. The past—what *was*—persists despite the failure to
represent it.

The tendency of the English Church to imitate life in its continual
resistance to authority remains a tendency of the *Sonnets* as well in
making the poet adjunct to his observations. Their "bold design," as
Wordsworth terms it in Sonnet XII—a poem he tellingly trans-
ferred to the sequence (and to Part III) in 1827—is not the province
of art, much less of the artist, but is rather like a river (in this case the
Rhine) on which the poet is "borne forward":

> The living landscapes greet him, and depart;
> Sees spires fast sinking—up again to start!
> And strives the towers to number, that recline
> O'er the dark steeps, or on the horizon line
> Striding with shattered crests his eye athwart.(3–8)[15]

In making parataxis, as it were, the best that he can do, Wordsworth
points to the limits of his art by attending (paradoxically) to its
mimetic function. Following the Church in its renunciative disposition, parataxis has become an organizing principle or, as Wordsworth terms it, the essence of "design" (1). Unlike structures that are
more willful or intentional, "design," like the sketches that comprise
it, derives its structure from what is "there" and visible. Thus, if the
Sonnets can be said follow a "bold design," it is in the way the poet is
"borne forward" by a force beyond his control: in refutation of
those narratives that make the visible invisible and render the real
ideal.

This point is made with particular force in the sonnets describing
the operation of the Church in the present, the particularity of
which often takes precedence over the invisible, or those aspects of
the Church that are symbolic. The descriptions of "pastoral character" (III, xviii) or the rites of baptism (III, xx) continually produce a
slippage between the "authority" to which these refer and the trace
to which God or Christ is increasingly tantamount. The Pastor, as
Wordsworth describes him, may well be "arrayed in Christ's authority" (10). But this "arrayment" owes less to his representation of
Christ than to actions or to a way of life to which Christ is immedi-

ately accessory. Further, by separating Christ from the man in his image, Wordsworth allows this imaging, those *human* structures that religion also masks and mystifies, to be similarly unnatural. Hence, the sonnet "Sponsors" (III, xxi) begins by exhorting the "father" as that image in which *God* was conceived ("Father! to God himself we cannot give / A holier name!") as a prelude to allowing their "con-j[unction]" (3) a demystifying function. The agent for this demys-tification is the "mother," who not only supersedes the father as the object of the speaker's address, but, in "striv[ing] / Against disheartening custom" (5–6), is charged finally with making "the Word" (potentially an "empty sound" [14]) more than a mere trace.

Similarly, the sonnets on catechizing and confirmation (III, xxii–xxiv) subordinate these practices to a more palpable "design" by allowing the "world" precedence over the "word." In "Catechising" the authority of the Pastor (before whom the speaker remembers "trembling" as a Child [xxii, 2–4]) is displaced by the memory of his "[b]eloved Mother" (9) whose ministry is more enduring. This ministry persists in the sonnets on confirmation, both of which have recourse to the maternal gaze. In the first of these (xxiii), the speaker actually adopts this gaze in witnessing the "gather[ing]" of "Young-ones . . . taking the baptismal Vow" (1–4). Noting the denaturing effect, by which "many a blooming, many a lovely, cheek / Under the holy fear of God turns pale" (7–8), the speaker cannot refrain either from the ironic observation that the "Omnipo-tent will raise / Their feeble Souls" (11–12) or, as a further measure of this irony, from offering his own "regrets" that "the Sun"—a figure for the Omnipotent—has somehow "se[t]" on "their child-hood." (12–14).

The second sonnet on confirmation is even more problematic. Observing a mother witnessing the confirmation of a daughter whose sister had earlier died, the speaker is moved to question the efficacy of an institution that would locate both children in another world:

Tell, if ye may, some star-crowned Muse, or Saint!
Tell what rushed in, from what she was relieved—
Then, when her Child the hallowing touch received,
And such vibration through the Mother went
That tears burst forth amain. Did gleams appear?
Opened a vision of that blissful place
Where dwells a Sister-child? And was power given
Part of her lost One's glory back to trace
Even to this Rite? (5–13)

The answer to these questions is as yet undecided. But a more a conclusive answer is not finally what the poem is after. Continuing by observing that the mother did, at any event, "kne[el]" throughout the ceremony, the speaker closes by also noting that she died shortly thereafter. Beyond the meaning of this death—whether it answers the question by attesting either to mother's faith or to her skepticism—the poem's ending protests the authority that would empower anyone, the poet included, to extrapolate meaning from appearance or to "tell" a story. Like the mother herself, we are left in the end with a nagging sense of disappearance, which only the present or, in the mother's case, her living daughter, can possibly relieve.

While the Church is being held culpable for its symbolizing posture, for adhering too strongly to a structure it had sometimes mitigated, it is for the purpose of *continuing* this mitigation by recalling the Church to its inherent feminization. The sudden recourse to the feminine gaze is neither accidental nor merely peevish at this juncture; indeed, by pointing up the discrepancy between the "world" and the "word," the gaze allows finally for the reintroduction of the "world" in such fashion that the Church is both recuperated and, in the process, made a paradigm for the function of art in the "present" time.[16] The poems with which Wordsworth concludes, beginning with the "Rural Ceremony" (xxxii) and culminating with the poems on various church structures, continue the project of introjecting the world as a way of rehabilitating the word. In "Rural Ceremony" the procession of children through the churchyard and into the Church reiterates the incorporation of the world into the poet's "Book" (1) and, following the garlands that the children bear as offerings, equates this "sacred Book" with the Church itself, whose narrative is pitched equally toward such "advance[ment]" (6).

This processional is more evident in the poems dealing with church structures. In "Old Abbeys" (xxxv), the "downward way" (1) of these structures, now in ruins, constitutes a "fall" that the poet admits to having "marked" (2) and, in marking, promotes. The "downward way" refers to more than the dissolution of physical structure; it signifies the leveling, or the dissolution of hierarchy, by which edifices that "once . . . were holy" are, the speaker assures us, "holy still" (13). That is, the continued holiness of the abbeys owes less to the permanence of human intention, and the hierarchies to which those intentions have referred, than to the permanence of a process whose "design" is forever present.

One might expect, therefore, that the sonnet devoted to "New Churches" (xxxviii) would contest this "downward way," for it commemorates the "rival haste" with which "the wished-for Temples rise!" (11). Yet the fact remains that just as the poet is careful to distinguish his wish from the too willful wish on the part of Parliament that new temples be built, so he concludes by observing that only by introjection of the world— through "that vale or hill" that "multiplies" their chime—do these churches' bells produce "the heavenliest of all sounds" (12–14). By the same right, the ensuing sonnets on the "Church To Be Erected" (xxxix–xl), prefer the prospect of a church "shelter[ed]" by surrounding nature ("where" the altar may justly "stand / For kneeling adoration" [xxxix, 8–12]), to the Continental counterpart, whose various embellishments occlude the world and privilege the word. The English church, of course, has its occlusions too, most notably a Cross. However, even this "symbol" is enhanced by nature:

> the Sun with his first smile
> Shall greet that symbol crowning the low Pile:
> And the fresh air of incense-breathing morn
> Shall wooingly embrace it; and green moss
> Creep round its arms through centuries unborn.
>
> (xl, 10–14)

Finally, in the climactic sonnets devoted to "Cathedrals" and to Kings College Chapel respectively (xlii–xlv), the priority that Wordsworth grants the world in its mitigation of symbol is reassigned to a Church reconciled to the limits of its referentiality. Earlier, in the Preface to *The Excursion,* Wordsworth had used the "gothic church" to symbolize his endeavor as an artist. Now, having transformed his art so that "his" church will be neither incomplete nor an edifice in ruins, Wordsworth can reenlist the metaphor without making too much of the structure's wholeness or of the fact that it is even a church. The "design" on which the cathedral is effectively based turns out to be no more (or less) of a whole than the world it imitates. No longer privileging the human imagination in its imitation of God, or in the performance of a recreative function, the cathedral no longer symbolizes God. Instead, the edifice in "Cathedrals" remains a place *beheld,* whose referent is not "celestial" (to use de Man's phrase), but, as Wordsworth appropriately terms it, "the world above" (xlii, 10).

The deference that Wordsworth grants the "world" in thus implying its equivalence to Heaven is a deference that the word— or, in this instance, the cathedral—must similarly reenact. It is the cathedral's function to consume the speaker by sensory means, to captivate his "eye" in a way that suspends time and, with it, the opposition ordinarily waged by the individual subject. ("Or down the nave to pace in motion slow; / Watching with upward eye, the tall tower grow / And mount, at every step . . ." [7–9].) No longer a mystification of human authority, the "world above" is more properly the world, the world beyond authority, to which both the word and the church are equally subordinate. If it is the case, therefore, that the interior of King's College Chapel is, as Wordsworth subsequently describes it, the "glorious Work of Fine intelligence," then such work and glory abide in the "reject[ion]" of intelligence—"of the nicely-calculated less or more" (xliii, 5–7). The "portraitures" and other traces of human authority that adorn the structure—those of "Martyr, or King, or sainted Eremite" (xliv, 5)—are made invisible by a "perspective" (1) that promotes the truly visible and "cast[s], before the eye, . . . a veil of ecstasy!" (13–14).

Although some of the sonnets I have discussed were added in 1827, I have not mentioned any of those composed between 1842–43 which were added to the sequence in 1845 and 1849. And I have declined for two reasons: first, because these later sonnets reverse the design of the earlier poems in apparently privileging the word over the world; and second, because this apparent rehabilitation of the word and of the poet's authority as its spokesman marks the final development in a poetry that is ever more ironic and indirect. We observed earlier how in the three Yarrow poems Wordsworth moves from initial doubt about the effects of imagination to a point where, in promoting imagination, he makes himself (in the image of Scott and "memory's shadowy moonshine") the object of some ridicule. A similar consequence prevails in the later *Ecclesiastical Sonnets*, which carry the ironization increasingly characteristic of the later poetry to its furthest extreme. Beyond the "traditional" authority these poems variously oppose, their irony requires an assumption of authority so utterly avuncular, and sufficiently blind to its own contradictions, that the reader has no choice but to regard this consequence and no other point as "the point at issue" (II, xxx).

To leave the reader in this situation departs in a significant way from the hermeneutic dispensation that, as Rajan describes it, empowers the reader in reestablishing authoritative meaning. For Wordsworth's charge to the reader in the late poems also acknowledges the speaker as the sole authority in these works. Thus, just as the speaker creates meaning, so he remains, much more than the reader, his own worst enemy. In contrast to nineteenth-century hermeneutics, which is restorative in function, Wordsworthian hermeneutics in the 1830s and 40s is more anomalous, more deconstructive. Now, the poet writes against himself (or against the speaker) without also promoting writing and also forcing the reader into a breach left by the disappearance of the author.

Two poems from Part III will suffice to make this point: "Visitation of the Sick" (xxviii) and "Funeral Service" (xxxi). Other sonnets in this group, as we have seen, describe the "present" in a way that introduces the world as an antidote to the symbolizing tendencies of both the Church and the hierarchy these represent. These two sonnets, by contrast, are determined to uphold the Church's mythologies at all costs. "Visitation of the Sick" does so by contrasting the very palpable healing effected by the "maternal" order, whose "zeal" the "ministers" appropriate (4–5), to the (implicitly superior) metaphysical or paternalistic healing that is the ministers' proper function. The contradiction here is not only in the ministers' subsumption of the "maternal" (which ceases afterwards to be that); it is also in the fact that without the maternal, whose genuine concern the Church initially mimes, the ministers could not function as ministers and "sustain with prayer, / And soothe the heart confession hath laid bare" (6–7).

In a similar way, the "Funeral Service" defends the efficacy of the Christian ritual by juxtaposing the inertness of the "Body" (3) and the equally palpable grief of its mourners with the "hope" that "comes reborn / At Jesu's bidding" (12–13). Again, however, this defense remains little more than testimony to the speaker's peculiarly myopic faith. His juxtapositions, confidently contrasting the "word" and *its* referent (6) to the "truth" and "[i]ts natural echo" (11–12), make the closing exclamation—"'O Death, / Where is thy Sting?—O Grave, where is thy Victory?'"—a question that founders on its own rhetoric.

The sonnets that follow this procedure most consistently, detaching the poet from his own language and from the authority of his own voice, are the *Sonnets Upon the Punishment of Death*, composed in 1839–1840 and published in 1842. Written in response to the debate in Parliament about the deterrent effects of capital punishment, a sentence that had recently been removed from approximately two hundred offenses, Wordsworth's poems appear to be a typically conservative effort to defend capital punishment against the well-meaning intentions of its more liberal opponents. On the surface the poems are clearly such an effort. Nevertheless, it is curious that the most sustained commentary on the sonnets, as well as the most sympathetic, Sir Henry Taylor's review for the *Quarterly Review* (which constituted the sonnets' first appearance) was not included in the version of the review that appeared revised in Taylor's *Collected Works* (1878).[17] The reasons for this omission may have had to do with the fact that the capital punishment debate was less pressing thirty years hence. But there is also a flatness to Taylor's defense, a tendency to read these sonnets as arguments rather than as poems, that is not the case with his general view of Wordsworth.

The question then must be asked: do Taylor's emendations reflect Wordsworth's failure always to accommodate the good intentions of posterity? Or, do they admit, however implicitly, the failure of criticism to comprehend its subject? My answer to both of these is "yes": the *Sonnets Upon the Punishment of Death* are at once failures (as their omission from Taylor's essay implies) and, as their omission simultaneously suggests, a challenge to the failings of posterity. But before demonstrating why this is necessarily the case, a look Taylor's other criticism of Wordsworth is in order.

Like many of his contemporaries, including Ruskin, Taylor adopted an encyclopedic view of Wordsworth that is not often appreciated by critics today.[18] In an essay for the *Quarterly Review* (1834) and later in his 1841 essay, Taylor observed in typically Victorian fashion that the totalizing tendency of Wordsworth's poetry depends paradoxically on the poet's aversion to an overarching view of things. Thus, Taylor is able to distinguish Wordsworth's philosophy, or such unity as may be inferred from his writing, from the unitary tendencies of philosophy in general. "Mr. Wordsworth," he writes, "is a philosophic writer in the sense in which any man must be so who writes from the impulses of a capacious and powerful mind, habituated to observe, to analyse, and to generalise." "But it does not follow," Taylor continues,

> that he should be supposed to have invented any peculiar ethical or metaphysical system, or to have discovered any new principles upon which such a system could be built. What is new and peculiar in him . . . consists not so much in the exposition of abstract truths as in his manner of his regarding the particulars of life as they arise and of generalising them into one truth

or according as the one or the other harmonises with his moral temperament and habitual and cherished states of feeling (*Works*, V 16–17).

Taylor's somewhat mystified sense of the harmony of subject and object, of the particulars of the world and the poet's moral disposition or temperament, belies his more compelling (if paradoxical) contention that the poetical disposition is comprehensive only by being subservient to "the particulars of life." The "unity of drift, which has given to [Wordsworth's] writings the character of embodying a peculiar system of philosophy," owes finally to the fact "that truth can only be shown piecemeal in its component parts, and that poetry, at all events, can do no more than cast partial lights upon it" (*Works*, V 17).

In making authority contingent upon its renunciation, Taylor is able similarly to explain the poet's "passionate love of Nature." Drawing on the poet's own observation that the mind—not nature—is "the haunt and the main region of his song," Taylor immediately qualifies this by noting paradoxically that "the mind of man, as exhibited by Mr. Wordsworth, hardly ever fails to be the mirror of natural objects, and more or less the creature of their power" (*Works*, V 25–26). The humanism, by which Taylor (in anticipation of such critics as Geoffrey Hartman) disabuses the more conventional sense of Wordsworth as "nature poet," is merely a pretext to a more unorthodox view: Wordsworth's nature poetry is suddenly a counterpoise, if not also a challenge, to the more mystified, romantic view of the power of the individual.

This post-humanist stance, demanding not only that the world be deferred to, but also that it be represented in paratactic or "piecemeal" fashion, similarly grounds Taylor's defense of Wordsworth's sonnets in 1841.[19] But there are new developments as well. Where Taylor's initial essay remains a typically Victorian effort to bring Wordsworth's earlier poetry in line with *The Excursion* (which in the two decades following its initially mixed reception had gradually become the poet's acknowledged masterpiece), the second essay seeks to promote a Wordsworthian aesthetic independent of that poem (*Works*, V 53–56). This exclusionary gesture poses immediate problems; without *The Excursion*, which looks backward at a nominally radical humanism so as to move beyond it, Taylor was obliged to promote an aesthetic without a *raison d'être*. Without the Wordsworth who supplements Wordsworth—the Wordsworth subject to his own revisability—it was impossible to explain the sonnets' most unique characteristic: their juxtaposition of tradition and individual talent in a way that each neutralized the other.

This is not to say that Taylor is altogether blind to the issue of corrigibility. In speaking of the way Wordsworth's sonnets show a "mind . . . open to nature with ever-wakeful susceptibility," or in noting the sonnets' resistance of a "romantic view of things" in deference to "the whole truth received," or even in his narrower, somewhat formal observation about their abstinence from false effects, particularly in matters of closure, Taylor consistently locates the sonnets' peculiar character in the impulse to characterlessness (*Works*, V 79, 107, 56). Nevertheless, Taylor is less able than before to justify this impulse by explaining Wordsworth's fascination with the sonnet form.

This liability is especially clear in his discussion of the sonnets on capital punishment. Rejecting, for all practical purposes, the assumption that these are even poems, that they reflect an aesthetic, much less an anti-aesthetic, Taylor places them entirely within the context of the parliamentary debate (*Quarterly Review* 39–50). And this is most unfortunate. More than any of Wordsworth's other poems, the sonnets on capital punishment require the context of Wordsworth's previous poems to be fully comprehended. The sonnets, to be sure, respond to the very real issue of law and punishment. But it is significant that Wordsworth was provoked to write sonnets in this occasion rather than pamphlets. In placing art at the service of politics in the public sphere Wordsworth did more than place his art beyond the reach of a critic like Taylor; he ultimately placed politics (as Taylor could not recognize) in the service of his art, which more than ever—at the terminus of his career—had become a private sphere.[20]

The hardening of sensibility with which the sonnets are customarily charged is not a hardening of sensibility per se; it represents, rather, an "escape" from the authority to which such hardening is manifestly equivalent. Only by being the "straight man," as he had done in "Yarrow Revisited" or in the sonnets later added to the *Ecclesiastical Sketches*, could Wordsworth finally resign his authority as a writer without having also to reappropriate it as the man who resigned it. As a measure of how completely he has relinquished authority, Wordsworth refuses to relinquish it at all. His refusal becomes something, then, that only the reader—someone *not* the poem's authority—can possibly interpret. To the extent they are ironic, the sonnets on capital punishment are ironic beyond the reach of intentionality. They are poems whose meaning is quite literally in search of an author, permitting no one, neither the man speaking nor the men reading him, the responsibility of authorizing it.

There is plenty in the way of contradiction in these sonnets to justify such a claim. The very first sonnet, in fact, sets the tone for the entire sequence by setting the speaker against himself without his apparent consent. Delighting in the prospect of Lancaster Castle (a "sight so fair / Of sea and land, with yon grey towers that still / Rise up as if to lord it over air" [1– 3]), the speaker next views the same "spot" from a different perspective: it now bears the surprising name "Weeping Hill." The very prospect that "[m]ight soothe in human breasts the sense of ill" or "fill / The heart with joy and gratitude to God" (4–6) is reimagined as one that affords prisoners headed for the castle "[f]or lingering durance or quick death with shame" (11) a "first look" (13) at their final residence. This second perspective is broached with a kind of wide-eyed curiosity. Having just noted both the apparent and potential beauty of the scene, the speaker is moved suddenly to ask: "Why bears [this spot] then the name of 'Weeping Hill'?" (8).

The answer turns out to be more complicated than the one he provides. Not only does the hill bear the name because of those who have "[s]hed [tears] on their chains" (13–14) upon seeing the castle for the first time; it also bears the name in conjunction with the visible imposition of Lancaster castle and its "lord[ly]" towers on the landscape. If the speaker's question is intended simply to remember those who have regarded this prospect differently, it simultaneously recalls his difference and deference to authority ("Why . . . then"), making *him* the imposition—and his *question* a protest to what he advocates.

It is the arbitrariness of human authority, at once imposed and resisted, that the *Sonnets Upon the Punishment of Death* document. The third sonnet notes the parallel between the Roman Consul who "doomed his sons to die" for having "betrayed their country" (1–2) and the repentant criminal who passes sentence on himself and eagerly solicits death. Just as the speaker's question in Sonnet I has the ironic effect of adumbrating a world where there are neither castles nor the impositions of authority of which the question is more immediately an index, so the defense of "Duty" (8) in Sonnet III serves a similar function of showing duty to be unnatural. Neither the execution of one's sons nor of the already penitent criminal remains, in the context of the poem, a necessary act. Instead, each reflects (particularly in tandem) the overkill that culture warrants. By way of justifying the punishment of these acts as absolutely necessary, Wordsworth's poem ironically justifies the acts themselves in terms of the arbitrariness they otherwise redress.

In no way, of course, can the speaker of these sonnets be credited with having consciously initiated such subversions. If anything, these subversions emerge because of his unwillingness to admit them. The second sonnet, which discourages sympathy for the condemned criminal in favor of sympathy for the victim (and the punishment it dictates) as being from a "higher source" (11), nevertheless promotes a structure of authority that sanctions the crime as well as its punishment. The speaker's distinction between "Nature's law" (1), urging sympathy "[f]or worst offenders" (2), and "man's" law (which discourages such sympathy in deference to God) returns us, ironically, to the scene of the crime. That is, in the very way that civilization discourages "nature's law" as inappropriate, so the lack of sympathy in the murderer "with the unforewarned, who died / Blameless" (12–13) marks a representation of authority—of "Him who stood in awe / Neither of God nor man" (4–5)—of which *his* punishment is a recapitulation.

The distinction in these sonnets between culture and Nature is a gender distinction as well. And it is through this difference, more than any other perhaps, that the source of the speaker's "higher source," those human structures from which God is extrapolated in order that "He" may be served by "man," is exposed. In his profile of the "wise Legislator" in Sonnet V, the speaker observes that "all Authority in earth depends / On . . . [c]opying with awe the one Paternal mind" (6–8). That the "paternal" is more properly a copy of the human order hardly concerns the speaker, whose main interest is that the "State" remain subservient to authority's wisdom. But while the speaker may be blind to the implications of his mythologies, the poem is not. In addition to identifying the source of "all authority" as belonging properly to the earth rather than to God, the poem suggests, as do almost all of the sonnets on capital punishment, that the earth might be better off without God and the "authority" that the mythology of "Him" underwrites. The basis of this suggestion lies, as usual, in the introduction of the "State," synonymous here with both woman and Nature (11–14). In bringing up the "State," Wordsworth does two things. He broaches a "state" of nature of which that human collective, the "state," is "naturally" a reflection; and he suggests, by returning "all authority" to the "earth," that we need not "depend" on God—a mystification of paternalism—for our salvation.

It must be emphasized that the speaker does not authorize this meaning or the feminization it projects. Nevertheless, the speaker is little capable of managing those contradictions to which his position is therefore vulnerable. There is, in fact, a link in these poems between their feminization, which the "paternal" speaker undoubtedly opposes, and their ironization, where meaning is authorized independent of the "paternal mind" or voice of the man speaking. This assault on voice, which anticipates Derrida's subsequent refusal to privilege speech over writing, simultaneously exceeds Derrida in allowing for a meaning that comes to more than the mere subversion of meaning. Statements are made in the *Sonnets*, but in a way that no one, certainly no single figure or presence, can be charged with making them. Instead, there is a rupture or slippage in the speaker's argument from which meaning simply emanates.[21] Thus, in tracing the origins of law from the initial "precept eye for eye, and tooth for tooth" (VII, 3), the speaker is typically caught between the goal of law, which he claims is "love," and the fact that law has demonstrably failed in the interim to effect that "end" (8). In opposition to those who would "strain" the "mandates" (9–10) that the "Master meek / Proscribed" (5–6), the speaker's history lesson offers a most ironic possibility: only with the "end" of "*his* law, . . . *his* school" (7), will the "end" of law—love—be achieved.

It is the prospect of a different world—one released from the very strictures of authority promoted and represented by the speaker—that is released in turn by this "revolution in poetic language." The image of "guilt escaping" (VIII, 12), by which the speaker threatens those who would eliminate the "terrors" intended to discourage "wrongful acts" (4–5), imagines an escape from the vicious circle where retribution bears virtually the same onus as the crime it would correct. Nor is it always a pun, such as the "end" of law or "escape" from guilt, that makes the speaker an unwitting millenarian. This function is more often accomplished by the speaker's blindness to a situation that, by his description, elicits an altogether different response.

Such blindness is particularly evident in Sonnet XI ("Ah, think how one compelled for life to abide"), where the speaker enlists civilization as a cure for the very discontents that can be laid at civilization's door. It is not surprising that in discussing this particular poem Henry Taylor deliberately avoided its argument—that capital punishment is preferable to life imprisonment—and argued instead against certain "secondary punishments" which reduce the "mind" to "a weak, blank, and negative condition" (*Quarterly Review* 46–47). However not even this excursus was sufficient to mask

Taylor's distress. "Independently, however, of these considerations," he concludes, "and on the ground of a moral preference in respect of the criminal, Mr. Wordsworth would inflict death rather than transportation or imprisonment for life" (48). Taylor then quotes the sonnet as if the poem were its own best advocate, and needed no further defense, not even paraphrasing.

And this, in a peculiar sense, is his most percipient criticism; for it is the sonnet itself, again, that is the speaker's severest critic. In contrast to the "guilt" that a prisoner must eventually visit on himself for life, death, the speaker insists, is more merciful, since it "[l]eav[es]"

> the final issue in *His* hands
> Whose goodness knows no change, whose love is sure,
> Who sees, foresees; who cannot judge amiss,
> And wafts at will the contrite soul to bliss. (11–14)

The speaker's final recourse to God seems to clinch his point, but it also betrays a weariness with a world whose strictures prevent neither crime nor crimes of stricture—crimes that only the punishment of death can ultimately set right. And yet, the issue does not come to a critique of human judgment, as the delegation of responsibility to God might suggest; it comes rather to a vindication of judgment as a representation, however inadequate, of God's will. The "earthly" authority, which "the one Paternal mind" merely magnifies, follows the example of punishment in being summoned in the end to heal itself.

In the "Apology" appended to the *Sonnets*, Wordsworth's speaker suggests (with considerable justification) that the aim of these poems has been something other than a mere defense of capital punishment. Indicating that his "utterance" has found an "ampler scope" (2–3) despite the "barriers" with which the poet's "labour" often "meets" (7), he closes by expressing hope that "whatsoe'er the way / Each takes in this high matter," let us all be "[c]heer[ed]" by "the prospect of a brighter day" (12–14).

It is clearly the "Apology"'s purpose to recuperate the sonnets' speaker by granting him a circumspection he has previously lacked. Nevertheless, only by changing the speaker is Wordsworth able to effect this rehabilitation. While there is a great deal of wisdom in the apology, particularly in the effort to distinguish poetic utterance from the "prospect" that still eludes it, the apology has the curious effect of making irony (or what was previously irony) subject to the supplement of apology. To admit to having meant something other than what was said is more than a retraction at this point; it is a recuperation of voice at the expense of the very "prospect" that both the subversion of voice and the deferral of meaning have kept alive. The speaker's statement that his goal has been a "brighter day" has the sudden effect of removing that day by returning it to an intentional structure or narrative. The very day or possibility adumbrated by agency of irony is displaced by agency of intention. Initially contesting the sonnets' voice in apparent confirmation of their ironic function, the "Apology" immediately reverses that function by assimilating an authority (the "guidance" of "Wisdom's heavenly Father" [10–11]) from "whom" another meaning issues: the poems *didn't* mean what they said. Acceding to those structures on which meaning customarily depends, Wordsworth's "Apology" defers writing to an authority to which reading is also secondary.

Fortunately, there are numerous occasions, including the *Sonnets* themselves, where Wordsworth knows better than to be apologetic. But in the case of a poem such as the "Apology," there is a sufficiently humanistic legacy to convince most critics that the poet was undoubtedly right to solicit our pardon. Solicitations of this sort are rare in the late Wordsworth, and not because Wordsworth was too ossified to admit them; they are rare because they resist the "anti-climax" whereby authority is relinquished rather than reassigned. Wordsworth's anti-climax is no mere abstraction, no attack simply on the indulgences of poetic voice. It is a real politics where the vitiation of speech is also a vitiation of culture.

In meeting the "hundreds of strangers" who came to Rydal Mount as if to a shrine, the aging Wordsworth would, as Harriet Martineau observed, "go the round of his garden and terraces, relating to persons whose very names he had not attended to, particulars about his writing and other affairs which each stranger flattered himself was a confidential communication to himself." Indeed, when two friends of Martineau's accompanied her on a visit to "Mrs. Wordsworth," "much wishing to obtain some testimony from the old poet on behalf of popular education," Wordsworth "received them precisely after his usual manner with strangers":

He marched them off to his terraces; and Mrs. Wordsworth and I sat down on a garden seat. I told her the state of the case; and she said she would take care that, when they returned, Mr. Wordsworth should understand who his guests were. This was more easily promised than done, however. When they appeared, Mr. Wordsworth uncovered his grey head as usual, wished the gentlemen improved health and much enjoyment of the lake scenery, and bowed us out. My friends told me (what I could have told them) that Mr. Wordsworth had related many interesting things about his poems, but that they doubted whether he had any idea who they were.[22]

It is customary to take an anecdote like this one as evidence of the word made flesh, of the erstwhile Romantic, bloated with the approbation of the Victorians and the Oxford movement, hardening in sensibility. And in a way this is all very true: Wordsworth, as Martineau describes him, is very much *the Wordsworth* to whom visitors would pay homage.

Yet from another angle this Wordsworth is sufficiently detached from Wordsworth the man to make the act of being "Wordsworth" a performance that, to Martineau's eyes, seems almost a self-reflexive gesture. The performance undoubtedly had its advantages; it would have been difficult, if not impossible, to have treated each pilgrim individually. But the greater advantage is the criticism, both of the individual subject/visitor and the mystified individual—"Wordsworth"—that the performance implicitly admits. Wordsworth might not have treated his guests in the manner that some, including Emerson, would have wished.[23] However, it is not unlikely that their disappointment remained a trace of Wordsworth's own.

NOTES

1. In his influential essay, "Structure and Style in the Greater Romantic Lyric" (*From Sensibility to Romanticism,* 527– 60), M. H. Abrams underscores the subjective, authoritative bearing of such poems: specifically, that they "all manifest a transaction between subject and object in which the thought incorporates and makes explicit what was already implicit in the outer scene" (551).

2. In a related (if ultimately contrary) argument, Hartman stresses the "capable negativity" of Wordsworth's later style: how the recourse to a more conventionally sublime or classicizing style, recovers a more imaginative sublime that resists "domestication" in language ("Blessing the Torrent: On Wordsworth's Later Style," *PMLA,* 93 [1978]: 196–204). While Hartman rightly notes the humanization to which "tradition" in the later Wordsworth is frequently put, he views this as a tension rather a token of a possibly greater affinity. My view of Wordsworth's later poetry may also be set in contrast to Stuart Curran's argument, in *Poetic Form and British Romanticism* (New York: Oxford University Press, 1986), 29–55, that the sonnet's re-

vival in the late eighteenth century "was a genuine artistic movement with much of the fervor, the aggressive creation and dismantling of conventions . . . that accompanied its predecessor in the sixteenth century" (31). This may well be true, but it is not, on balance, true of Wordsworth. Thus, in his discussion of Wordsworth as a poet who sets out "to recapture the tone and ethos of the Miltonic sonnet" (41), Curran typically concentrates on the sonnets written earlier and published in 1807, and can only lament the "programmatic" aspects of the later sonnets which inhibit their originality (49).

3. "Creative Fantasy and Matter-of-Fact Reality in Wordsworth's Poetry," *JEGP*, 75 (1976): 1.

4. Moorman, *William Wordsworth: The Later Years*, 258–93. With this in mind, the rather indulgent gesture to publish *The White Doe of Rylstone* in quarto seven years after it was written seems both a defensive and possibly even a self-critical gesture and not at all a measure of the poet's admiration for that work. Such exclusivity, in fact, was not generally characteristic of Wordsworth's behavior. He may have been remote in manner, but he sought, as recently as *The Excursion*, as wide an audience as possible (*The Later Years*, 260).

5. Although some of the *River Duddon* sonnets were composed as early as 1806 (and possibly even earlier), the majority were written no earlier than 1818 and, more importantly, in a concentration of creative energy that apparently drove the poet to "exhaustion" (*Poetical Works*, vol. 3, 506). At all events, save for Sonnet XIV ("O Mountain Stream") and Sonnet XX ("The Plain of Donnerdale"), none of the remaining sonnets in the sequence is listed by Reed as having been composed *before* 1815.

6. For the issue of "unrepresentability," particularly its relation to the anti-aesthetic of postmodernism, see Ihab Hassan, "Pluralism in a Postmodern Perspective," *Critical Inquiry*, 12 [1986]: 506. It is characteristic of postmodern literature, according to Hassan, to "see[k] its limits . . . in forms of "articulate 'silence'" that "repel mimesis," "contesting the modes of its own representation." The "articulate silence" toward which Wordsworth's poems aspire, then—whereby the visionary is made vulnerable to the visible, is compatible as well (as Hassan suggests) with Kristeva's specifically feminist or maternal notions of "unrepresentability"—"[t]hat which, through language, is of no particular language," and thus in no way aligned with a more conventional symbolic order. ("Postmodernism?", in *Bucknell Review: Romanticism, Modernism, Postmodernism*, ed. Harry R. Garvin [Lewisburg, PA: Bucknell University Press, 1980], 136–41.)

7. The choice of Chaucer's Pastor is especially revealing. Although often thought to be an idealized portrait, the account of the Pastor in the General Prologue reveals a man who clearly enjoys his privileged, indeed "golden," status as shepherd to his flock.

8. "Wordsworth at St. Bees: Scandals, Sisterhoods, and Wordsworth's Later Poetry," *ELH*, 52 (1985): 33–58. See also Batho, *The Later Wordsworth* (Cambridge: Cambridge University Press, 1933), 234–311.

9. The closest thing to a critical manifesto for the "new historicism,"

especially in romantic studies, remains McGann's, *The Romantic Ideology: A Critical Investigation.*

10. See, for example, Manning, "Placing Poor Susan: Wordsworth and the New Historicism," *SIR,* 25 (1986): 351–69, and with particular attention to that poem's contention with "the vicious circle within which the likes of Poor Susan are trapped—servants becoming prostitutes and creating the demand for more servants," David Simpson, "What Bothered Charles Lamb About Poor Susan?", *SEL,* 26 (1986): 589–612. See also McGann, *The Romantic Ideology,* 81–92, and Levinson, *Wordsworth's Great Period Poems.*

11. For an account of the campaign against Brougham and its relationship to the war against Bonaparte, see Moorman, *Wordsworth: The Later Years,* 330–63. Moorman argues for Wordsworth's independent-mindedness over the prevailing view of his so-called conservatism. Thus, she attempts (as did Batho before her) to defend Wordsworth against the charge of apostasy by preserving him as the liberal he is generally believed not to have remained. The new historical view adopts a somewhat different approach. Here, as both Manning ("Wordsworth at St. Bees") and James K. Chandler (*Wordsworth's Second Nature: A Study of the Poetry and Politics* [Chicago: University of Chicago Press, 1984]) observe, the radicalism inherent in the poet's *Letter to the Bishop of Llandaff* (1793) marks a temporary aberration from a more consistently conservative or consistently non-radical posture. Thus, the new historical approach to Wordsworth is also a critique of the liberalism by which the poet has been both excoriated and, in recent years, defended.

12. My view may be distinguished from two recent studies which trace the trajectory of Wordsworth's politics toward conservatism: Chandler's *Wordsworth's Second Nature* and Michael Friedman's *The Making of a Tory Humanist: William Wordsworth and the Idea of Community.* For Friedman the problem is largely psychoanalytic: Wordsworth's patron, the Earl of Londsdale, becomes a surrogate father (after the death of the poet's father). It is against Londsdale that the poet next engages in an Oedipal struggle in the course of which he is forced finally to become the "father" (and to become loyal to the fatherland) following his early opposition. Chandler, who is concerned with Wordsworth's fundamental Englishness, takes even less stock in the poet's radicalism, particularly in regard to the French Revolution. Tracing the poet's relationship with Burke as it is manifest in the revolutionary books in *The Prelude,* Chandler notes a parallel reflection on the revolution which, "like Burke's moral sentiments, [are] strongly allied with early prejudice, insensibly formed in particular circumstances, and profoundly indebted to the English past" (61). Such loyalty to the "past" is just as prevalent in Wordsworth's later posture to which Burkean "traditionalism"—the concern over "the preservation of social practices and values"—is similarly analogous. Thus, there is a continuity between poems such as "Michael," which promotes "the moral life of the ancestors" (166), and such later poems as the *River Duddon Sonnets* which, in Chandler's reading, endeavor to the make the reader "profit from a vision of the

'far-off past'" (170). I, too, am determined to de-center Wordsworth's radicalism, but am less convinced that Wordsworth need be ancillary to the process. *The Convention of Cintra* (1809), urging the "just and necessary" war against Napoleon can certainly be seen, along with Friedman and Chandler, as indicative of a traditionally British posture. But the pamphlet also registers an opposition to authority that is in many ways self-reflexive—as in the vivid example of the Boy of Saragossa who, in laying his captured banner "upon the Altar of the Virgin," registers his "hatred of oppression" in a renunciation of authority and in the refusal to imitate his oppressor's example (*Prose Works*, vol. 1, 224–343.) Similar self-reflexive tendencies can be observed in such ostensibly "conservative" actions as *The Guide to the Lakes* (1809), which boasted the absence of royalty and lamented the impress of the human on the environment (*Prose Works*, vol. 2, 151–253), as well as in such seemingly incidental actions as Wordsworth's complaint about educators who deemed nature the work of God (Moorman, *The Later Years*, 222–29) or even in his opposition to his superiors in the civil service (251).

13. For discussion of the way many of Wordsworth's allegedy conservative gestures—the *Cintra* essay, *The Guide to the Lakes*, the campaign against Brougham—actually "complicate the popular myth of the 'two Wordsworths', early and later" by adherence to a less apostate "agrarian idealism," see Simpson, *Wordsworth's Historical Imagination*, 56–78. Perhaps, the most visible instance of this "consistency" remains *The Prelude*, which with relatively few exceptions remained essentially the same poem as the one completed in 1805. Moreover, when one realizes that the majority of the revisions were undertaken throughout the 1830s, the fact that *The Prelude* remained intact, must in itself force a reassessment of Wordsworth's disposition at this time.

14. This point is reaffirmed by Barbara T. Gates ("Wordsworth's Mirror of Morality: Distortions of Church History," *TWC*, 12 [1981]: 129–32), who notes Wordsworth's failure both to present "a Christian history which is obviously and at once both the history of a Christian institution operating in time and of personal Christian salvation," and also to write "a symbolically satisfying sonnet series" (131–32). Gates is surely right to document Wordsworth's failure in the *Ecclesiastical Sonnets*, but she is insufficiently attentive (in my view) to the point of these deficiencies. Wordsworth's failure, that is, to "make the most of the [sonnets'] dramatic potential" by "minimizing conflict," or, as Gates further observes, to exploit a narrative "perspective on both time and history, on individual and collective salvation," whereby "Christianity . . . is both already at hand and an *eschaton* still to be realized" (129–31), represents a resistance first and foremost to an authoritarian or otherwise aestheticized stance *already* characteristic of the poet's high romantic phase.

15. "Down a swift Stream" was initially composed sometime between 1820 and 1821 and was first published in 1822 in *Memorials of a Tour on the Continent* (*Poetical Works*, vol. 3, 390).

16. Again, the "revolution" that, as Kristeva warrants, may be endemic to "poetic language" is especially relevant here. For it is the function of this revolution to dismantle a symbolizing tendency, which is fundamentally patriarchal—that is, predicated on a "bar" between sign and meaning (*Revolution*, 63) interposed, as Lacan observed, by the father or Other—by agency of a poetic, non-symbolic orientation that is "maternal" in origin (*Powers of Horror*, 208).

17. *The Collected Works of Sir Henry Taylor* (London: C. Kegan Paul, 1878), vol. 5, 53–122. Taylor's review of Wordsworth's collected *Sonnets* (which marked the the first appearance and also the first criticism of the sonnets on capital punishment) appeared in the December, 1841 *Quarterly Review* (1–51), which was published by John Murray in 1842.

18. A notable exception is Lawrence Poston, whose two essays "Wordsworth Among the Victorians: The Case of Sir Henry Taylor" (*SIR*, 17 [1978]: 293–305) and " 'Worlds Not Realised': Wordsworthian Poetry in the 1830s" (*TSLL*, 28 [1986]: 51–80) initially brought Taylor to my attention. Yet where Poston is concerned chiefly with the uniqueness of Taylor's viewpoint, the ways his more formal observations may be distinguished from those of Arnold, Aubrey De Vere and the more "impressionistic Victorians," I hold Taylor to be representative of the Victorian viewpoint. This is evident not only in his admiration for *The Excursion*, but also in Taylor's reluctance to distinguish Wordsworth's "major period," thereby staying the assault on "periodization," particularly the "romantic" period, that the completed Wordsworth represents. I discuss the implications of reading the "whole" Wordsworth on nineteenth-century periodization in "Anti-Romanticism, Victorianism, and the Case of Wordsworth," *VP*, 24 (1986): 357–71.

19. References to this essay, exclusive of the observations on the sonnets "on punishment by death," are to the "Essay on Mr. Wordsworth's Sonnets" in *Collected Works*, vol. 5, 53–122.

20. This point was made with particular, if still ironic, force the same year when in *Poems, Chiefly of Early and Late Years* (1842) the capital punishment sonnets were placed in the same context as *Guilt and Sorrow* (initially titled *Salisbury Plain*)—a poem which dates from the poet's early, radical phase (1793–95), and had remained unpublished. The very idea of juxtaposing poems of the early and late years is itself revealing—as revealing, certainly, as the problematic edition of 1815. But the use of the capital punishment poems, presumably to correct or to supplement the rather different view of punishment in the earlier poem, immediately invites consideration of the obverse: the corrigibility to which, as merely conservative or non-radical documents, the sonnets are equally prone. The arc, in short, that can be traced through all of Wordsworth's poetry is highlighted by the decision finally to juxtapose works from the extremities of the poet's career.

21. It is important, once more, to distinguish this view from the somewhat similar claim for reading advanced by Rajan in "The Supplement of Reading." For Rajan the priority granted reading in nineteenth-century

hermeneutics and in high romantic texts is proto-deconstructive, founded chiefly on the recognition that there was indeed a gap between signifier and signified. In my view, reading—though similarly aligned with the "dises-tablishment of authoritative meaning"—is more structural at base, deriving from a systematic recognition of the arbitrary, hierarchical structures that authorize poetic voice, prior to its deauthorization. This recognition, par-ticularly involving the structure of authority, is prevalent in texts that are customarily associated with Wordsworth's romantic phase, but it is only after this period that Wordsworth is able to recuperate meaning through reading (and through irony)—instead of merely using reading as a mea-sure of (or even as a stay against) poetry's inadequacy.

22. Harriet Martineau, *Autobiography, Vol. II* (London: Smith Elder, 1877), 240–42. See also Moorman, *Wordsworth: The Later Years,* 576.

23. See Emerson's accounts of his visits to Wordsworth in Merton M. Sealts, Jr., ed., vol. 10 of *The Journals of Ralph Waldo Emerson* (Cambridge, MA: The Belknap Press of Harvard University Press, 1973), 554–60.

INDEX

Boldface numerals indicate pages where specific issues are discussed in depth.